THE
HUMANISTIC
TRADITION

THIRD EDITION

3 The European
Renaissance, the
Reformation, and
Global Encounter

Et commence le livre de la mutacion de fortune

Omment seut ce possible
A moy simple et pou sensible
De proprement copmier
Ce quon ne peut estimer
onnement ne bien comprendre
ontant ait homs sceu aprendre
uentierement peust desaire
e que bien voulsisse escripre
ant sont ses diuersitez
mudes des aduersitez
artailleuses et faus
ompris es tres pesans faiz
ue linfluence muable
e fortune decenable
ait par la reflection

e satiunt reflection
ui droite abisme est sanz faille
ne peut que ie ne faille
emprendre si tiunt ouurage
om de desaire sombrage
aaistre de sa fallace
ort seroit que ien parlasse
proprement presentement
si peut sentement
omme iay quant mains uaillans
ny ont escript qui faillans
nt este de tout noter
uanque on peut delle noter
mais ne sauray ia pour tant
ant mest fortune apportant
e ses mes que matiere ay
en parler si ne tauray
rien ou mal quel sache due
out y ait il a uedue
e que de son fait compris
u temps que ses tours appris
ar diuers cas qui mauint
ar elle par quoy deuint
on sens plus soubtil assez
ueste not es temps passez
auenu ne fust ne sceusse
e son fait tant napperceusse
our ce a bon droit on raisonne
ue a qlque chose est bonne
alcune auaine fois
ar elle apprent a la fois
i ne pense dire bourdes
qui sans oreilles sourdes
car il a son droit entendre

THE HUMANISTIC TRADITION

THIRD EDITION

3 The European Renaissance, the Reformation, and Global Encounter

Gloria K. Fiero

McGraw
Hill

New York St. Louis San Francisco Auckland Bogotá Caracas
Lisbon London Madrid Mexico City Milan Montreal New Delhi
San Juan Singapore Sydney Tokyo Toronto

McGraw-Hill

A Division of The McGraw·Hill Companies

THE HUMANISTIC TRADITION, BOOK 3

Copyright © 1998 by The McGraw-Hill Companies, Inc.
Previous editions © 1995, 1992 by William C. Brown Communications, Inc.
All rights reserved. Except as permitted under the United States Copyright Act
of 1976, no part of this publication may be reproduced or distributed in any
form or by any means, or stored in a data base or retrieval system, without
the prior written permission of the publisher.

Permissions Acknowledgments appear on page 170,
and on this page by reference.

Library of Congress Catalog Card Number: 97–071269
ISBN 0–697–34070–8

Editorial Director *Phillip Butcher*
Senior Sponsoring Editor *Cynthia Ward*
Director of Marketing *Margaret Metz*
National Sales Manager *Jerry Arni*

This book was designed and produced by
CALMANN & KING LTD
71 Great Russell Street, London WC1B 3BN

Editors *Ursula Payne, Richard Mason*
Designer *Karen Osborne*
Cover Designer *Karen Stafford*
Timeline Designer *Richard Foenander*
Picture Researcher *Carrie Haines*
Maps by Oxford Illustrators Ltd.

Developmental Editing by M. J. Kelly for McGraw-Hill

Typeset by Fakenham Photosetting, Norfolk
Printed in Hong Kong

10 9 8 7 6 5 4 3 2 1

http://www.mhhe.com

Front cover
Main image: Sandro Botticelli, detail of *Birth of Venus*, after 1482. Tempera on
canvas, full image 5 ft. 9 in. × 9 ft. ½ in. Uffizi Gallery, Florence. Scala, Florence.
Insets: (top) Red-figure *kylix* showing man and youth debating. The Metropolitan Museum of Art,
Rogers Fund, 1952 52.11.4. Photograph © 1984 The Metropolitan Museum of Art, New York.
(center) Head of Theodora, detail of *Empress Theodora and Retinue*, ca. 547 C.E. Mosaic. San Vitale,
Ravenna. Photo: © Dagli Orti, Paris.
(bottom) Detail of *Seated Buddha*, from the Gandharan region of Northwest Pakistan,
ca. 200 C.E. Gray schist, 51 × 31 in. The Cleveland Museum of Art. Leonard Hanna, Jr. Bequest.
CMA 61.418.

Frontispiece
Frontispiece to Christine de Pisan's *Livre de la Mutacion de Fortune*, early fifteenth century.
Bibliothèque Royale, Brussels, MS9508, f.2r.

Series Contents

Book 3
Contents

PART II

A Brave New World   77

19 Africa, the Americas, and Cross-Cultural Encounter *134*

MUSIC LISTENING SELECTIONS

MAPS

Preface

"It's the most curious thing I ever saw in all my life!" exclaimed Lewis Carroll's Alice in Wonderland, as she watched the Cheshire Cat slowly disappear, leaving only the outline of a broad smile. "I've often seen a cat without a grin, but a grin without a cat!" A student who encounters an ancient Greek epic, a Yoruba mask, or a Mozart opera—lacking any context for these works—might be equally baffled. It may be helpful, therefore, to begin by explaining how the artifacts (the "grin") of the humanistic tradition relate to the larger and more elusive phenomenon (the "cat") of human culture.

The Humanistic Tradition and the Humanities

In its broadest sense, the term *humanistic tradition* refers to humankind's cultural legacy—the sum total of the significant ideas and achievements handed down from generation to generation. This tradition is the product of responses to conditions that have confronted all people throughout history. Since the beginnings of life on earth, human beings have tried to ensure their own survival by achieving harmony with nature. They have attempted to come to terms with the inevitable realities of disease and death. They have endeavored to establish ways of living collectively and communally. And they have persisted in the desire to understand themselves and their place in the universe. In response to these ever-present and universal challenges—*survival, communality*, and *self-knowledge*—human beings have created and transmitted the tools of science and technology, social and cultural institutions, religious and philosophic systems, and various forms of personal expression, the sum total of which we call culture.

Even the most ambitious survey cannot assess all manifestations of the humanistic tradition. This book therefore focuses on the creative legacy referred to collectively as *the humanities*: literature, philosophy, history (in its literary dimension), architecture, the visual arts (including photography and film), music, and dance. Selected examples from each of these disciplines constitute our *primary sources*. Primary sources (that is, works original to the age that produced them) provide first-hand evidence of human inventiveness and ingenuity. The primary sources in this text have been chosen on the basis of their authority, their beauty, and their enduring value. They are, simply stated, the great works of their time and, in some cases, of all time. Universal in their appeal, they have been transmitted from generation to generation. Such works are, as well, the landmark

examples of a specific time and place: They offer insight into the ideas and values of the society in which they were produced. The drawings of Leonardo da Vinci, for example, reveal a passionate determination to understand the operations and functions of nature. And while Leonardo's talents far exceeded those of the average individual of his time, his achievements may be viewed as a mirror of the robust curiosity that characterized his time and place—the age of the Renaissance in Italy. *The Humanistic Tradition* surveys such landmark works, but joins "the grin" to "the cat" by examining them within their political, economic, and social contexts.

The Humanistic Tradition explores a living legacy. History confirms that the humanities are integral forms of a given culture's values, ambitions, and beliefs. Poetry, painting, philosophy, and music are not, generally speaking, products of unstructured leisure or indulgent individuality; rather, they are tangible expressions of the human quest for the good (one might even say the "complete") life. Throughout history, these forms of expression have served the domains of the sacred, the ceremonial, and the communal. And even in the waning days of the twentieth century, as many time-honored traditions have come under assault, the arts retain their power to awaken our imagination in the quest for survival, communality, and self-knowledge.

The Scope of the Humanistic Tradition

The humanistic tradition is not the exclusive achievement of any one geographic region, race, or class of human beings. For that reason, this text assumes a global and multicultural rather than exclusively Western perspective. At the same time, Western contributions are emphasized, first, because the audience for these books is predominantly Western, but also because in recent centuries the West has exercised a dominant influence on the course and substance of global history. Clearly, the humanistic tradition belongs to all of humankind, and the best way to understand the Western contribution to that tradition is to examine it in the arena of world culture.

As a survey, *The Humanistic Tradition* cannot provide an exhaustive analysis of our creative legacy. The critical reader will discover many gaps. Some aspects of culture that receive extended examination in traditional Western humanities surveys have been pared down to make room for the too often neglected contributions of

Islam, Africa, and Asia. This book is necessarily selective—it omits many major figures and treats others only briefly. Primary sources are arranged, for the most part, chronologically, but they are presented as manifestations of *the informing ideas of the age* in which they were produced. The intent is to examine the evidence of the humanistic tradition thematically and topically, rather than to compile a series of mini-histories of the individual arts.

Studying the Humanistic Tradition

To study the creative record is to engage in a dialogue with the past, one that brings us face to face with the values of our ancestors, and, ultimately, with our own. This dialogue is (or should be) a source of personal revelation and delight; like Alice in Wonderland, our strange, new encounters will be enriched according to the degree of curiosity and patience we bring to them. Just as lasting friendships with special people are cultivated by extended familiarity, so our appreciation of a painting, a play, or a symphony depends on close attention and repeated contact. There are no shortcuts to the study of the humanistic tradition, but there are some techniques that may be helpful. It should be useful, for instance, to approach each primary source from the triple perspective of its *text*, its *context*, and its *subtext*.

The Text: The *text* of any primary source refers to its *medium* (that is, what it is made of), its *form* (its outward shape), and its *content* (the subject it describes). All literature, for example, whether intended to be spoken or read, depends on the medium of words—the American poet Robert Frost once defined literature as "performance in words." Literary form varies according to the manner in which words are arranged. So poetry, which shares with music and dance rhythmic organization, may be distinguished from prose, which normally lacks regular rhythmic pattern. The main purpose of prose is to convey information, to narrate, and to describe; poetry, by its freedom from conventional patterns of grammar, provides unique opportunities for the expression of intense emotions. Philosophy (the search for truth through reasoned analysis) and history (the record of the past) make use of prose to analyze and communicate ideas and information. In literature, as in most kinds of expression, content and form are usually interrelated. The subject matter or the form of a literary work determines its *genre*. For instance, a long narrative poem recounting the adventures of a hero constitutes an *epic*, while a formal, dignified speech in praise of a person or thing constitutes a *eulogy*.

The visual arts—painting, sculpture, architecture, and photography—employ a wide variety of media, such as wood, clay, colored pigments, marble, granite, steel, and (more recently) plastic, neon, film, and computers.

The form or outward shape of a work of art depends on the manner in which the artist manipulates the formal elements of color, line, texture, and space. Unlike words, these formal elements lack denotative meaning. The artist may manipulate form to describe and interpret the visible world (as in such genres as portraiture and landscape painting); to generate fantastic and imaginative kinds of imagery; or to create imagery that is nonrepresentational—without identifiable subject matter. In general, however, the visual arts are spatial, that is, they operate and are apprehended in space.

The medium of music is sound. Like literature, music is durational: It unfolds over the period of time in which it occurs. The formal elements of music are melody, rhythm, harmony, and tone color—elements that also characterize the oral life of literature. As with the visual arts, the formal elements of music are without symbolic content, but while literature, painting, and sculpture may imitate or describe nature, music is almost always nonrepresentational—it rarely has meaning beyond the sound itself. For that reason, music is the most difficult of the arts to describe in words. It is also (in the view of some) the most affective of the arts. Dance, the artform that makes the human body itself a medium of expression, resembles music in that it is temporal and performance-oriented. Like music, dance exploits rhythm as a formal tool, but, like painting and sculpture, it unfolds in space as well as time.

In analyzing the text of a work of literature, art, or music, we ask how its formal elements contribute to its meaning and affective power. We examine the ways in which the artist manipulates medium and form to achieve a characteristic manner of execution and expression that we call *style*. And we try to determine the extent to which a style reflects the personal vision of the artist and the larger vision of his or her time and place. Comparing the styles of various artworks from a single era, we may discover that they share certain defining features and characteristics. Similarities (both formal and stylistic) between, for instance, golden age Greek temples and Greek tragedies, between Chinese lyric poems and landscape paintings, and between postmodern fiction and pop sculpture, prompt us to seek the unifying moral and aesthetic values of the cultures in which they were produced.

The Context: We use the word *context* to describe the historical and cultural environment. To determine the context, we ask: In what time and place did the artifact originate? How did it function within the society in which it was created? Was the purpose of the piece decorative, didactic, magical, propagandistic? Did it serve the religious or political needs of the community? Sometimes our answers to these questions are mere guesses. Nevertheless, understanding the function of an artifact often serves to clarify the nature of its form (and vice versa). For instance, much of the literature produced prior to the fifteenth century was spoken or sung rather than read; for that reason, such literature tends to feature repetition and rhyme, devices that facilitate memorization. We can assume that literary works embellished with frequent repetitions, such as the *Epic of Gilgamesh* and the Hebrew Bible, were products of an oral tradition. Determining the original function of an artwork also permits us to assess its significance in its own time and place: The paintings on the walls of Paleolithic caves, which are among the most compelling animal illustrations in the history of world art, are not "artworks" in the modern sense of the term but, rather, magical signs that accompanied hunting rituals, the performance of which was essential to the survival of the community. Understanding the relationship between text and context is one of the principal concerns of any inquiry into the humanistic tradition.

The Subtext: The *subtext* of the literary or artistic object refers to its secondary and implied meanings. The subtext embraces the emotional or intellectual messages embedded in, or implied by, a work of art. The epic poems of the ancient Greeks, for instance, which glorify prowess and physical courage in battle, suggest that such virtues are exclusively male. The state portraits of the seventeenth-century French ruler Louis XIV carry the subtext of unassailable and absolute power. In our own century, Andy Warhol's serial adaptations of soup cans and Coca-Cola bottles offer wry commentary on the supermarket mentality of postmodern American culture. Identifying the implicit message of an artwork helps us to determine the values and customs of the age in which it was produced and to assess those values against others.

Beyond *The Humanistic Tradition*

This book offers only small, enticing samples from an enormous cultural buffet. To dine more fully, students are encouraged to go beyond the sampling presented at this table; and for the most sumptuous feasting, nothing can substitute for first-hand experience. Students, therefore, should make every effort to supplement this book with visits to art museums and galleries, concert halls, theaters, and libraries. *The Humanistic Tradition* is designed for students who may or may not be able to read music, but who surely are able to cultivate an appreciation of music in performance. The clefs that appear in the text refer to the forty-five Music Listening Selections found on two accompanying cassettes, available from the publishers. Lists of suggestions for further reading are included at the end of each chapter, while a selected general bibliography of humanities resources appears at the end of each book.

The Third Edition

On the threshold of the new millennium, this third edition of *The Humanistic Tradition* brings increased attention to the theme of global cross-cultural encounter and, in particular, to the interaction of the West with the cultures of Islam, East Asia, and Africa. In this connection, a full chapter has been devoted to the Islamic World, and the chapter on ancient Rome has been expanded to provide parallels between the cultures of the Roman Empire and Han China. Chapter 1 now includes a carefully chosen selection of creation myths. There are new readings from *Beowulf*, Christine de Pisan, Murasaki Shikibu, Ibn Battuta, Hernán Cortés, Jonathan Swift, Mary Shelley, and Alice Walker. Excerpts from the *Iliad* (in chapter 6) appear in the 1990 English translation by Robert Fagles. Sufi poetry, the transatlantic slave trade, Japanese theater, and contemporary computer art add new perspectives to this, the latest version of the text.

The third edition also features two new study aids, both of which are designed to facilitate an appreciation of the arts in relation to their time and place: *Science and Technology Boxes*, which appear throughout the chapters, list key scientific and technological developments that have directly or indirectly affected the history of culture. *Locator Maps* (keyed to the map that appears on p. xii) assist readers in linking specific cultural events with the geographic region in which they occurred. This edition also expands on the number of color illustrations and large color maps, renumbers the Readings by book, and updates the Suggestions for Reading and Selected General Bibliography. Finally, in the transcription of the Chinese language, the older Wade-Giles system has been replaced by the more modern Hanyu Pinyin.

A Note to Instructors

The key to successful classroom use of *The Humanistic Tradition* is *selectivity*. Although students may be assigned to read whole chapters that focus on a topic or theme, as well as complete works that supplement the abridged readings, the classroom should be the stage for a selective treatment of a single example or a set of examples. The organization of this textbook is designed to emphasize themes that cut across geographic boundaries—themes whose universal significance prompts students to evaluate and compare rather than simply memorize and repeat lists of names and places. In an effort to assist readers in achieving global cultural literacy, every effort has been made to resist isolating (or "ghettoizing") individual cultures and to avoid the inevitable biases we bring to our evaluation of relatively unfamiliar cultures.

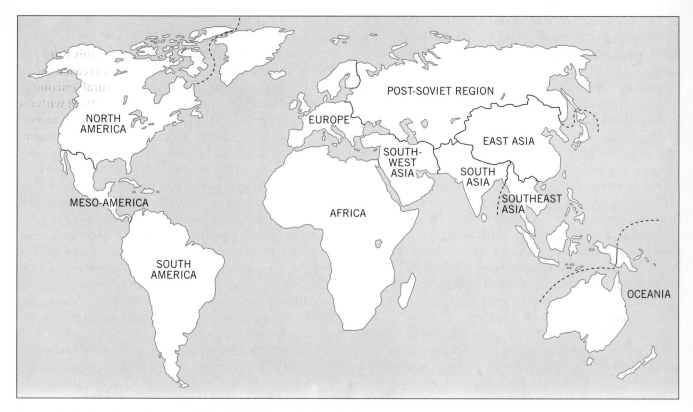

Keymap Indicating Areas Shown as White Highlights on the Locator Maps.

Acknowledgments

Writing *The Humanistic Tradition* has been an exercise in humility. Without the assistance of learned friends and colleagues, assembling a book of this breadth would have been an impossible task. James H. Dormon read all parts of the manuscript and made extensive and substantive editorial suggestions; as his colleague, best friend, and wife, I am most deeply indebted to him. I owe thanks to the following faculty members of the University of Southwestern Louisiana: for literature, Allen David Barry, Darrell Bourque, C. Harry Bruder, John W. Fiero, Emilio F. Garcia, Doris Meriwether, and Patricia K. Rickels; for history, Ora-Wes S. Cady, John Moore, Bradley Pollack, and Thomas D. Schoonover; for philosophy, Steve Giambrone and Robert T. Kirkpatrick; for geography, Tim Reilly; for the sciences, Mark Konikoff and John R. Meriwether; and for music, James Burke and Robert F. Schmalz.

The following readers and viewers generously shared their insights in matters of content and style: Michael K. Aakhus (University of Southern Indiana), Vaughan B. Baker (University of Southwestern Louisiana), Katherine Charlton (Mt. San Antonio Community College), Bessie Chronaki (Central Piedmont Community College), Debora A. Drehen (Florida Community College—Jacksonville), Paula Drewek (Macomb Community College), William C. Gentry (Henderson State University), Kenneth Ganza (Colby College), Ellen Hofman (Highline Community College), Burton Raffel (University of Southwestern Louisiana), Frank La Rosa (San Diego City College), George Rogers (Stonehill College), Douglas P. Sjoquist (Lansing Community College), Howard V. Starks (Southeastern Oklahoma State University), Ann Wakefield (Academy of the Sacred Heart—Grand Coteau), Sylvia White (Florida Community College—Jacksonville), and Audrey Wilson (Florida State University).

In the preparation of the third edition, I have benefited from the suggestions and comments generously offered by numerous readers, only some of whom are listed below. Rodney D. Boyd (Collin County Community College), Arnold Bradford (Northern Virginia Community College), Patricia L. Brace (Southwest State University), Orville V. Clark (University of Wisconsin—Green Bay), Carolyn Copeland (Bethune Cookman), Susan Cornett (St. Petersburg Junior College—Tarpon Center), Anthony M. Coyne (University of North Carolina), Kenneth Ganza (Colby College), Margaret Hasselman (Virginia Polytechnic Institute and State University), Victor Hébert (Fayetteville State University), Ellen Hofmann (Highline Community College), Enid Housty (Hampton University), Mabel Khawaja (Hampton University), James W. Mock (University of

Central Oklahoma), Lewis Parkhill (East Central University), Joseph G. Rahme (University of Michigan—Flint), David Simmons (Brevard Community College), J. Paul De Vierville (St. Phillip's College), Bertha L. Wise (Oklahoma City Community College), and Jon Young (Fayetteville State University). I am grateful to Julia Girouard, who provided research assistance for the

third edition, and to Timothy Reilly, who generously assisted in the preparation of the Locator Maps.

The burden of preparing the third edition has been lightened by the assistance of M. J. Kelly, Developmental Editor, and by the editorial vigilance of Ursula Payne and Richard Mason at Calmann & King.

SUPPLEMENTS FOR THE INSTRUCTOR AND THE STUDENT

A number of useful supplements are available to instructors and students using *The Humanistic Tradition*. Please contact your sales representative or call 1-800-338-3987 to obtain these resources, or to ask for further details.

Audiocassettes
Two ninety-minute audiocassettes containing a total of forty-five musical selections have been designed exclusively for use with *The Humanistic Tradition*. Cassette One corresponds to the music listening selections discussed in books 1–3 and Cassette Two contains the music in books 4–6. Each selection on the cassettes is discussed in the text and includes a voice introduction for easier location. Instructors may obtain copies of the cassettes for classroom use by calling 1-800-338-3987. Individual cassettes may be purchased separately; however, upon the request of instructors who place book orders, Cassette One or Two can be packaged with any of the six texts, so that students may use the musical examples *along with* the text.

Slide Sets
A set of fifty book-specific slides is available to qualified adopters of *The Humanistic Tradition*. These slides have been especially selected to include many of the less well-known images in the books, and will be a useful complement to your present slide resources. A larger set of two hundred book-specific slides is available for purchase from Sandak, Inc. For more information, contact your McGraw–Hill representative.

Instructor's Resource Manual
The Instructor's Resource Manual is designed to assist instructors as they plan and prepare for classes. Course outlines and sample syllabuses for both semester and quarter systems are included. The chapter summaries emphasize key themes and topics that give focus to the primary source readings. The study questions for each chapter may be removed and copied as handouts for student discussion or written assignments. A Test Item File follows each chapter along with a correlation list that directs instructors to the appropriate music examples, slides, transparencies, and software sections of the other supplements. A list of suggested videotapes, recordings, videodiscs, CD-ROMs, and their suppliers is included.

MicroTest III
The questions in the Test Item File are available on MicroTest III, a powerful but easy-to-use test generating program. MicroTest is available for DOS, Windows, and Macintosh personal computers. With MicroTest, an instructor can easily select the questions from the Test Item File and print a test and answer key. You can customize questions, headings, and instructions and add or import questions of your own.

Humanities Transparencies
A set of seventy-one acetate transparencies is available with *The Humanistic Tradition*. These show examples of art concepts, architectural styles, art media, maps, musical notation, musical styles, and musical elements.

Culture 3.0 CD-ROM
Culture 3.0 CD-ROM is a unique Macintosh reference tool that emphasizes the interaction of varied disciplines. It contains 40 historical maps, 120 signature melodies, 50,000 hypertext links, and 170 essays on topics ranging from Greek gods and goddesses to the Cold War. Thirty-two CultureGrids are arranged chronologically from the biblical era to the twentieth century, organizing people, places, and events by country, discipline, and generation. (*Culture 2.0* is also available in a seven-disk set for Mac and IBM.)

Student Study Guides, Volumes 1 and 2
Written by Gloria K. Fiero, two new Student Study Guides are now available to help students gain a better understanding of subjects found in *The Humanistic Tradition*. Volume 1 accompanies books 1–3 and Volume 2 accompanies books 4–6. Each chapter contains: a Chapter Objective; a Chapter Outline; Key Terms, Names, and Dates; Vocabulary Building; Multiple Choice Questions; and Essay Questions. Many chapters also contain a Visual/Spatial Exercise and Bonus Material. At the end of each Part, Synthesis material helps students draw together ideas from a set of chapters.

The Art Historian CD-ROM, Volumes 1 and 2
This flexible two-volume series on dual platform (Mac and Windows) CD-ROMs is designed to supplement introductory level art history education. Volume 1 covers ancient and medieval art, and Volume 2 covers Renaissance to modern art. The images included on the CD were gathered from over three hundred museums, galleries, and private collections throughout the world, and the text and test questions were written by current scholars from universities across the United States. With *The Art Historian*, students may listen to multimedia presentations, review full-color high-resolution images, and test their knowledge with flashcards and essay questions. *The Art Historian* is flexible, allowing students to take notes, compare two images on the screen at the same time, and create personalized collections of images for study and review. With *The Art Historian*, we place the power of multimedia *and* art at your fingertips.

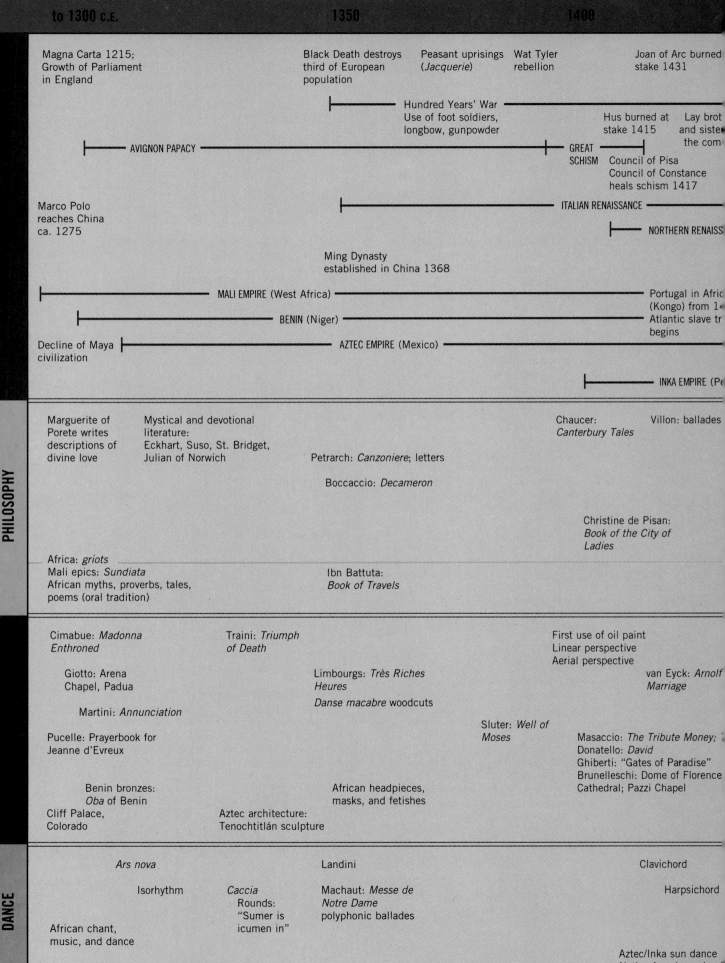

Magna Carta 1215;
Growth of Parliament
in England

Black Death destroys
third of European
population

Peasant uprisings
(*Jacquerie*)

Wat Tyler
rebellion

Joan of Arc burned
stake 1431

Hundred Years' War
Use of foot soldiers,
longbow, gunpowder

Hus burned at
stake 1415

Lay brot
and siste
the com

AVIGNON PAPACY

GREAT
SCHISM

Council of Pisa
Council of Constance
heals schism 1417

Marco Polo
reaches China
ca. 1275

ITALIAN RENAISSANCE

NORTHERN RENAISS

Ming Dynasty
established in China 1368

MALI EMPIRE (West Africa)

Portugal in Afric
(Kongo) from 1

BENIN (Niger)

Atlantic slave tr
begins

Decline of Maya
civilization

AZTEC EMPIRE (Mexico)

INKA EMPIRE (Pe

LITERATURE AND PHILOSOPHY

Marguerite of
Porete writes
descriptions of
divine love

Mystical and devotional
literature:
Eckhart, Suso, St. Bridget,
Julian of Norwich

Chaucer:
Canterbury Tales

Villon: ballades

Petrarch: *Canzoniere*; letters

Boccaccio: *Decameron*

Christine de Pisan:
*Book of the City of
Ladies*

Africa: *griots*
Mali epics: *Sundiata*
African myths, proverbs, tales,
poems (oral tradition)

Ibn Battuta:
Book of Travels

ART AND ARCHITECTURE

Cimabue: *Madonna
Enthroned*

Traini: *Triumph
of Death*

First use of oil paint
Linear perspective
Aerial perspective

Giotto: Arena
Chapel, Padua

Limbourgs: *Très Riches
Heures*

van Eyck: *Arnolf
Marriage*

Martini: *Annunciation*

Danse macabre woodcuts

Sluter: *Well of
Moses*

Pucelle: Prayerbook for
Jeanne d'Evreux

Masaccio: *The Tribute Money;*
Donatello: *David*
Ghiberti: "Gates of Paradise"
Brunelleschi: Dome of Florence
Cathedral; Pazzi Chapel

Benin bronzes:
Oba of Benin

African headpieces,
masks, and fetishes

Cliff Palace,
Colorado

Aztec architecture:
Tenochtitlán sculpture

MUSIC AND DANCE

Ars nova

Landini

Clavichord

Isorhythm

Caccia
Rounds:
"Sumer is
icumen in"

Machaut: *Messe de
Notre Dame*
polyphonic ballades

Harpsichord

African chant,
music, and dance

Aztec/Inka sun dance
Native American chant

...alius: *Anatomy*
...pernicus: *On the*
...volution of the
...avenly Spheres*

Global exploration:
Columbus reaches
America 1492
da Gama, Magellan

European
witch-hunts

Spanish
Armada
defeated
1588

Globe
Theatre,
London

...evotio moderna*

Pope Leo X
Luther posts *Ninety-Five Theses*

...utenberg: printing
...ress perfected 1450

THE PROTESTANT REFORMATION

Henry VIII breaks with
Roman Catholic Church
Calvin in Geneva
Zwingli: Anabaptists

Charles V, Holy Roman Emperor

HIGH RENAISSANCE

Medici rule Florence
Fall of Constantinople to
the Turks 1453
Platonic Academy founded
in Florence

Patronage: Pope
Julius II commissions
Raphael, Michelangelo,
and Bramante

First Spanish
colony in
Florida 1565

Benin civilization at its peak

Cortés in Mexico 1519 ——— Jesuits in "New Spain"

Portuguese in India
and Brazil

Tokugawa Shogunate
in Japan 1603

Pizarro conquers Peru 1531

...icino: Neoplatonism
Pico: *Oration on the*
Dignity of Man

Castiglione: *The*
Book of the Courtier

Rabelais: *Gargantua*
and Pantagruel

Cervantes: *Don Quijote*

Montaigne: *Essays*

Alberti: *On the*
Family

Machiavelli: *The Prince*

Luther: *Address to the*
German Nobility

Shakespeare: *Othello*;
sonnets and other
plays

...homas à
...empis:
...nitatio Christi*

Erasmus: *The Praise of Folly*
More: *Utopia*

Vasari: *Lives of the*
Artists

Maya: *Popol Vuh*
(excerpt in
chapter 1)

...tive America:
...ths, tales, poems
...al tradition)

Cortés: *Letters*
from Mexico

Benzoni: *History of*
the New World

...lberti: *Ten Books*
...n Architecture*;
...Santa Maria Novella

Pollaiuolo: *Hercules and*
Antaeus
Botticelli: *Birth of Venus*

Raphael: *Alba Madonna*;
School of Athens

Titian: *Pastoral*
Concert; *Venus of*
Urbino

Michelangelo: *David*;
Sistine Chapel ceiling;
dome of St. Peter's

...errocchio:
...Colleoni

Laurana: *Battista Sforza*
Studiolo at Urbino

Bellini: *Procession in*
Piazza San Marco

Palladio: *Four*
Books on
Architecture,
Villa Rotonda

Leonardo: notebooks;
Mona Lisa; *Last Supper*

Cranach
Holbein: *Erasmus*

Brueghel: *Triumph*
of Death: *Wedding*
Dance

Bramante:
Tempietto

Baldung ("Grien"):
Witches

...Aztec "Calendar
...Stone"

Dürer: landscapes, portraits,
printmaking
Bosch: *Garden of Earthly Delights*
Grünewald: Isenheim Altarpiece

...ufay: *chansons*;
Missa L'homme armé

Printed music

Josquin des Prez:
masses, motets

Renaissance madrigals:
Lassus: "Matona, mia cara"
Dowland

Ebreo: *Art of Dance*;
balli (ballet)

Lutheran chorales:
"A Mighty Fortress is
Our God"

Morley: "My bonny lass she
smileth"

Italian court dances:
basse danse,
saltarello, *piva*

Word painting
Imitation

Town pageants, festival displays, theatrical dance

PART

I

THE AGE OF THE RENAISSANCE

The three hundred years between 1300 and 1600 brought Western Europe out of the Middle Ages and onto the threshold of modernity. In economic life, manorialism succumbed to entrepreneurial capitalism. In political life, feudalism gave way to centralized forms of government and the advent of national states. Ascendant individualism, secularism, and rationalism challenged devotional sentiment and religious fervor. The printing press made liberal education available to an increasingly literate population, while the science of navigation and advancing technology encouraged European expansion and cross-cultural contacts. By 1600, Europe would assume a dominant presence in parts of the world whose geography had only recently been mapped with any accuracy.

The Renaissance, or "rebirth" of classicism, was the cultural hinge between medieval and modern times. Originating in fourteenth-century Italy, and spreading northward during the fifteenth and sixteenth centuries, this dynamic movement shaped some of the West's most fundamental political, economic, and cultural values—values associated with the rise of nation-states, the formation of the middle class, and the advancement of classically based education and classically inspired art.

The first three chapters of this unit are devoted to an examination of the age of the Renaissance. Chapter 15, "Adversity and Challenge: The Fourteenth-Century Transition," treats the century of change that ushered in the Renaissance. During this time, the struggle for survival against the devastating bubonic plague, the trials of a long and debilitating war between England and

France, and the series of events leading to the decline of the Roman Catholic Church radically altered all aspects of Western European life and cultural expression. In the writings of Boccaccio, Chaucer, and Christine de Pisan, in the paintings of Giotto, and in the *ars nova* of music, there are distinct signs of a revived self-consciousness, increasing fidelity to nature, and a growing preoccupation with gender and class.

Chapter 16, "Classical Humanism in the Age of the Renaissance," examines evidence of the cultural revival that motivated the finest literature and art of this era. Classical humanism—the movement to recover, study, and disseminate ancient Greek and Latin texts—stimulated in Italy, the birthplace of the Renaissance, a sense of individualism, a boundless vitality, and an optimistic view of the human potential for fulfillment on earth. The writings of Petrarch, Alberti, Pico, Castiglione, and Machiavelli are viewed as evidence of the Renaissance effort to apply classical precepts to matters of education, diplomacy, politics, and social life.

Chapter 17, "Renaissance Artists: Disciples of Nature, Masters of Invention," charts the visual arts and music of the fifteenth and sixteenth centuries. Renaissance artists sought new ways of representing the physical world with greater accuracy. They looked to classical Greece and Rome as sources of aesthetic authority, but competed with their classical predecessors in the search for unity of design and heroic individualism. In this chapter, we meet many of the giants of Renaissance art and architecture, including Donatello, Brunelleschi, Masaccio, Leonardo, Raphael, and Michelangelo. The chapter also surveys the high points of Renaissance music and dance, including the development of the madrigal, the rise of instrumental music, and the beginnings of choreography.

15
Adversity and Challenge:
The Fourteenth-Century Transition

Traditions normally undergo modification only over long periods of time. However, natural disasters, epidemic disease, and protracted warfare generally accelerate cultural change. The fourteenth century provides a case in point, for during that dramatic time all of these catalytic phenomena occurred in Western Europe, causing widespread havoc and wrenching medieval customs and practices out of their steady, dependable rhythms. As a result, the period between roughly 1300 and 1400 became a time of transition between medieval and early modern history. During this age, many medieval traditions were revised or discarded and new cultural patterns contributed to the formation of a modern world system dominated by the rise of the West.

The Black Death

The most devastating natural catastrophe of the early modern era was the bubonic plague, which struck Europe in 1347 and destroyed one third to one half of its population within less than a century. Originating in Asia and spread by the Mongol tribes that dominated that vast area, the disease devastated China and the Middle East, interrupting long-distance trade and cross-cultural encounters that had flourished for two centuries. The plague was carried into Europe by flea-bearing black rats infesting the commercial vessels that brought goods to Mediterranean ports. Within two years of its arrival it ravaged much of the Western world. In its early stages, it was transmitted by the bite of either the infected flea or the host rat; in its more severe stages, it was passed on by those infected with the disease. The symptoms of the malady were terrifying: Buboes (or abscesses) that began in the lymph glands of the groin or armpits of the afflicted slowly filled with pus, turning the body a deathly black, hence the popular label "the Black Death." Once the boils and accompanying fever appeared, death

usually followed within two to three days. Traditional treatments, such as the bleeding of victims and fumigation with vapors of vinegar, proved useless. No connection was perceived between the ubiquitous rats and the plague itself, and in the absence of a clinical understanding of bacterial infection, the medical profession of the day was helpless. (Indeed, the bacillus of the bubonic plague was not isolated until 1894.)

The plague hit hardest in the towns, where a concentration of population and the lack of sanitation made the disease all the more difficult to contain. Four waves of bubonic plague spread throughout Europe between 1347 and 1375, infecting some European cities several times and nearly wiping out their entire populations (Figure **15.1**). The virulence of the plague and the mood of mounting despair horrified the Florentine writer Giovanni Boccaccio (1313–1375). In his preface to the *Decameron*, a collection of tales told by ten young people who abandoned plague-ridden Florence for the safety of a country estate, Boccaccio described the physical conditions of the pestilence, as well as its psychological consequences. He recorded with somber precision how widespread death had forced Florentine citizens to abandon the traditional forms of grieving and the rituals associated with death and burial. The stirring vernacular prose captured the mood of dread that prevailed in Florence, as people fled their cities, homes, and even their families.

READING 3.1

From Boccaccio's Introduction to the *Decameron*

. . . In the year of Our Lord 1348 the deadly plague broke   1
out in the great city of Florence, most beautiful of Italian
cities. Whether through the operation of the heavenly
bodies or because of our own iniquities which the just
wrath of God sought to correct, the plague had arisen in
the East some years before, causing the death of
countless human beings. It spread without stop from one
place to another, until, unfortunately, it swept over the
West. Neither knowledge nor human foresight availed
against it, though the city was cleansed of much filth by   10

Figure 15.1 *The Black Death*, miniature from a rhymed Latin chronicle of the events of 1349–1352 by Egidius, abbot of Saint Martin's, Tournai, France, ca. 1355. Manuscript illumination. Bibliothèque Royale, Brussels, MS13076–77, f.24v.

chosen officers in charge and sick persons were forbidden to enter it, while advice was broadcast for the preservation of health. Nor did humble supplications serve. Not once but many times they were ordained in the form of processions and other ways for the propitiation of God by the faithful, but, in spite of everything, toward the spring of the year the plague began to show its ravages in a way short of miraculous.

It did not manifest itself as in the East, where if a man bled at the nose he had certain warning of inevitable [20] death. At the onset of the disease both men and women were afflicted by a sort of swelling in the groin or under the armpits which sometimes attained the size of a common apple or egg. Some of these swellings were larger and some smaller, and all were commonly called boils. From these two starting points the boils began in a little while to spread and appear generally all over the body. Afterwards, the manifestation of the disease changed into black or livid spots on the arms, thighs and [30] the whole person. In many these blotches were large and far apart, in others small and closely clustered. Like the boils, which had been and continued to be a certain indication of coming death, these blotches had the same meaning for everyone on whom they appeared.

Neither the advice of physicians nor the virtue of any medicine seemed to help or avail in the cure of these diseases. Indeed, whether the nature of the malady did not suffer it, or whether the ignorance of the physicians could not determine the source and therefore could take no preventive measures against it, the fact was that not [40] only did few recover, but on the contrary almost everyone died within three days of the appearance of the signs— some sooner, some later, and the majority without fever or other ill. Moreover, besides the qualified medical men, a vast number of quacks, both men and women, who had never studied medicine, joined the ranks and practiced cures. The virulence of the plague was all the greater in that it was communicated by the sick to the well by contact, not unlike fire when dry or fatty things are brought near it. But the evil was still worse. Not only did [50] conversation and familiarity with the diseased spread the malady and even cause death, but the mere touch of the clothes or any other object the sick had touched or used, seemed to spread the pestilence. . . .

Because of such happenings and many others of a like sort, various fears and superstitions arose among the survivors, almost all of which tended toward one end—to flee from the sick and whatever had belonged to them. In this way each man thought to be safeguarding his own health. Some among them were of the opinion that by [60] living temperately and guarding against excess of all kinds, they could do much toward avoiding the danger;

and forming a band they lived away from the rest of the world. Gathering in those houses where no one had been ill and living was more comfortable, they shut themselves in. They ate moderately of the best that could be had and drank excellent wines, avoiding all luxuriousness. With music and whatever other delights they could have, they lived together in this fashion, allowing no one to speak to them and avoiding news either of death or sickness from 70 the outer world.

Others, arriving at a contrary conclusion, held that plenty of drinking and enjoyment, singing and free living and the gratification of the appetite in every possible way, letting the devil take the hindmost, was the best preventative of such a malady; and as far as they could, they suited the action to the word. Day and night they went from one tavern to another drinking and carousing unrestrainedly. At the least inkling of something that suited them, they ran wild in other people's houses, and 80 there was no one to prevent them, for everyone had abandoned all responsibility for his belongings as well as for himself, considering his days numbered. Consequently most of the houses had become common property and strangers would make use of them at will whenever they came upon them even as the rightful owners might have

done. Following this uncharitable way of thinking, they did their best to run away from the infected.

Meanwhile, in the midst of the affliction and misery that had befallen the city, even the reverend authority of divine 90 and human law had almost crumbled and fallen into decay, for its ministers and executors, like other men, had either died or sickened, or had been left so entirely without assistants that they were unable to attend to their duties. As a result everyone had leave to do as he saw fit.

[Others, in an effort to escape the plague, abandoned the city, their houses, their possessions, and their relatives.] The calamity had instilled such horror into the hearts of men and women that brother abandoned brother, uncles, sisters and wives left their dear ones to 100 perish, and, what is more serious and almost incredible, parents avoided visiting or nursing their very children, as though these were not their own flesh. . . . So great was the multitude of those who died in the city night and day, what with lack of proper care and the virulence of the plague, that it was terrible to hear of, and worse still to see. Out of sheer necessity, therefore, quite different customs arose among the survivors from the original laws of the townspeople.

It used to be common, as it is still, for women, friends 110

Figure 15.2 Attributed to Francesco Traini, detail of *Triumph of Death*, 1330s (state prior to 1944). Fresco, whole wall 18 ft. 6 in. × 49 ft. 2 in. Camposanto, Pisa. Alinari/Art Resource, New York.

and neighbors of a dead man, to gather in his house and mourn there with his people, while his men friends and many other citizens collected with his nearest of kin outside the door. Then came the clergy, according to the standing of the departed, and with funereal pomp of tapers and singing he was carried on the shoulders of his peers to the church he had elected before death. Now, as the plague gained in violence, these customs were either modified or laid aside altogether, and new ones were instituted in their place, so that, far from dying among a   120 crowd of women mourners, many passed away without the benefit of a single witness. Indeed, few were those who received the piteous wails and bitter tears of friends and relatives, for often, instead of mourning, laughter, jest and carousal accompanied the dead—usages which even naturally compassionate women had learned to perfection for their health's sake. It was a rare occurrence for a corpse to be followed to church by more than ten or twelve mourners—not the usual respectable citizens, but a class of vulgar grave-diggers who called themselves "sextons"   130 and did these services for a price. They crept under the bier and shouldered it, and then with hasty steps rushed it, not to the church the deceased had designated before death, but oftener than not to the nearest one. . . .

More wretched still were the circumstances of the common people and, for a great part, of the middle class, for, confined to their homes either by hope of safety or by poverty, and restricted to their own sections, they fell sick daily by thousands. There, devoid of help or care, they died almost without redemption. A great many breathed their   140 last in the public streets, day and night; a large number perished in their homes, and it was only by the stench of their decaying bodies that they proclaimed their death to their neighbors. Everywhere the city was teeming with corpses. A general course was now adopted by the people, more out of fear of contagion than of any charity they felt toward the dead. Alone, or with the assistance of whatever bearers they could muster, they would drag the corpses out of their homes and pile them in front of the doors, where often, of a morning, countless bodies might be seen. Biers   150 were sent for. When none was to be had, the dead were laid upon ordinary boards, two or three at once. It was not infrequent to see a single bier carrying husband and wife, two or three brothers, father and son, and others besides. . . .

So many bodies were brought to the churches every day that the consecrated ground did not suffice to hold them, particularly according to the ancient custom of giving each corpse its individual place. Huge trenches were dug in the crowded churchyards and the new dead were piled in them, layer upon layer, like merchandise in the hold of a   160 ship. A little earth covered the corpses of each row, and the procedure continued until the trench was filled to the top. . . .

———————————◆———————————

The Effects of the Black Death

Those who survived the plague tried to fathom its meaning and purpose. Some viewed it as the manifestation of God's displeasure with the growing worldliness of contemporary society, while others saw it as a divine warning to all Christians, but especially to the clergy,

Figure 15.3 *Dance of Death*, ca. 1490. Woodcut. Library of Congress, Washington, D.C. Lessing J. Rosenwald Collection.

whose profligacy and moral laxity were commonly acknowledged facts (as we shall see in the next section). Those who perceived the plague as God's scourge urged a return to religious orthodoxy, and some devised fanatic kinds of atonement. Groups of Flagellants, for instance, wandered the countryside lashing their bodies with whips in frenzies of self-mortification. At the other extreme, there were many who resolved to "eat, drink, and be merry" in what might be the last hours of their lives; while still others, in a spirit of doubt and inquiry, questioned the very existence of a god who could work such evils on humankind.

The abandonment of church-directed rituals of funeral and burial described by Boccaccio threatened tradition and shook the confidence of medieval Christians. Inevitably, the old medieval regard for death as a welcome release from earthly existence began to give way to a gnawing sense of anxiety and a new self-consciousness. Some of these changes are mirrored in the abundance of death-related pictorial images, including purgatorial visions and gruesome depictions of death and burial, that appeared during the century of the Black Death (Figure 15.2). Of all plague-related themes, the most popular was the "Dance of Death." Set forth in both poetry and the visual arts, the Dance of Death or *danse macabre* portrayed death as a grinning skeleton or cadaver shepherding his victims to the grave (Figure 15.3). The procession (which might have originated in conjunction with popular dances) included men, women, and children from all walks of life and social classes: peasants and kings, schoolmasters and merchants, priests and nuns—all succumb to Death's ravishment. The Dance of Death objectified the new regard for death as "the Great Equalizer," that is, as an impartial phenomenon threatening every individual, regardless of status or wealth. This vulnerability of humankind is a prevailing motif in fourteenth- and fifteenth-century verse. Note, for example, these lines written by

François Villon (1431–ca. 1463), the greatest French poet of his time.

> I know this well, that rich and poor
> Fools, sages, laymen, friars in cowl,
> Large-hearted lords and each mean boor,[1]
> Little and great and fair and foul,
> Ladies in lace, who smile or scowl,
> From whatever stock they stem,
> Hatted or hooded, prone to prowl,
> Death seizes every one of them.

The theme of the Dance of Death captured the imagination of fourteenth-century artists and appeared in almost every medium of expression, including woodcut and engraving, for two centuries thereafter. In the medieval morality play *Everyman* (see chapter 12), Death is a powerful antagonist. But in visual representations, he assumes subtle guises—ruler, predator, and seducer—and is a sly and cajoling figure who mocks the worldly pursuits of his unsuspecting victims.

If the psychological impact of the Black Death was traumatic, its economic effects were equally devastating. Widespread death among the poor caused a shortage of labor, which in turn created a greater demand for workers. The bargaining power of those who survived the plague was thus improved. In many parts of Europe, workers pressed to raise their status and income. Peasants took advantage of opportunities to become tenant farmers on lands leased by lords in need of laborers. Others fled their rural manors for cities where jobs were readily available. This exodus from the countryside spurred urban growth and contributed to the disintegration of manorialism.

All of Europe, however, continued to be disadvantaged by the climatic disasters that caused frequent crop failure and famine, and by the continuing demands of financially threatened feudal overlords. Violent working-class revolts—the first examples of labor rebellion in Western history—broke out in France and England in the mid-fourteenth century. In 1358, French peasants (known as *jacques*) staged an angry protest (the *Jacquerie*) that took the lives of hundreds of noblemen before it was suppressed by the French king. In England, the desperation of the poor was manifested in the Wat Tyler rebellion of 1381, an event described in the *Chronicles* of the French historian Jean Froissart (1338–1410). Despite their ultimate failure, these revolts left their imprint on the social history of the West. They frightened landowners everywhere and lent an instability to class relationships that hastened the demise of the old feudal order.

Europe in Transition

England's Constitutional Monarchy

While the peasant rebellions achieved no immediate reforms, the lower classes had taken a major step toward demanding equality with the rest of society. England's laboring classes were not the first, however, to have contested the absolute authority of the English monarch. As early as the year 1215, the barons of the realm had forced King John of England to sign a document called the Magna Carta (Latin, meaning "great charter"), which forbade the king from levying additional feudal taxes without the consent of his royal council. The Magna Carta, which was also interpreted to guarantee such other freedoms as trial by jury, asserted the primacy of law above the will of the ruler—a principle that paved the way for the development of constitutional monarchy.

Only fifty years after the signing of the Magna Carta, the English nobility, demanding equal authority in ruling England, imprisoned King Henry III and invited middle-class representatives to participate in the actions of the Great Council (Parliament), thus initiating the first example of representative government among the burgeoning nation-states of the West. During the fourteenth century, as Parliament met frequently to raise taxes for England's wars with France, it bargained for greater power, including the right to initiate legislation. Peasants, laborers, and members of the lower middle class still exercised no real political influence, but by the end of the century the English had laid the groundwork for a constitutional monarchy that would bridge the gap between medieval feudalism and modern democracy.

The Hundred Years' War

In France, the ills of plague, famine, and civil disturbance were compounded by a war with England that lasted more than one hundred years (1337–1453) and was fought entirely on French soil. Larger and more protracted than any previous medieval conflict, the Hundred Years' War was the result of a longstanding English claim to continental lands: From the time of the Norman Conquest, the kings of England had held land in France, a situation that caused chronic resentment among the French. But the immediate cause of the war was the English claim to the French throne, occasioned by the death of Charles IV, the last of the male heirs in a long line of French kings that had begun with Hugh Capet in 987.

1300s	mechanical clocks appear in Europe
1346	gunpowder and longbows are utilized by the English army at the Battle of Crécy
1370	the steel crossbow is adopted as a weapon of war

---

[1]Peasant; a rude and illiterate person.

Figure 15.4 *The End of the Siege of Ribodane: English Soldiers Take a French Town*, late fifteenth century. Manuscript illumination. Note longbow and light cannon. By permission of the British Library, London, MS Roy.14.E.IV, f.281v.

The war that began in 1337 was marked by intermittent battles, in many of which the French outnumbered the English by three or four to one. Nevertheless, the English won most of the early battles of the war, owing to their use of three new "secret" weapons: the foot soldier, the longbow, and gunpowder—the invisible enemy that would ultimately eliminate the personal element in military combat. Along with the traditional cavalry, the English army depended heavily on foot soldiers armed with longbows (Figure 15.4). The thin, steel-tipped arrows of the 6-foot longbow could be fired more quickly and at a longer range than those of the traditional crossbow. Because the thin arrows of the longbow easily pierced the finest French chain mail, plate mail soon came to replace chain mail. However, within the next few centuries, even plate mail became obsolete, since it proved useless against artillery that employed gunpowder.

Introduced into Europe by the Muslims, who borrowed it from the Chinese, gunpowder was first used in Western combat during the Hundred Years' War. In the first battle of the war, however, the incendiary substance proved too potent for the poorly cast English cannons, which issued little more than terrifying noise. Still, gunpowder constituted an advance in military technology, one that ultimately outmoded hand-to-hand combat and rendered obsolete the medieval code of chivalry. Froissart's account of the Hundred Years' War—which reads like a Crusade chronicle—glorifies the performance of chivalric deeds, even though many of the methods of combat Froissart describes clearly anticipate a new era. For instance, because the English were greatly outnumbered by the French, they resorted to ambush, thus violating medieval rules of war. It can be said, then, that the Hundred Years' War inaugurated the impersonal style of combat that has come to dominate modern warfare.

Figure 15.5 *King Charles VII of France Receiving Joan of Arc at Chinon in March 1429*, late fourteenth century. Fragment of a German tapestry. The legend on the banner reads "Here comes 'La Pucelle' ['the maiden,' Joan's nickname] sent by God to the Dauphin in his land." Orléans-Musée Historique et Archéologique de l'Orléanais. Photo: Lauros-Giraudon, Paris.

Although throughout the Hundred Years' War the English repeatedly devastated the French armies, the financial and physical burdens of garrisoning French lands ultimately proved too great for the English, who, facing a revitalized army under the charismatic leadership of Joan of Arc, finally withdrew from France in 1429. Of peasant background, the seventeen-year-old Joan begged the French king to allow her to obey the voices of the Christian saints who had directed her to expel the English (Figure **15.5**). Donning armor and riding a white horse, she led the French into battle. Her success, which forced the English to withdraw from Orléans, initiated her martyrdom; in 1431, she was condemned as a heretic and burned at the stake.

The Hundred Years' War dealt the death blow to feudalism. By the mid-fifteenth century, the French nobility was badly depleted, and those knights who survived the war found themselves "outdated." In France, feudal allegiances were soon superseded by systems of national conscription, and in the decades following the English withdrawal, both countries were ready to move in separate directions, politically and culturally.

The Decline of the Church

The growth of the European nation-states contributed to the weakening of the Christian commonwealth, especially where Church and state competed for influence and authority. The two events that proved most damaging to the prestige of the Catholic Church were the Avignon Papacy (1309–1377) and the Great Schism (1378–1417). The term "Avignon Papacy" describes the relocation of the papacy to the city of Avignon in Southern France (see Map 16.1). While the move from Rome to Avignon occurred in response to political pressure from the French king Philip IV ("the Fair"), the relocated papacy proceeded to establish a luxurious and powerful court. The Avignon popes attempted to compete in prestige and political influence with the secular rulers of Europe, and used stringent (and occasionally corrupt) means to accomplish their purpose. The increasing need for Church revenue led some of the Avignon popes to sell Church office (a practice known as **simony**), to levy additional taxes upon clergymen, to elect members of their own families to ecclesiastical office, and to step up the sale of **indulgences** (pardons from temporal penalties for sins committed by lay Christians). From the twelfth century on, the Church had sold these certificates of grace—drawn from the "surplus" of good works left by the saints—to lay Christians who bought them as a means of speeding their own progress to Heaven or to benefit their relatives and friends in Purgatory. While the seven popes who ruled from Avignon were able administrators, their unsavory efforts at financial and political aggrandizement damaged the reputation of the Church.

The return of the papacy to Rome in 1377 was followed by one of the most devastating events in Church history: A rift between French and Italian factions of the College of Cardinals led to the election of two popes, one who ruled from Avignon, the other who ruled from Rome. This schism produced two conflicting claims to universal sovereignty and violent controversy within the Church. As each pope excommunicated the other, lay people questioned whether any Christian soul might enter Heaven. The Great Schism proved even more detrimental to Church prestige than the Avignon Papacy, for while the latter had prompted strong anticlerical feelings—even shock—in Christians who regarded Rome as the traditional home of the papacy, the Schism violated the very sanctity of the Holy Office. The ecumenical council at Pisa in 1409 tried to remedy matters by deposing both popes and electing another (the "Pisan pope"), but, when the popes at Rome and Avignon refused to step down, the Church was rent by *three* claims to the throne of Christ, a disgraceful situation that nevertheless lasted for almost a decade.

Anticlericalism and the Rise of Devotional Piety

In 1417, the Council of Constance healed the Schism, authorizing Pope Martin V to rule from Rome, but ecclesiastical discord continued. Fifteenth-century popes refused to acknowledge limits to papal power, thus hampering the efforts of church councils to exercise authority over the papacy. The Avignon Papacy and the Great Schism drew criticism from uneducated Christians and intellectuals alike. Two of the most vocal Church critics were the Oxford scholar John Wycliffe (ca. 1320–1384) and the Czech preacher Jan Hus (1373–1415). Wycliffe and Hus attacked papal power and wealth. They called for the abolition of pilgrimages and relic worship, insisting that Christian belief and practice must rest solidly in the Scriptures, which they sought to translate into the vernacular. The Church vigorously condemned Wycliffe and his bands of followers, who were called Lollards. Hus stood trial for heresy and was burned at the stake in 1415. Disenchanted with the institutional Church, lay Christians increasingly turned to private forms of devotional piety and to mysticism—the effort to know God directly and intuitively.

By its very nature, mysticism challenged the authority of the institutional Church and threatened its corporate hold over Catholicism. Throughout the Middle Ages, mystics—many of whom came from the cloister—had voiced their passionate commitment to Christ in writings that had incurred ecclesiastical disapproval. The Church condemned the lyrical descriptions of divine love penned by the thirteenth-century mystic Marguerite of Porete, for instance, and Marguerite herself was burned at the stake in 1310. Nonetheless, during the fourteenth century a flood of mystical and devotional literature engulfed Europe. The writings of the great fourteenth-century German mystics Johannes Eckhart (1260–1327) and Heinrich Suso, of the English Julian of Norwich, and of the Swedish Saint Bridget describe—in language that is at once intimate and ecstatic—the heightened personal experience of God. Such writings—the expression of pious individualism—mark an important shift from the scholastic reliance on religious authority to modern assertions of faith based on inner conviction.

Literature in Transition

The Social Realism of Boccaccio

Fourteenth-century Europeans manifested an unprecedented preoccupation with differences in class, gender, and personality. Both in literature and in art, there emerged a new fidelity to nature and to personal experience in the everyday world. This close, objective attention to human society and social interaction may be described as "social realism." The new realism is visible in the fourteenth-century Pisan fresco the *Triumph of Death*, which pictures a group of elegantly dressed men and women as they encounter three rotting corpses (see Figure 15.2). It is also evident in the many woodcuts of the Dance of Death (see Figure 15.3), where class differences are clearly drawn, and in the one hundred lively vernacular tales that make up Boccaccio's *Decameron* (part of the preface to which appeared earlier in this chapter). The framework for the *Decameron* is provided by the plague itself: Eager to escape the contagion, seven young women and three young men retreat to a villa in the suburbs of Florence, where, to pass the time, each tells a story on each of ten days. The stories, designed to distract the listeners from the horrors of the pandemic, are, in effect, amusing secular entertainments. They provide insight, however, into the social concerns and urban affairs of both the fictional narrators and Boccaccio's reading public.

Boccaccio borrowed many stories in the *Decameron* from popular fables, *fabliaux*, and contemporary incidents. His characters resemble neither the allegorical figures of *Everyman* nor the courtly stereotypes of *Lancelot*. Rather, they are realistically conceived, high-spirited individuals who prize cleverness, good humor, and the world of the flesh over the classic medieval virtues of chivalry, piety, and humility. A case in point is "The Tale of Filippa," a delightful story that recounts how a woman from the Italian town of Prato shrewdly escapes legal punishment for committing adultery. The heroine, Madame Filippa, candidly confesses that she has a lover; however, she bitterly protests the city ordinance that serves a double standard of justice: one law for men, another for women. Filippa's proposal that women should not waste the passions unclaimed by their husbands but, rather, be allowed to enjoy the "surplus" with others—a view that might enlist the support of modern-day feminists—rings with good-humored defiance. Boccaccio's Filippa strikes a sharp note of contrast with the clinging heroines of the medieval romance. While Guinevere, for instance, wallows in longing for Lancelot (see chapter 11), Filippa boldly defends her right to sexual independence. Like many a male protagonist, she fearlessly challenges and exploits fortune to serve her own designs.

The *Decameron* must have had special appeal for men and women who saw themselves as the heroes and heroines of precarious and rapidly changing times. And although toward the end of his life, Boccaccio repented writing what he himself called his "immoral tales," his stories, as the following example illustrates, remain a lasting tribute to the varieties of human affection and desire.

READING 3.2
Boccaccio's "Tale of Filippa" from the *Decameron*

Once upon a time, in the town of Prato, there used to be a law in force—as pernicious, indeed, as it was cruel, to the effect that any woman caught by her husband in the act of adultery with a lover, was to be burned alive, like any vulgar harlot who sold herself for money. 1

While this statute prevailed, a beautiful lady called Filippa, a devout worshiper of Cupid, was surprised in her bedroom one night by her husband, Rinaldo de' Pugliesi, in the arms of Lazzarino de' Guazzagliotri, a high-born Adonis of a youth of that city, whom she loved as the apple of her eye. 10

Burning with rage at the discovery, Rinaldo could scarcely forbear running upon them, and slaying them on the spot. Were it not for the misgivings he had for his own safety, if he gave vent to his wrath, he would have followed his impulse. However, he controlled his evil intent, but could not abandon his desire to demand of the town's statute, what it was unlawful for him to bring about—in other words, the death of his wife.

As he had no lack of evidence to prove Filippa's guilt, 20 he brought charges against her, early in the morning, at daybreak, and without further deliberation, had her summoned before the court.

Now Filippa was a high-spirited woman, as all women are who truly love, and though many of her friends and relatives advised her against going, she resolved to appear before the magistrate, preferring a courageous death, by confessing the truth, to a shameful life of exile, by a cowardly flight that would have proved her unworthy of the lover in whose arms she had lain that night. 30

Accordingly, she presented herself before the provost, with a large following of men and women who urged her to deny the charges. She asked him firmly and without moving a muscle what he desired of her. The provost, seeing her so beautiful, courteous and so brave—as her words demonstrated—felt a certain pity stirring in his heart at the thought that she might confess a crime for which he would be obliged to sentence her to death to save his honor. But then, seeing he could not avoid cross-questioning her on the charge proffered against 40 her, he said:

"Madam, here as you see, is Rinaldo, your husband, who is suing you on the grounds of finding you in the act of adultery with another man, and who therefore demands that I sentence you to death for it, as the law, which is in force, requires. I cannot pass sentence if you do not confess your guilt with your own lips. Be careful of your answers, then, and tell me if what your husband charges you with is true."

Filippa, not at all daunted, replied in a very agreeable 50 voice: "Your honor, it is true that Rinaldo is my husband, and that last night he found me in the arms of Lazzarino, where I had lain many another time, out of the great and true love I bear him. Far be it from me ever to deny it.

"As you are doubtless aware, laws should be equal for all, and should be made with the consent of those whom they affect. Such is not the case with this particular statute, which is stringent only with us poor women, who, after all, have it in our power to give pleasure to many more people than men ever could. Moreover, when this 60 law was drawn up, not a single woman gave her consent or was so much as invited to give it. For all these reasons, it surely deserves to be considered reprehensible. If you insist upon enforcing it, not at the risk of my body, but of your immortal soul, you are at liberty to do so; but before you proceed to pass judgment, I beg you to grant me a small request. Simply ask my husband whether I have ever failed to yield myself to him entirely, whenever he chose, and as often as he pleased."

Without waiting for the magistrate to question him, 70 Rinaldo immediately answered that there was no doubt Filippa had always granted him the joy of her body, at each and every request of his.

"That being the case, your honor," she went on, directly, "I'd like to ask him, since he has always had all he wanted of me and to his heart's content, what was I to do with all that was left over? Indeed, what am I to do with it? Throw it to the dogs? Isn't it far better to let it give enjoyment to some gentleman who loves me more than his life, than to let it go to waste or ruin?" 80

As it happened, the whole town had turned out to attend the sensational trial that involved a lady of such beauty and fame, and when the people heard her roguish question, they burst into a roar of laughter, shouting to a man that she was right and had spoken well.

That day, before court was adjourned, that harsh statute was modified at the magistrate's suggestion to hold only for such women as made cuckolds of their husbands for love of money.

As for Rinaldo, he went away crest-fallen at his mad venture, while Filippa returned home victorious, feeling in her joy that she had, in a sense, been delivered from the flames.

90

◆

The Feminism of Christine de Pisan

Just decades after Boccaccio took the woman's view in the "Tale of Filippa," the world's first feminist writer, Christine de Pisan (1365–1428?), emerged in France. The daughter of an Italian physician, Christine wedded a French nobleman when she was fifteen—medieval women usually married in their mid to late teens. Ten years later, when her husband died, Christine was left to support three children, a task she met by becoming the first female professional writer (Figure 15.6; see also Frontispiece, p. ii). Christine attacked the long antifemale

Figure 15.6 *Christine de Pisan at Her Writing Desk*, frontispiece to Christine's *Livre de la Mutacion de Fortune*, early fifteenth century. Bibliothèque Royale, Brussels, MS9508, f.2r.

tradition that had demeaned women and denied them the right to a university education. Her feminism is all the more significant because it occurred in a time in which men were making systematic efforts to restrict female inheritance of land and female membership in the guilds. In an early poem, the "Epistle to the God of Love" (1399), she protested the persistent antifemale bias of churchmen and scholars with these words:

> Some say that many women are deceitful,
> Wily, false, of little worth;
> Others that too many are liars,
> Fickle, flighty, and inconstant;
> Still others accuse them of great vices,
> Blaming them much, excusing them nothing,
> Thus do clerics, night and day,
> First in French verse, then in Latin,
> Based on who knows what books
> That tell more lies than drunkards do.

Christine was keenly aware of the fact that Western literary tradition did not offer a representative picture of women's importance to society. Eager to correct this inequity, she became a spokesperson for female achievements and talents. In her *Book of the City of Ladies* (1405), Christine attacks male misogyny and exalts the accomplishments of famous women throughout the ages. Patterned as an allegorical debate, *The City of Ladies* pictures Christine herself "interviewing" three goddesses—Lady Reason, Lady Rectitude, and Lady Justice—as she seeks moral guidance on matters such as whether women can and should be educated in the same manner as men (I.27) and why men claim it is not good for women to be educated at all (II.36). Excerpts from these two portions of Christine's landmark feminist work follow.

READING 3.3

From Christine de Pisan's
Book of the City of Ladies

Book I. 27 Christine Asks Reason Whether God Has Ever Wished to Ennoble the Mind of Woman With the Loftiness of the Sciences; and Reason's Answer.

. . . please enlighten me again, whether it has ever pleased this God, who has bestowed so many favors on women, to honor the feminine sex with the privilege of the virtue of high understanding and great learning, and whether women ever have a clever enough mind for this. I wish very much to know this because men maintain that the mind of women can learn only a little."

She answered, "My daughter, since I told you before, you know quite well that the opposite of their opinion is true, and to show you this even more clearly, I will give you proof through examples. I tell you again—and don't doubt the contrary—if it were customary to send daughters to school like sons, and if they were then taught the natural sciences, they would learn as thoroughly and

1

10

understand the subtleties of all the arts and sciences as well as sons. And by chance there happen to be such women, for, as I touched on before, just as women have more delicate bodies than men, weaker and less able to perform many tasks, so do they have minds that are freer and sharper whenever they apply themselves." 20

"My lady, what are you saying? With all due respect, could you dwell longer on this point, please. Certainly men would never admit this answer is true, unless it is explained more plainly, for they believe that one normally sees that men know more than women do."

She answered, "Do you know why women know less?"

"Not unless you tell me, my lady."

"Without the slightest doubt, it is because they are not involved in many different things, but stay at home, where it is enough for them to run the household, and 30 there is nothing which so instructs a reasonable creature as the exercise and experience of many different things."

"My lady, since they have minds skilled in conceptualizing and learning, just like men, why don't women learn more?"

She replied, "Because, my daughter, the public does not require them to get involved in the affairs which men are commissioned to execute, just as I told you before. It is enough for women to perform the usual duties to which they are ordained. As for judging from experience, since 40 one sees that women usually know less than men, that therefore their capacity for understanding is less, look at men who farm the flatlands or who live in the mountains. You will find that in many countries they seem completely savage because they are so simple-minded. All the same, there is no doubt that Nature provided them with the qualities of body and mind found in the wisest and most learned men. All of this stems from a failure to learn, though, just as I told you, among men and women, some possess better minds than others. . . . 50

Book II. 36 Against Those Men Who Claim It Is Not Good for Women to Be Educated.

Following these remarks, I, Christine, spoke, "My lady, I realize that women have accomplished many good things and that even if evil women have done evil, it seems to me, nevertheless, that the benefits accrued and still accruing because of good women—particularly the wise and literary ones and those educated in the natural science whom I mentioned above—outweigh the evil. Therefore, I am amazed by the opinion of some men who claim that they do not want their daughters, wives, or kinswomen to be educated because their mores would be ruined as a result." 60

She responded, "Here you can clearly see that not all opinions of men are based on reason and that these men are wrong. For it must not be presumed that mores necessarily grow worse from knowing the moral sciences, which teach the virtues, indeed, there is not the slightest doubt that moral education amends and ennobles them. How could anyone think or believe that whoever follows good teaching or doctrine is the worse for it? Such an opinion cannot be expressed or maintained. I do not mean that it would be good for a man or a woman to 70 study the art of divination or those fields of learning which are forbidden—for the holy Church did not remove them from common use without good reason—but it

should not be believed that women are the worse for knowing what is good.

"Quintus Hortensius,[1] a great rhetorician and consummately skilled orator in Rome, did not share this opinion. He had a daughter, named Hortensia, whom he greatly loved for the subtlety of her wit. He had her learn letters and study the science of rhetoric, which she 80 mastered so thoroughly that she resembled her father Hortensius not only in wit and lively memory but also in her excellent delivery and order of speech—in fact, he surpassed her in nothing. As for the subject discussed above, concerning the good which comes about through women, the benefits realized by this woman and her learning were, among others, exceptionally remarkable. That is, during the time when Rome was governed by three men, this Hortensia began to support the cause of women and to undertake what no man dared to 90 undertake. There was a question whether certain taxes should be levied on women and on their jewelry during a needy period in Rome. This woman's eloquence was so compelling that she was listened to, no less readily than her father would have been, and she won her case.

"Similarly, to speak of more recent times, without searching for examples in ancient history, Giovanni Andrea, a solemn law professor in Bologna not quite sixty years ago, was not of the opinion that it was bad for women to be educated. He had a fair and good daughter, 100 named Novella, who was educated in the law to such an advanced degree that when he was occupied by some task and not at leisure to present his lectures to his students, he would send Novella, his daughter, in his place to lecture to the students from his chair. And to prevent her beauty from distracting the concentration of her audience, she had a little curtain drawn in front of her. In this manner she could on occasion supplement and lighten her father's occupation. He loved her so much that, to commemorate her name, he wrote a book 110 of remarkable lectures on the law which he entitled *Novella super Decretalium*, after his daughter's name.

"Thus, not all men (and especially the wisest) share the opinion that it is bad for women to be educated. But it is very true that many foolish men have claimed this because it displeased them that women knew more than they did. Your father, who was a great scientist and philosopher, did not believe that women were worth less by knowing science; rather, as you know, he took great pleasure from seeing your inclination to learning. The 120 feminine opinion of your mother, however, who wished to keep you busy with spinning and silly girlishness, following the common custom of women, was the major obstacle to your being more involved in the sciences. But just as the proverb already mentioned above says, 'No one can take away what Nature has given,' your mother could not hinder in you the feeling for the sciences which you, through natural inclination, had nevertheless gathered together in little droplets. I am sure that, on account of these things, you do not think you are worth 130 less but rather that you consider it a great treasure for yourself; and you doubtless have reason to."

And I, Christine, replied to all of this, "Indeed, my lady, what you say is as true as the Lord's Prayer."

————————◆————————

[1]Quintus Hortensius (114–50 B.C.E.).

The Social Realism of Chaucer

Geoffrey Chaucer (1340–1400) was a contemporary of Boccaccio and Christine de Pisan and one of the greatest masters of fourteenth-century vernacular literature. A middle-class civil servant, soldier, and diplomat, and a citizen of the bustling city of London, Chaucer left an indelible image of his time in a group of stories known as the *Canterbury Tales*. Modeled broadly on Boccaccio's *Decameron*, this versified human comedy was framed by Chaucer in the setting of a pilgrimage whose participants tell stories to entertain each other while traveling to the shrine of Saint Thomas à Becket in Canterbury. Chaucer's twenty-nine pilgrims, who include a miller, a monk, a plowman, a knight, a priest, a scholar, and a prioress, provide a literary cross-section of late medieval society. Although they are type characters, they are also individual personalities. (The Pardoner, for instance, is portrayed as effeminate, while the Wife of Bath is lusty.) Chaucer characterizes them by description, by their lively and humorous conversations, and by the twenty stories they tell, which range from moral tales and beast fables to *fabliaux* of the most risqué and bawdy sort.

Like his medieval predecessors, Chaucer tended to moralize, reserving special scorn for clerical abuse and human hypocrisy. But unlike his forebears, whose generalized view of human nature often produced stereotypes, Chaucer brought his characters to life by means of memorable details. His talent in this direction is best realized through a brief comparison. In a twelfth-century verse narrative called *Equitan*, written by Marie de France, a poet in the Norman court of England, we find the following description of the heroine:

> Very desirable was the lady; passing tender of body and sweet of vesture, coiffed and fretted with gold. Her eyes were blue, her face warmly colored, with a fragrant mouth, and a dainty nose. Certainly she had no peer in all the realm.

Compare Chaucer's descriptions of the Wife of Bath and the Miller (from the "Prologue"). Then, in direct comparison with the lines from *Equitan*, consider Chaucer's evocation of Alison (the Miller's wife) in "The Miller's Tale" which, though too long to reproduce here, is recommended to all who might enjoy a spicy yarn.

READING 3.4

From Chaucer's "Prologue" and "The Miller's Tale" in the *Canterbury Tales*

There was a good Wife from near Bath, but she was   1
somewhat deaf, which was a shame. She had such skill in clothmaking that she surpassed the weavers of Ypres and Ghent. In all her parish there was no woman who could go before her to the offertory; and if someone did, the Wife of Bath was certainly so angry that she lost all charitable feeling. Her kerchiefs were of fine texture; those she wore upon her head on Sunday weighed, I swear, ten pounds. Her fine scarlet hose were carefully tied, and her shoes were uncracked and new. Her face was bold and fair and red.   10
All of her life she had been an estimable woman: she had had five husbands, not to mention other company in her youth—but of that we need not speak now. And three times she had been to Jerusalem; she had crossed many a foreign river; she had been to Rome, to Bologna, to St. James' shrine in Galicia, and to Cologne. About journeying through the country she knew a great deal. To tell the truth she was gap-toothed. She sat her gentle horse easily, and wore a fine headdress with a hat as broad as a buckler or a shield, a riding skirt about her large hips, and a pair of sharp   20
spurs on her heels. She knew how to laugh and joke in company, and all the remedies of love, for her skill was great in that old game.

. . . .

The Miller was a very husky fellow, tremendous in bone and in brawn which he used well to get the best of all comers; in wrestling he always won the prize. He was stocky, broad, and thickset. There was no door which he could not pull off its hinges or break by ramming it with his head. His beard was as red as any sow or fox, and as broad as a spade. At   the right on top of his nose he had a wart, from which there   30
grew a tuft of hairs red as the bristles of a sow's ears, and his nostrils were wide and black. A sword and a shield hung at his side. His mouth was as huge as a large furnace, and he was a jokester and a ribald clown, most of whose jests were of sin and scurrility. He knew quite well how to steal grain and charge thrice over, but yet he really remained reasonably honest. The coat he wore was white and the hood blue. He could play the bagpipe well and led us out of town to its music.

. . . .

The young wife was pretty, with a body as neat and graceful   40
as a weasel. She wore a checked silk belt, and around her loins a flounced apron as white as fresh milk. Her smock was white also, embroidered in front and in back, inside and outside and around the collar, with coal-black silk. The strings of her white hood were of the same material as her collar; her hair was bound with a wide ribbon of silk set high on her head. And, truly, she had a wanton eye. Her eyebrows were plucked thin and were arched and black as any sloe.[1] She was even more delightful to look at than a young, early-ripe pear tree, and she was softer than lamb's   50
wool. A leather purse, with a silk tassel and metal ornaments, hung from her belt. In all the world there is no man so wise that, though he looked far and near, he could imagine so gay a darling or such a wench. Her coloring was brighter than that of a coin newly forged in the Tower, and her singing was as loud and lively as a swallow's sitting on a barn. In addition, she could skip about and play like any kid or calf following its mother. Her mouth was as sweet as honey or mead, or a pile of apples laid up in hay or heather. She was as skittish as a young colt, and tall and straight   60
as a mast or wand. On her low collar she wore a brooch as broad as the boss on a shield. Her shoes were laced high on her legs. She was a primrose, a trillium,[2] fit to grace the bed of any lord or to marry any good yeoman. . . .

───────────── ◆ ─────────────

[1] A small, dark berry.   [2] A lily.

Figure 15.7 Giotto, *Madonna Enthroned*, ca. 1310. Tempera on panel, 10 ft. 8 in. × 6 ft. 8 in.
Uffizi Gallery, Florence. Scala/Art Resource, New York.

Chaucer uses sprightly similes ("graceful as a weasel," "as sweet as honey") and vivid details ("a checked silk belt," "high laced" shoes) to bring alive the personality and physical presence of the Miller's wife. (He also hints at the contradiction between her chaste exterior and her sensual nature, a major feature in the development of the story in which she figures.) By comparison, Marie de France's portrait is a pallid and stereotypical adaptation of the standard medieval female image: the courtly lady, the Virgin Mary, and the female saint. Chaucer's humanizing techniques bring zesty realism to both his pilgrim-narrators and the characters featured in their tales. Writing in the everyday language of his time (Middle English, as distinguished from the more Germanic Old English that preceded it), Chaucer shaped the development of English literature, much as Dante, a century earlier, had influenced Italian poetry.

Art and Music in Transition

Giotto's New Realism

A half century before Boccaccio and Chaucer began to write, the Florentine artist Giotto (1266–1337) anticipated the shift to realism that accompanied the transition from medieval to modern times. A comparison of Cimabue's *Madonna Enthroned*, completed around 1290 (see chapter 13), with Giotto's rendering of the same subject executed in 1310 (Figure **15.7**), provides visual evidence of that shift. Cimabue's Virgin looks back to the flat, decorative, and idealized style of Byzantine icons, while Giotto's Madonna—robust, lifelike, and set in deep space—anticipates the pictorialism and humanism of Italian Renaissance painting (see chapter 17). As with Cimabue, Giotto shows an oversized Virgin on a Gothic throne that is set against a gold background. But Giotto renounces the graceful Gothic line that etherealizes Cimabue's Madonna. Instead, by means of *chiaroscuro* (the use of light and shade), Giotto invests the form with an imposing three-dimensional presence (note the forward projection of her knees, which gives the sense of physical support for the baby Jesus). Instead of placing the angels above one another around the throne, Giotto arranges them in positions that define their presence in three-dimensional space. In contrast with Cimabue's stylized and idealized Madonna, Giotto has created a natural and lifelike image.

Giotto brought this same naturalism to his frescoes. In 1303, the wealthy banker Enrico Scrovegni commissioned Giotto to paint a series of frescoes for the family

Figure 15.8 Giotto, *Lamentation*, 1305–1306. Fresco, 7 ft. 7 in. × 7 ft. 9 in. Arena Chapel, Padua.

chapel in Padua. On the walls of the Arena Chapel, Giotto illustrated familiar episodes from the narrative cycle that recounts the lives of the Virgin and Christ (Figure 15.9). While wholly traditional in subject matter (see chapter 9), the enterprise constituted an innovative approach to representation: Giotto transformed the tiny chapel into a theater in which individual events, as viewed from the center of the chapel and lit from the west, appear to take place in real space. This illusionistic approach to representation is also evident in the individual scenes in the cycle. For the Lamentation over Jesus (Figure 15.8), Giotto gave weight and volume to figures whose nobility and dignity call to mind classical sculpture (see chapter 6). Giotto placed these figures in a shallow but carefully defined theatrical space delimited by craggy rocks and a single, barren tree. He enhanced dramatic expression by subtly varying the gestures of lament among the ten principal witnesses and by introducing emphatically grief-stricken responses among the ten angels that flutter above the scene. Like the characters in Boccaccio's *Decameron* and Chaucer's *Canterbury Tales*, Giotto's figures are convincingly human: While they are not individualized to the point of portraiture, neither are they stereotypes. Giotto's style advanced the trend toward realism already evident in late Gothic sculpture (see chapter 13). At the same time, it gave substance to the spirit of lay piety and individualism that marked the fourteenth century.

Devotional Realism and Portraiture

In all of the arts, realism enhanced the devotional mood of the age. Traditional scenes of the lives of Christ and the Virgin became at once more pictorial and detailed, a reflection of the new concern with Christ's human nature and his suffering. The image of the crucified Christ, which had been a popular object of veneration since the tenth century, was now depicted with a new expressive intensity. One anonymous German artist of the mid-fourteenth century rendered the crucified Jesus with an emaciated torso, wiry hair, and arms as rigid as the wood from which they were carved (Figure 15.10). The sculpture captures the torment of Christ's martyrdom with a fierce energy more frequently found in African wood sculpture (see Figures 19.7, 19.9) than in traditional European art.

The most notable personality in the domain of fourteenth-century monumental sculpture was the Dutch artist Claus Sluter (1380–1406). Sluter's *Well of Moses*, executed between 1395 and 1406 for the Carthusian monastery at Champmol just outside of Dijon,

Figure 15.10 *Crucifixion*, from Cologne, ca. 1380. Walnut, height 16⅛ in., armspan 14½ in. The Cleveland Museum of Art. Andrew R. and Martha Holden Jennings Fund. CMA 81.52.

France, was originally part of a 25-foot-tall stone fountain designed to celebrate the sacraments of Eucharist and Baptism. The Crucifixion group that made up the superstructure is lost, but the pedestal of the fountain with its six Old Testament prophets—Moses, David, Jeremiah, Zachariah, Daniel, and Isaiah—survives in its entirety (Figure 15.11). However, time has robbed the piece of the brightly colored paint and metal accessories (the scholarly Jeremiah bore a pair of copper spectacles) that once gave it a startlingly lifelike presence. Carrying scrolls engraved with their messianic texts, the life-sized prophets are swathed in deeply cut, voluminous draperies. Facial features are individualized so as to render each prophet with a distinctive personality. As in Giotto's *Lamentation*, mourning angels (at the corners of the pedestal above the heads of the prophets) cover their faces or wring their hands in gestures of anguish and despair. So intensely theatrical is the realism of the Champmol ensemble that scholars suspect Sluter might have been inspired by contemporary mystery plays, where Old Testament figures regularly appeared between the acts to "prophesy" New Testament events.

Devotional realism is equally apparent in illuminated manuscripts, and especially in the type of manuscript known as the Book of Hours. This guide to private prayer featured traditional recitations for the canonical hours—the sets of prayers recited daily at three-hour

Figure 15.9 (oppposite) Arena Chapel (Cappella Scrovegni), Padua, interior looking toward the choir. Height 42 ft., width 27 ft. 10 in., length 96 ft. Scala, Florence.

Figure 15.12 Jean Pucelle, *Betrayal* and *Annunciation* from the *Book of Hours of Jeanne d'Evreux, Queen of France*, 1325–1328. Miniature on vellum, each folio 3½ × 2⁷⁄₁₆ in. The Metropolitan Museum of Art, New York. The Cloisters Collection, 1954 (54.1.2. ff.15v and 16r).

intervals: matins, lauds, prime, terce, sext, none, vespers, and compline—as well as prayers to the Virgin and the saints. As manuals for personal piety and alternatives to daily Church ritual, Books of Hours were in great demand, especially among prosperous Christians. In the miniatures of these prayer books, scenes from sacred history are filled with realistic and homely details drawn from everyday life. Even miraculous events are made more believable as they are presented in lifelike settings and given new dramatic fervor. Such is the case with the animated *grisaille* (gray-toned) miniatures found in a prayer book executed around 1325 for Jeanne d'Evreux, Queen of France, by the French court painter Jean Pucelle (Figure 15.12). The Betrayal of

Christ, in contrast with a thirteenth-century version discussed earlier (see chapter 13), features accurately proportioned figures modeled in subtle *chiaroscuro*. In the Annunciation illustrated above, Pucelle employed receding diagonal lines to create the illusion of a "doll's house" that holds an oversized Madonna.

Pucelle's experiments in empirical perspective and his dramatic renderings of traditional subjects were carried further by the three brothers Jean, Pol, and Herman Limbourg, who flourished between 1385 and 1415. Their generous patron Jean, Duke of Berry and brother of the King of France, commissioned from them a remarkable series of Books of Hours illustrated with religious and secular subjects. For the calendar pages of the *Très Riches Heures* ("Very Precious Hours"), the Limbourgs painted scenes illustrating the mundane activities and labors peculiar to each month of the year. In the scene for the month of February—the first snowscape in Western art—three peasants warm themselves by the

Figure 15.11 (opposite) Claus Sluter, figure of Moses on the *Well of Moses*, Carthusian Monastery of Champmol, Dijon, France, 1395–1406. Painted stone, height approx. 6 ft. Photo: © James Austin, Cambridge, U.K., 1995.

fire, while others hurry to complete their chores (Figure 15.13). The Limbourgs show a new fascination with natural details: dovecote and beehives covered with new-fallen snow, sheep that huddle together in a thatched pen, smoke curling from a chimney, and even the genitalia of two of the laborers who warm themselves by the fire.

Devotional realism also overtook the popular subject of the Madonna and Child: The new image of the Virgin as a humble matron tenderly nurturing the Infant Jesus (Figure 15.14) replaced earlier, more hieratic representations of Mary as Queen of Heaven (see chapter 13). In paintings of the Virgin as humble matron and as "Nursing Madonna," the Infant is shown as a lively baby, not as the miniature adult of previous renderings. Fourteenth-century artists frequently introduced narrative details from mystery plays or from the writings of mystics like Saint Bridget of Sweden.

Figure 15.13 Limbourg brothers, *February*, plate 3 from the *Très Riches Heures* ("Very Precious Hours") *du Duc de Berry*, ca. 1413–1416. Illumination, 8¾ × 5⁵⁄₁₆ in. Musée Condé, Chantilly, France. Giraudon, Paris.

Figure 15.14 Ambrogio Lorenzetti, *Madonna del Latte* ("Nursing Madonna"), ca. 1340. Fresco. San Francesco, Siena, Italy. Alinari/Art Resource, New York.

Indeed, the interchange of imagery between devotional literature, medieval drama, and the visual arts was commonplace.

In light of the growing interest in the human personality—so clearly revealed in the literature of Boccaccio and Chaucer—it is no surprise that fourteenth-century artists produced the first portrait paintings since classical antiquity. Many such portraits appear in manuscripts. In panel painting, the anonymous portrait of John the Good, King of France (Figure 15.15), documents the new consciousness of the particular as opposed to the generalized image of humankind.

Figure 15.15 *King John the Good*, ca. 1356–1359(?). Canvas on panel, 21⅞ × 13⅜ in. Louvre, Paris. Photo: © R.M.N., Paris.

The *Ars Nova* in Music

Imagination and diversity characterized fourteenth-century music, which composers of that era self-consciously labeled the *ars nova* ("new art"). The music of the *ars nova* featured increased rhythmic complexity and aural expressiveness, achieved in part by **isorhythm** (literally, "same rhythm"): the close repetition of identical rhythmic patterns in different portions of a composition. Isorhythm, which gave unprecedented unity to a musical composition, reflected a new interest in the manipulation of pitches and rhythms.

In France, the leading proponent of the *ars nova* was the French poet, priest, and composer Guillaume de Machaut (1300–1377). Like the Limbourg brothers, Machaut held commissions from the French aristocracy, including the Duke of Berry. Machaut's most important musical achievement was his *Messe de Notre Dame* (*Mass*

of Our Lady). Departing from the medieval tradition of treating the Mass as five separate compositions (based on Gregorian chant), he unified the parts into a single musical composition. He is the first known composer to have provided this type of unified setting for the textually fixed portions of the Mass. Machaut's effort at coherence of design is clear evidence that composers had begun to rank musical effect as equal to liturgical function. He also added to the Mass a sixth movement, the "Ite missa est."♪ Machaut's new treatment of the Catholic liturgy set a precedent for such composers as the sixteenth-century Palestrina and the baroque master Johann Sebastian Bach (see chapter 21). Machaut's sacred compositions represent only a small part of his total musical output. Typical of the trend toward secular music are his polyphonic **ballades** (secular songs), which look back to the music of the *trouvères*. They introduce new warmth and lyricism, as well as vivid poetic imagery—features that parallel the humanizing currents in fourteenth-century art and literature.

Although fourteenth-century polyphony involved both voices and instruments, manuscripts of the period did not usually specify whether a given part of a piece was instrumental or vocal. Custom probably dictated the performance style, not only for vocal and instrumental ensembles, but for dance as well. Outside France, polyphonic music flourished. The blind Italian composer Francesco Landini (ca. 1325–1397) produced graceful instrumental compositions and eloquent two- and three-part songs. Landini's 150 works constitute more than one third of the surviving music of the fourteenth century—evidence of his enormous popularity. Italian composers anticipated Renaissance style (see chapter 17) with florid polyphonic compositions that featured a close relationship between musical parts. The *caccia* (Italian for "chase"), for instance, which dealt with such everyday subjects as hunting, was set to lively music in which one voice part "chased" another. Another popular fourteenth-century polyphonic composition, the **round**, featured successive voices that repeated a single melody (as in "Row, Row, Row Your Boat"). The English round "Sumer is icumen in"♪ is an example of fourteenth-century polyphony at its freshest and most buoyant.

SUMMARY

The fourteenth century witnessed the transition from medieval to early modern culture in the West. During this era, violence uprooted tradition, corruption bred cynicism, and widespread death generated insecurity and fear. The two great catalysts of the age—the Black

---

♪ See Music Listening Selections at end of chapter.

Death and the Hundred Years' War—brought about a collapse of the medieval synthesis marked by distinct political, military, and economic changes, including the decline of feudalism and manorialism. By the end of the century, the population of Western Europe had declined by approximately sixty percent. At the same time, as a result of the Avignon Papacy and the Great Schism, the Church of Rome lost, in great measure, its aura of sanctity. Demands for Church reform echoed throughout the fourteenth century (though actual reform would not occur for nearly two more centuries).

Rising secularism paralleled the decline of the Church. In the wake of the Black Death and during the Great Schism, Boccaccio and Chaucer penned vernacular tales to entertain urban audiences. Rejecting literary stereotypes, allegorical intent, and religious purpose, these writers brought to life the personalities of self-motivated, contemporary men and women. In France, Chaucer's contemporary Christine de Pisan ushered in the birth of feminism in Western literature.

The new realism of fourteenth-century literature was also evident in the visual arts, both in the rise of portraiture and in a more humanized and personal approach to traditional religious subjects such as that seen in the art of Giotto. In manuscript illumination and in devotional sculpture, as in panel and fresco painting, true-to-life narrative detail and emotional expressiveness came to replace Gothic abstraction and stylization. The term *ars nova*, coined by composers of that time to describe the trend toward novel rhythmic and harmonic patterns in music, is, therefore, equally appropriate for all of the arts of the fourteenth century.

If medieval people thought and acted communally, as members of a manor, a guild, or the Holy Church, fourteenth-century Westerners began to see themselves in terms of class, gender, and personality—categories that are essentially secular and modern. An era of turmoil and yet of remarkable artistic productivity, the fourteenth century challenged the feudal and corporate traditions of medieval life in the West, introducing new kinds of warfare, new forms of political organization, and a general retreat from the all-embracing spirituality of medieval Christendom.

GLOSSARY

ars nova (Latin, "new art") a term used for the music of fourteenth-century Europe to distinguish it from that of the old art (*ars antiqua*); it featured new rhythms, new harmonies, and more complicated methods of musical notation

ballade a secular song that tells a story in simple verse, usually repeating the same music for each stanza

caccia (Italian, "chase") a lively fourteenth-century Italian musical form that deals with everyday subjects, such as hunting and fishing

chiaroscuro (Italian, "light-dark") in drawing and painting, the manipulation of light and shade to produce the illusion of three-dimensional form

grisaille (French, "gray-toned") the use of exclusively gray tones in painting or drawing

indulgence a Church pardon from the temporal penalties for sins; the remission of purgatorial punishment

isorhythm the close repetition of identical rhythmic patterns in different sections of a musical composition

round a type of polyphonic composition that features successive voices repeating exactly the same melody and text

simony the buying or selling of Church office (see Simon Magus, Acts of the Apostles 8:9–24)

SUGGESTIONS FOR READING

Cole, Bruce. *Giotto: The Scrovegni Chapel, Padua*. New York: Braziller, 1993.

Gottfried, R. S. *The Black Death: Natural and Human Disaster in Medieval Europe*. New York: Free Press, 1984.

Howard, Donald. *The Idea of the Canterbury Tales*. Berkeley, Calif.: University of California Press, 1977.

Lerner, Robert E. *The Age of Adversity: The Fourteenth Century*. Ithaca, N.Y.: Cornell University Press, 1968.

Robertson, D. W. *A Preface to Chaucer, Studies in Medieval Perspectives*. Princeton, N.J.: Princeton University Press, 1963.

Stejskal, Karel. *European Art in the Fourteenth Century*, translated by T. Gottheinerová. London: Octopus Books, 1978.

Tuchman, Barbara. *A Distant Mirror: The Calamitous 14th Century*. New York: Ballantine, 1979.

Warner, Marina. *Joan of Arc: The Image of Female Heroism*. New York: Knopf, 1981.

Ziegler, Philip. *The Black Death*. London: Collins, 1969.

MUSIC LISTENING SELECTIONS

Cassette I Selection 13 Machaut, *Messe de Notre Dame* (*Mass of Our Lady*), "Ite missa est, Deo gratias" 1364.

Cassette I Selection 14 Anonymous, English round, "Sumer is icumen in," fourteenth century.

16
Classical Humanism in the Age of the Renaissance

While humanism, in its most general sense, describes an attitude centered on human interests and values, the term *classical humanism* refers to the revival of Greco-Roman culture—a phenomenon that gave the Renaissance (the word literally means "rebirth") its distinctly secular stamp. Classical culture did not disappear altogether with the fall of Rome in 476 C.E. It was preserved by countless Christian and Muslim scholars, revived by Charlemagne in the early Middle Ages, and championed by such medieval intellectuals as Aquinas (who took Aristotle as his master) and Dante (who chose Virgil as his guide). But the classical revival of the fourteenth to sixteenth centuries—the age of the Renaissance—generated new and more all-embracing attitudes toward Greco-Roman antiquity than any that had preceded it.

Renaissance humanists advocated the recovery and uncensored study of the entire body of Greek and Latin manuscripts and the self-conscious imitation of classical art and architecture. They regarded classical authority not exclusively as a means of clarifying Christian truths, but as the basis for a new appraisal of the role of the individual in the world order. Thus, although Renaissance humanists still prized the Liberal Arts as the basis for intellectual advancement, they approached the classics from a different point of view than that of their scholastic predecessors. If the Scholastics had studied the Greco-Roman legacy as the foundation for Christian dogma and faith, Renaissance humanists discovered in the Greek and Latin classics a rational guide to the fulfillment of human potential. Moreover, the Renaissance revival of humanism differed from earlier revivals because it attracted the interests of a broad base of the population and not a mere handful of theologians, as was the case, for instance, in Carolingian or later medieval times.

The humanists of the Renaissance were the cultural archeologists of their age. They uncovered new evidence of the splendor of Greco-Roman antiquity and consumed the fruits of their Western heritage. Unattached to any single school or university, this new breed of humanists pursued what the ancient Romans had called *studia humanitatis*, a program of study that embraced grammar, rhetoric, history, poetry, and moral philosophy. These branches of learning fostered training in the moral and aesthetic areas of human knowledge—the very areas of experience with which this textbook is concerned. While such an educational curriculum was assuredly not antireligious—indeed, most Renaissance humanists were devout Catholics—its focus was secular rather than religious. For these humanists, life on earth was not a vale of tears but, rather, an extended occasion during which human beings might cultivate their unique talents and abilities. Classical humanists saw no conflict, however, between humanism and religious belief. They viewed their intellectual mission as both pleasing to God and advantageous to society in general. Humanism, then, grounded in a reevaluation of classical literature and art, represented a shift in emphasis rather than an entirely new pursuit; it involved a turning away from exclusively otherworldly preoccupations to a robust, this-worldly point of view.

Italy: Birthplace of the Renaissance

The Renaissance designates that period in European history between roughly 1300 and 1600, during which time the revival of classical humanism spread from its birthplace in Florence, Italy, throughout Western Europe. Italy was the homeland of Roman antiquity, the splendid ruins of which stood as reminders of the greatness of classical civilization. The least feudalized part of the medieval world and Europe's foremost commercial and financial center, Italy had traded with Southwest Asian cities even in the darkest days of the Dark Ages. It had also maintained cultural contacts with Byzantium, the heir to Greek culture. The cities of Italy, especially Venice and Genoa (Map 16.1), had profited financially from the Crusades (see chapter 11) and—despite the ravages of the plague—continued to enjoy a high level of commercial prosperity. In fourteenth-

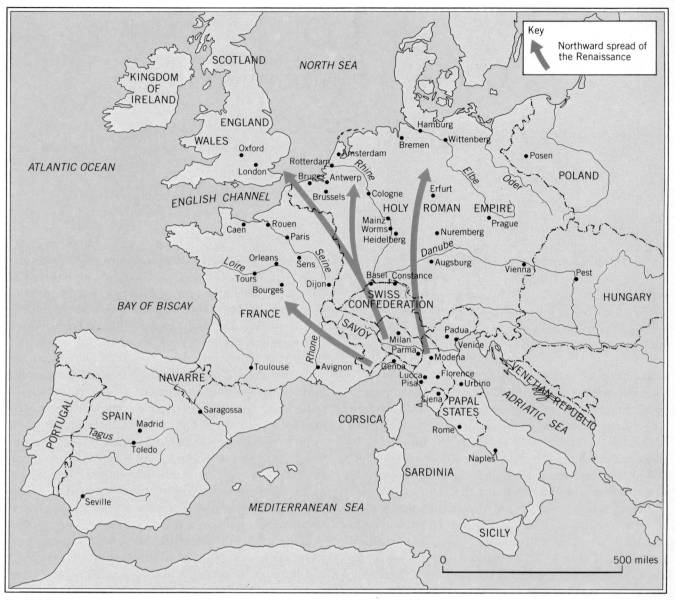

Map 16.1 Renaissance Europe, ca. 1500.

century Florence, shopkeepers invented double-entry bookkeeping to maintain systematic records of transactions in what was the soundest currency in the West: the Florentine gold florin.

The pursuit of money and leisure, rather than a preoccupation with feudal and chivalric obligations, marked the lifestyle of merchants and artisans who lived in the bustling city-states of Italy. Here especially, the Avignon Papacy and the Great Schism had produced a climate of anticlericalism and intellectual skepticism. Middle-class men and women challenged canonical sources of authority that frowned upon profit-making and the accumulation of wealth. In this materialistic and often only superficially religious society, the old medieval values no longer made sense, while those of pre-Christian antiquity seemed more compatible with

the secular interests and ambitions of the rising merchant class. The ancient Greeks and Romans were indeed ideal historical models for the enterprising citizens of the Italian city-states.

Politically, Renaissance Italy had much in common with ancient Greece. Independent and disunited, the city-states of Italy, like those of ancient Greece, were fiercely competitive. As in golden-age Greece, commercial rivalry among the Italian city-states led to frequent civil wars. In Italy, however, such wars were not always fought by citizens (who, as merchants, were generally ill prepared for combat), but by *condottieri* (professional soldiers) whose loyalties, along with their services, were bought for a price. The papacy, a potential source of political leadership, made little effort to unify the rival Italian communes. Rather, as temporal governors of the

Papal States (the lands located in central Italy), Renaissance popes joined in the game of power politics, often allying with one group of city-states against another.

Italian Renaissance cities were ruled either by members of the petty nobility, by mercenary generals, or—as in the case of Florence and Venice—by wealthy middle-class families. In Florence, some one hundred families dominated political life. The most notable of these was the Medici, a wealthy banking family that rose to power during the fourteenth century and proceeded to take over the reins of state. Partly because the commercial ingenuity of the Medici enhanced the material status of the Florentine citizens, and partly because strong, uninterrupted leadership guaranteed local economic stability, the Medici ruled Florence for four generations. The Medici merchant-princes, especially Cosimo (1389–1464) and Lorenzo "the Magnificent" (1449–1492) (Figure 16.1; see also Part Opener, p. xvi), supported scholarship and patronized the arts. Affluence coupled with intellectual discernment and refined taste inspired the Medici to commission works from such artists as Brunelleschi, Botticelli, Verrocchio, and Michelangelo, who produced some of the West's most brilliant works of art. The Renaissance was a period when scholars, poets, painters, and civic leaders shared common interests, acknowledging one another as leaders of a vigorous cultural revival.

Figure 16.1 Andrea del Verrocchio, *Lorenzo de' Medici*, ca. 1478. Terra-cotta, 25⅞ × 23¼ × 12⅞ in. © 1998 Board of Trustees, National Gallery of Art, Washington, D.C. Samuel H. Kress Collection.

Petrarch: Father of Humanism

The most famous of the early Florentine humanists was the poet and scholar Francesco Petrarch (1304–1374). Often called the Father of Humanism, Petrarch devoted his life to the recovery, copying, and editing of Latin manuscripts. In quest of these ancient sources of wisdom, he traveled all over Europe, hand-copying manuscripts he could not beg or buy from monastic libraries, borrowing others from friends, and gradually amassing a private library of more than two hundred volumes. Petrarch was a tireless popularizer of classical studies. Reviving the epistolary (letter-writing) tradition that had practically disappeared since Roman times, he wrote hundreds of letters describing his admiration for antiquity and his enthusiasm for the classics, especially the writings of the Roman statesman Cicero (see chapter 7). In his letters, Petrarch eulogized and imitated Cicero's polished prose style, which stood in refined contrast to the corrupt Latin of his own time.

The intensity of Petrarch's passion for antiquity and his eagerness to rescue it from neglect come across powerfully in a letter addressed to his friend Lapo da Castiglionchio. Here, he laments the scarcity and incompetence of copyists, bemoans the fact that books that are difficult to understand have "sunk into utter neglect," and defends his ambition to preserve them, despite the inordinate amount of time it takes to copy them. (Such fervor, shared by his successors, surely motivated the invention of print technology within one hundred years of his death.) In the letter to Lapo, part of which is reproduced below, Petrarch vows to sacrifice the precious hours of his old age to the pleasures of copying Cicero (whom he calls fondly by his middle name, Tullius).

READING 3.5

From Petrarch's Letter to Lapo da Castiglionchio

Your Cicero has been in my possession four years and   1
more. There is a good reason, though, for so long a delay;
namely, the great scarcity of copyists who understand
such work. It is a state of affairs that has resulted in an
incredible loss to scholarship. Books that by their nature
are a little hard to understand are no longer multiplied,
and have ceased to be generally intelligible, and so have
sunk into utter neglect, and in the end have perished.
This age of ours consequently has let fall, bit by bit, some
of the richest and sweetest fruits that the tree of   10
knowledge has yielded; has thrown away the results of the
vigils and labors of the most illustrious men of genius,
things of more value, I am almost tempted to say, than
anything else in the whole world. . . .

But I must return to your Cicero. I could not do without
it, and the incompetence of the copyists would not let me
possess it. What was left for me but to rely upon my own

resources, and press these weary fingers and this worn and ragged pen into service? The plan that I followed was this. I want you to know it, in case you should ever have to grapple with a similar task. Not a single word did I read except as I wrote. But how is that, I hear someone say; did you write without knowing what it was that you were writing? Ah! but from the very first it was enough for me to know that it was a work of Tullius, and an extremely rare one too. And then as soon as I was fairly started I found at every step so much sweetness and charm, and felt so strong a desire to advance, that the only difficulty which I experienced in reading and writing at the same time came from the fact that my pen could not cover the ground so rapidly as I wanted it to, whereas my expectation had been rather that it would outstrip my eyes, and that my ardor for writing would be chilled by the slowness of my reading. So the pen held back the eye, and the eye drove on the pen, and I covered page after page, delighting in my task, and committing many and many a passage to memory as I wrote. For just in proportion as the writing is slower than the reading does the passage make a deep impression and cling to the mind.

And yet I must confess that I did finally reach a point in my copying where I was overcome by weariness; not mental, for how unlikely that would be where Cicero was concerned, but the sort of fatigue that springs from excessive manual labor. I began to feel doubtful about this plan that I was following, and to regret having undertaken a task for which I had not been trained; when suddenly I came across a place where Cicero tells how he himself copied the orations of—someone or other; just who it was I do not know, but certainly no Tullius, for there is but one such man, one such voice, one such mind. These are his words: "You say that you have been in the habit of reading the orations of Cassius[1] in your idle moments. But I," he jestingly adds, with his customary disregard of his adversary's feelings, "have made a practice of *copying* them, so that I might *have* no idle moments." As I read this passage I grew hot with shame, like a modest young soldier who hears the voice of his beloved leader rebuking him. I said to myself, "So Cicero copied orations that another wrote, and you are not ready to copy his? What ardor! what scholarly devotion! what reverence for a man of godlike genius!" These thoughts were a spur to me, and I pushed on, with all my doubts dispelled. If ever from my darkness there shall come a single ray that can enhance the splendor of the reputation which his heavenly eloquence has won for him, it will proceed in no slight measure from the fact that I was so captivated by his ineffable sweetness that I did a thing in itself most irksome with such delight and eagerness that I scarcely knew I was doing it at all.

So then at last your Cicero has the happiness of returning to you, bearing you my thanks. And yet he also stays, very willingly, with me; a dear friend, to whom I give the credit of being almost the only man of letters for whose sake I would go to the length of spending my time, when the difficulties of life are pressing on me so sharply and inexorably and the cares pertaining to my literary labors make the longest life seem far too short, in transcribing

compositions not my own. I may have done such things in former days, when I thought myself rich in time, and had not learned how stealthily it slips away: but I now know that this is of all our riches the most uncertain and fleeting; the years are closing in upon me now, and there is no longer any room for deviation from the beaten path. I am forced to practice strict economy; I only hope that I have not begun too late. But Cicero! he assuredly is worthy of a part of even the little that I have left. Farewell.

———————◆———————

Nothing in the letter to Lapo suggests that Petrarch was a devout Christian; yet, in fact, Petrarch's affection for Cicero was matched only by his devotion to Saint Augustine and his writings. Indeed, in their introspective tone and their expression of intimate feelings and desires, Petrarch's letters reveal the profound influence of Augustine's *Confessions*, a work that Petrarch deeply admired. Torn between Christian piety and his passion for classical antiquity, Petrarch experienced recurrent psychic conflict. In his writings we detect a gnawing and unresolved dissonance between the dual imperatives of his heritage: the Judeo-Christian will to believe and the classical will to reason. Such self-torment—evident in Petrarch's poetry, over three hundred examples of which make up the *Canzoniere* ("Songbook")—implies that Petrarch remained, in part, a medieval man. Yet it did not prevent him from pursuing worldly fame. At Rome in 1341, he proudly received the laurel crown for outstanding literary achievement (Figure **16.2**). The tradition, which looks back to the ancient Greek practice of honoring victors in the athletic games with wreaths made from the foliage of the laurel tree, survives in our modern honorary title "poet *laureate*."

The object of Petrarch's affection and the inspiration for the *Canzoniere* was a married Florentine woman named Laura de Sade. To Laura, Petrarch dedicated more than three hundred love lyrics, many of which were written after she died of bubonic plague in 1348. While Petrarch used Latin, the language of learning, for his letters and essays, he wrote his poems and songs in vernacular Italian. His favorite poetic form was the **sonnet**, a fourteen-line lyric poem. The sonnet form originated among the poets of Sicily, but it was Petrarch who brought it to perfection. Influenced by the "sweet style" of his Italian forebears and, more generally, by *troubadour* songs and Islamic lyric verse, Petrarch's sonnets are a record of his struggle between the flesh and the spirit. In their self-reflective and even self-indulgent tone, they are strikingly modern, especially where they explore Petrarch's love for Laura—and for love itself. In the first of the two sonnets below, Petrarch explores the conflicting emotional states evoked by his unfulfilled desire. These are phrased intriguingly in contrasting sets: peace/war, burn/freeze, tears/laughter, and so on.

---

[1]More probably Lucius Licenius Crassus (140–91 B.C.E.), one of the great Roman orators and a principal figure in Cicero's treatise *On Oratory*.

Figure 16.2 *Petrarch*, from a copy by Mrs. Arthur Lemon of the portrait in the Laurentian Library, Florence. Frontispiece from H. C. Hallow-Calthrop, *Petrarch, His Life and Times*. Putnam, 1907.

In the second sonnet, Petrarch employs vivid imagery— "a field without flowers," "[a] ring without gem"—to picture the void left by Laura's death.

READING 3.6
From Petrarch's *Canzoniere*

Sonnet 132

I find no peace and I am not at war;   1
I fear and hope, and I burn and I freeze;
I rise up to the sky, lie on earth's floor;
And I grasp nothing and I hug the trees.

She has jailed me, and nor opens nor shuts,   5
Nor keeps me for her own, nor tears the noose,
Love does not slay and does not set me loose,
He wants me nor alive nor out of ruts.

I see and have no eyes; no tongue, and cry;
I wish to perish and call help to fly;   10
And I abhor myself and love another.

I feed on grief, in tears and laugh I smother;
Death and life are the objects of my hate:
Lady, because of you, such is my state.

Sonnet 338

Death, you have left the world without its sun,   1
Gloomy and cold, Love blind and without arms,
Loveliness bare, and sick all beauty's charms,
Myself distressed and by this load undone,

Courtesy banished, honesty pretext: 5
I alone mourn, though not alone I should;
For you uprooted a clear shoot of good.
Torn the first valour, which will be the next?

They ought to weep, the earth, the sea, the air,
The human lineage that without her is   10
Like a field without flowers, ring without gem.

They did not know her while she was with them;
I did, who am left here and weep for this,
And the sky did, that with my grief grows fair.

———————————◆———————————

In his own time, Petrarch was acclaimed as the finest practitioner of the sonnet form. His sonnets were translated by Chaucer and set to music by Landini (see chapter 15). During the sixteenth century, Michelangelo Buonarroti in Italy and the English poets Thomas Wyatt, Edmund Spenser, and William Shakespeare (see chapter 18) wrote sonnets modeled on those of Petrarch. Petrarch's influence as a classical humanist was equally significant: He established the standards for the study of the Latin classics, and, by insisting on the union of ethics and eloquence, he pioneered the modern ideal of the educated individual. Although Petrarch never learned to read Greek, he encouraged his contemporaries and friends (including Boccaccio) to master the language of the first philosophers. Petrarch's passion for classical learning initiated something of a cult, which at its worst became an infatuation with everything antique, but which at its best called forth a diligent examination of the classical heritage.

Italian Renaissance Humanism

The effort to recover, copy, and produce accurate editions of classical writings dominated the early history of the Renaissance in Italy. By the middle of the fifteenth century, almost all of the major Greek and Latin manuscripts of antiquity were available to scholars. Throughout Italy, the small study retreat, or *studiolo*, filled with manuscripts, musical instruments, and the artifacts of scientific inquiry, came to be considered essential to the advancement of intellectual life; and wealthy patrons like Federico da Montefeltro, Duke of Urbino, commissioned elaborately designed private studies for their villas and palaces (Figure 16.3). Among the humanists of Italy, classical writings kindled new attitudes concerning the importance of active participation in civic life. Aristotle's view of human beings as

Figure 16.3 The *studiolo* of Federico da Montefeltro in the Palazzo Ducale, Urbino, Italy, 1476. Scala, Florence. Intarsia.

"political animals" (see chapter 4) and Cicero's glorification of duty to the state (see chapter 7) encouraged humanists to perceive that the exercise of civic responsibility was the hallmark of the cultivated individual. Such civic humanists as Leonardo Bruni and Coluccio Salutati, who served Florence as chancellors and historians during the Renaissance, defended the precept that one's highest good was activity in the public interest.

After the fall of Constantinople in 1453, Greek manuscripts and Greek scholars poured into Italy, contributing to the efflorescence of what the humanist philosopher Marsilio Ficino (1433–1499) called "a golden age." Encouraged by the availability of Greek resources and supported by his patron Cosimo de' Medici, Ficino translated the entire corpus of Plato's writings from Greek into Latin, making them available to Western scholars for the first time since antiquity. Ficino's translations and the founding of the Platonic Academy in Florence (financed by Cosimo) launched a reappraisal of Plato and the neoplatonists that had major consequences in the domains of art and literature. Plato's writings—especially the *Symposium*, in which love is exalted as a divine force—advanced the idea, popularized by Ficino, that "platonic" (or spiritual) love attracted the soul to God. Platonic love became a major theme among Renaissance poets and painters, who held that such love was inspired by physical beauty.

While Ficino was engaged in popularizing Plato, one of his most learned contemporaries, Giovanni Pico della Mirandola (1463–1494), undertook the translation of ancient literary works in Hebrew, Arabic, Latin, and Greek. Humanist, poet, and theologian, Pico sought not only to bring to light the entire history of human thought, but to prove that all intellectual expression shared the same divine purpose and design. This effort to discover a "unity of truth" in all philosophic thought—similar to but more comprehensive than the medieval quest for synthesis and so dramatically different from our own modern pluralistic outlook—dominated the arts and ideas of the High Renaissance (see chapter 17).

Pico's monumental efforts to recover the past and his reverence for the power of human knowledge typified Renaissance *individualism*—the assertion of the uniqueness of the human being. In Rome, at the age of twenty-four, Pico boldly challenged the Church to debate some nine hundred theological propositions. The young scholar did not get the chance to debate his theses, which blatantly challenged the institutional Church; indeed, he was persecuted for heresy and forced to flee Italy. As an introduction to the disputation, Pico had prepared the piece that has come to be called the *Oration on the Dignity of Man*. In this preface, Pico boldly affirms the perfectibility of the individual. The Renaissance idea of the rational person at the center of a rational universe is nowhere better described than in the following excerpt.

READING 3.7

From Pico's *Oration on the Dignity of Man*

. . . At long last . . . I feel that I have come to some 1
understanding of why man is the most fortunate of living things and, consequently, deserving of all admiration; of what may be the condition in the hierarchy of beings assigned to him, which draws upon him the envy, not of the brutes alone, but of the astral beings and of the very intelligences which dwell beyond the confines of the world. A thing surpassing belief and smiting the soul with wonder. Still, how could it be otherwise? For it is on this ground that man is, with complete justice, 10
considered and called a great miracle and a being worthy of all admiration.

Hear then, oh Fathers, precisely what this condition of man is; and in the name of your humanity, grant me your benign audition as I pursue this theme.

God the Father, the Mightiest Architect, had already raised, according to the precepts of His hidden wisdom, this world we see, the cosmic dwelling of divinity, a temple most august. He had already adorned the supercelestial region with Intelligences, infused the 20
heavenly globes with the life of immortal souls and set the fermenting dung-heap of the inferior world teeming with every form of animal life. But when this work was done, the Divine Artificer still longed for some creature which might comprehend the meaning of so vast an achievement, which might be moved with love at its beauty and smitten with awe at its grandeur. When, consequently, all else had been completed, . . . in the very last place, He bethought Himself of bringing forth man. Truth was, however, that there remained no 30
archetype according to which He might fashion a new offspring, nor in His treasure-houses the wherewithal to endow a new son with a fitting inheritance, nor any place, among the seats of the universe, where this new creature might dispose himself to contemplate the world. All space was already filled; all things had been distributed in the highest, the middle and the lowest orders. Still, it was not in the nature of the power of the Father to fail in this last creative élan; nor was it in the nature of that supreme Wisdom to hesitate through lack 40
of counsel in so crucial a matter; nor, finally, in the nature of His beneficent love to compel the creature destined to praise the divine generosity in all other things to find it wanting in himself.

At last, the Supreme Maker decreed that this creature, to whom He could give nothing wholly his own, should have a share in the particular endowment of every other creature. Taking man, therefore, this creature of indeterminate image, He set him in the middle of the world and thus spoke to him: 50
"We have given you, Oh Adam, no visage proper to yourself, nor any endowment properly your own, in order that whatever place, whatever form, whatever gifts you may, with premeditation, select, these same you may have and possess through your own judgment and decision. The nature of all other creatures is defined and restricted within laws which We have laid down; you, by contrast, impeded by no such restrictions, may, by your own free will, to whose custody We have assigned you, trace for yourself the lineaments of your own nature. I 60
have placed you at the very center of the world, so that from that vantage point you may with greater ease glance round about you on all that the world contains. We have made you a creature neither of heaven nor of earth, neither mortal nor immortal, in order that you may, as the free and proud shaper of your own being, fashion yourself in the form you may prefer. It will be in your power to descend to the lower, brutish forms of life; [or] you will be able, through your own decision, to rise again to the superior orders whose life is divine. . . ." 70

————————————◆————————————

Alberti and Renaissance *Virtù*

Although Pico's *Oration* was not circulated until after his death, its assertion of free will and its acclamation of the unlimited potential of the individual came to symbolize the collective ideals of the Renaissance humanists. In words hauntingly reminiscent of Sophocles (compare the choral eulogy for humankind in *Antigone*; see chapter 4), Pico gave voice to the optimistic view of the individual as free and perfectible. This view—basic to so much Renaissance literature—was central to the life and thought of the Florentine humanist Leon Battista Alberti (1404–1474) (Figure **16.4**). A mathematician, architect, engineer, musician, and playwright, Alberti's most original literary contribution (and that for which he was best known in his own time) was his treatise *On the Family*. Published in 1443, *On the Family* is the first sociological inquiry into the structure, function, and responsibilites of the family. It is also a moralizing treatise that defends the importance of a classical education and hard work as prerequisites for worldly success. In Alberti's view, skill, talent, fortitude, ingenuity, and the ability to determine one's destiny—qualities summed up in the single Italian word *virtù*—are essential to human enterprise. *Virtù*, Alberti observes, is not inherited; rather, it must be cultivated. Not to be confused with the English word "virtue," *virtù* describes the self-confident vitality of the self-made Renaissance individual.

In *On the Family*, Alberti warns that idleness is the enemy of human achievement, while the performance of "manly tasks" and the pursuit of "fine studies" are sure means to worldly fame and material fortune. Pointing to the success of his own family, he defends the acquisition of wealth as the reward of free-spirited *virtù*. The buoyant optimism so characteristic of the age of the Renaissance is epitomized in Alberti's statement that "man can do anything he wants." Alberti himself—architect, mathematician, and scholar—was living proof of that viewpoint.

Figure 16.4 Leon Battista Alberti, *Self-Portrait*, ca. 1435. Bronze, 7²⁹⁄₃₂ × 5¹¹⁄₃₂ in. © 1998 Board of Trustees, National Gallery of Art, Washington, D.C. Samuel H. Kress Collection.

READING 3.8

From Alberti's *On the Family*

. . . Let Fathers . . . see to it that their sons pursue the   1
study of letters assiduously and let them teach them to understand and write correctly. Let them not think they have taught them if they do not see that their sons have learned to read and write perfectly, for in this it is almost the same to know badly as not to know at all. Then let the children learn arithmetic and gain a sufficient knowledge of geometry, for these are enjoyable sciences suitable to young minds and of great use to all regardless of age or social status. Then let them turn once more to   10
the poets, orators, and philosophers. Above all, one must try to have good teachers from whom the children may learn excellent customs as well as letters. I should want my sons to become accustomed to good authors. I should want them to learn grammar from Priscian and Servius and to become familiar, not with collections of sayings and extracts, but with the works of Cicero, Livy,

and Sallust above all, so that they might learn the perfection and splendid eloquence of the elegant Latin tongue from the very beginning. They say that the same   20
thing happens to the mind as to a bottle: if at first one puts bad wine in it, its taste will never disappear. One must, therefore, avoid all crude and inelegant writers and study those who are polished and elegant, keeping their works at hand, reading them continuously, reciting them often, and memorizing them. . . .

Think for a moment: can you find a man—or even imagine one—who fears infamy, though he may have no strong desire for glory, and yet does not hate idleness and sloth? Who can ever think it possible to achieve   30
honors and dignity without the loving study of excellent arts, without assiduous work, without striving in difficult manly tasks. If one wishes to gain praise and fame, he must abhor idleness and laziness and oppose them as deadly foes. There is nothing that gives rise to dishonor and infamy as much as idleness. Idleness has always been the breeding-place of vice. . . .

Therefore, idleness which is the cause of so many evils must be hated by all good men. Even if idleness were not a deadly enemy of good customs and the cause of every   40 vice, as everyone knows it is, what man, though inept, could wish to spend his life without using his mind, his limbs, his every faculty? Does an idle man differ from a tree trunk, a statue, or a putrid corpse? As for me, one who does not care for honor or fear shame and does not act with prudence and intelligence does not live well. But one who lies buried in idleness and sloth and completely neglects good deeds and fine studies is altogether dead. One who does not give himself body and soul to the quest for praise and virtue is to be deemed 50 unworthy of life. . . .

. . . [Man] comes into this world in order to enjoy all things, be virtuous, and make himself happy. For he who may be called happy will be useful to other men, and he who is now useful to others cannot but please God. He who uses things improperly harms other men and incurs God's displeasure, and he who displeases God is a fool if he thinks he is happy. We may, therefore, state that man is created by Nature to use, and reap the benefits of, all things, and that he is born to be happy. . . . 60

. . . I believe it will not be excessively difficult for a man to acquire the highest honors and glory, if he perseveres in his studies as much as is necessary, toiling, sweating, and striving to surpass all others by far. It is said that man can do anything he wants. If you will strive with all your strength and skill, as I have said, I have no doubt you will reach the highest degree of perfection and fame in any profession. . . .

. . . To those of noble and liberal spirit, no occupations seem less brilliant than those whose purpose is to make 70 money. If you think a moment and try to remember which are the occupations for making money, you will see that they consist of buying and selling, lending and collecting. I believe that these occupations whose purpose is gain may seem vile and worthless to you, for you are of noble and lofty spirit. In fact, selling is a mercenary trade; you serve the buyer's needs, pay yourself for your work, and make a profit by charging others more than you yourself have paid. You are not selling goods, therefore, but your labors; you are 80 reimbursed for the cost of your goods, and for your labor you receive a profit. Lending would be a laudable generosity if you did not seek interest, but then it would not be a profitable business. Some say that these occupations, which we shall call pecuniary, always entail dishonesty and numerous lies and often entail dishonest agreements and fraudulent contracts. They say, therefore, that those of liberal spirit must completely avoid them as dishonest and mercenary. But I believe that those who judge all pecuniary occupations in this 90 manner are wrong. Granted that acquiring wealth is not a glorious enterprise to be likened to the most noble professions. We must not, however, scorn a man who is not naturally endowed for noble deeds if he turns to these other occupations in which he knows he is not inept and which, everyone admits, are of great use to the family and to the state. Riches are useful for gaining friends and praise, for with them we can help those in need. With wealth we can gain fame and prestige if we use it munificently for great and noble projects. . . . 100

Castiglione and *"l'uomo universale"*

By far the most provocative analysis of Renaissance individualism is that found in *The Book of the Courtier*, a treatise written between 1513 and 1518 by the Italian diplomat and man of letters Baldassare Castiglione (1478–1529) (Figure **16.5**). Castiglione's *Courtier* was inspired by a series of conversations that had taken place among a group of sixteenth-century aristocrats at the court of Urbino, a mecca for humanist studies located in central Italy. The subject of these conversations, which Castiglione probably recorded from memory, concerned the qualifications of the ideal Renaissance man and woman. Debating this subject at length, the members of the court arrived at a consensus that afforded the image of *l'uomo universale*, the well-rounded person. Castiglione reports that the ideal man should master all the skills of the medieval warrior and display the physical proficiency of a champion athlete. But, additionally, he must possess the refinements of a humanistic education. He must know Latin and Greek (as well as his own native language), be familiar with the classics, speak and write well, and be able to compose verse, draw, and play a musical instrument. Moreover, all that the Renaissance gentleman does, he should do with an air of nonchalance and grace, a quality summed up in the Italian word *sprezzatura*. This unique combination of breeding and education would produce a cultured individual to serve a very special end: the perfection of the state. For, as Book Four of *The Courtier* explains, the primary duty of *l'uomo universale* is to influence the ruler to govern wisely.

Although, according to Castiglione, the goal of the ideal gentleman was to cultivate his full potential as a human being, such was not the case with the Renaissance gentlewoman. The Renaissance woman should have a knowledge of letters, music, and art—that is, like the gentleman, she should be privileged with a humanistic education—but in no way should she violate that "soft and delicate tenderness that is her defining quality." Castiglione's peers agreed that "in her ways, manners, words, gestures, and bearing, a woman ought to be very unlike a man." Just as the success of the courtier depended on his ability to influence those who ruled, the success of the lady rested with her skills in entertaining the male members of the court.

Castiglione's handbook of Renaissance etiquette was based on the views of a narrow, aristocratic segment of society. But despite its selective viewpoint, it was immensely popular: It was translated into five languages and went through fifty-seven editions before the year 1600. Historically, *The Book of the Courtier* is an index to cultural changes that were taking place between medieval and early modern times. It departs from exclusively feudal and Christian educational ideals and formulates a program for the cultivation of both mind *and* body that has become fundamental to modern Western education. Representative also of the shift from medieval to modern values is Castiglione's preoccupation with manners rather than morals, that is, with *how* individuals act and how their actions may impress their peers, rather than with the intrinsic moral value of those actions.

READING 3.9

From Castiglione's *Book of the Courtier*

[Count Ludovico de Canossa says:] "I am of opinion that the principal and true profession of the Courtier ought to be that of arms; which I would have him follow actively above all else, and be known among others as bold and strong, and loyal to whomsoever he serves. And he will win a reputation for these good qualities by exercising them at all times and in all places, since one may never fail in this without severest censure. And just as among women, their fair fame once sullied never recovers its first lustre, so the reputation of a gentleman who bears arms, if once it be in the least tarnished with cowardice or other disgrace, remains forever infamous before the world and full of ignominy. Therefore the more our Courtier excels in this art, the more he will be worthy of praise. . . .

"Then coming to the bodily frame, I say it is enough if this be neither extremely short nor tall, for both of these conditions excite a certain contemptuous surprise, and men of either sort are gazed upon in much the same way that we gaze on monsters. Yet if we must offend in one of the two extremes, it is preferable to fall a little short of the just measure of height than to exceed it, for besides often being dull of intellect, men thus huge of body are also unfit for every exercise of agility, which thing I should much wish in the Courtier. And so I would have him well built and shapely of limb, and would have him show strength and lightness and suppleness, and know all bodily exercises that befit a man of war; whereof I think the first should be to handle every sort of weapon well on foot and on horse, to understand the advantages of each, and especially to be familiar with those weapons that are ordinarily used among gentlemen; for besides the use of them in war, where such subtlety in contrivance is perhaps not needful, there frequently arise differences between one gentleman and another, which afterwards result in duels often fought with such weapons as happen at the moment to be within reach; thus knowledge of this kind is a very safe thing. Nor am I one of those who say that skill is forgotten in the hour of need; for he whose skill forsakes him at such a time, indeed gives token that he has already lost heart and head through fear.

"Moreover I deem it very important to know how to wrestle, for it is a great help in the use of all kinds of weapons on foot. Then, both for his own sake and for that of his friends, he must understand the quarrels and differences that may arise, and must be quick to seize

Figure 16.5 Raphael, *Portrait of Baldassare Castiglione*, ca. 1515. Oil on canvas, approx. 30¼ × 26½ in. Louvre, Paris.

an advantage, always showing courage and prudence in all things. Nor should he be too ready to fight except when honor demands it. . . .

"There are also many other exercises, which although not immediately dependent upon arms, yet are closely connected therewith, and greatly foster manly sturdiness; and one of the chief among these seems to me to be the chase [hunting], because it bears a certain likeness to war: and truly it is an amusement for great lords and befitting a man at court, and furthermore it is seen to have been much cultivated among the ancients. It is fitting also to know how to swim, to leap, to run, to throw stones, for besides the use that may be made of this in war, a man often has occasion to show what he can do in such matters; whence good esteem is to be won, especially with the multitude, who must be taken into account withal. Another admirable exercise, and one very befitting a man at court, is the game of tennis, in which are well shown the disposition of the body, the quickness and suppleness of every member, and all those qualities that are seen in nearly every other exercise. Nor less highly do I esteem vaulting on horse, which although it be fatiguing and difficult, makes a man very light and dexterous more than any other thing; and besides its utility, if this lightness is accompanied by grace, it is to my thinking a finer show than any of the others.

"Our Courtier having once become more than fairly expert in these exercises, I think he should leave the others on one side: such as turning summersaults, rope-walking, and the like, which savor of the mountebank and little befit a gentleman.

"But since one cannot devote himself to such fatiguing exercises continually, and since repetition becomes very tiresome and abates the admiration felt for what is rare, we must always diversify our life with various occupations. For this reason I would have our Courtier sometimes descend to quieter and more tranquil exercises, and in order to escape envy and to entertain himself agreeably with everyone, let him do whatever others do, yet never departing from praiseworthy deeds, and governing himself with that good judgment which will keep him from all folly; but let him laugh, jest, banter, frolic and dance, yet in such fashion that he shall always appear genial and discreet, and that everything he may do or say shall be stamped with grace."

[Cesare Gonzaga says:] "But having before now often considered whence this grace springs, laying aside those men who have it by nature, I find one universal rule concerning it, which seem to me worth more in this matter than any other in all things human that are done or said: and that is to avoid affectation to the uttermost and as it were a very sharp and dangerous rock; and, to use possibly a new word, to practice in everything a certain nonchalance that shall conceal design and show that what is done and said is done without effort and almost without thought. . . ."

[Count Ludovico says:] "I think that what is chiefly important and necessary for the Courtier, in order to speak and write well, is knowledge; for he who is ignorant and has nothing in his mind that merits being heard, can neither say it nor write it.

"Next he must arrange in good order what he has to say or write; then express it well in words, which (if I do not err) ought to be precise, choice, rich and rightly formed, but above all, in use even among the masses; because such words as these make the grandeur and pomp of speech, if the speaker has good sense and carefulness, and knows how to choose the words most expressive of his meaning, and to exalt them, to mould position and order that they shall at a glance show and make known their dignity and splendor, like pictures placed in good and proper light.

"And this I say as well of writing as of speaking: in which however some things are required that are not needful in writing,—such as a good voice, not too thin and soft like a woman's, nor yet so stern and rough as to smack of the rustic's,—but sonorous, clear, sweet and well sounding, with distinct enunciation, and with proper bearing and gestures; which I think consist in certain movements of the whole body, not affected or violent, but tempered by a calm face and with a play of the eyes that shall give an effect of grace, accord with the words, and as far as possible express also, together with the gestures, the speaker's intent and feeling.

"But all these things would be vain and of small moment, if the thoughts expressed by the words were not beautiful, ingenious, acute, elegant and grave,— according to the need.

"I would have him more than passably accomplished in letters, at least in those studies that are called the humanities, and conversant not only with the Latin language but with the Greek, for the sake of the many different things that have been admirably written therein. Let him be well versed in the poets, and not less in the orators and historians, and also proficient in writing verse and prose, especially in this vulgar tongue of ours; for besides the enjoyment he will find in it, he will by this means never lack agreeable entertainment with ladies, who are usually fond of such things. And if other occupations or want of study prevent his reaching such perfection as to render his writings worthy of great praise, let him be careful to suppress them so that others may not laugh at him. . . .

"My lords, you must know that I am not content with the Courtier unless he be also a musician and unless, besides understanding and being able to read notes, he can play upon divers instruments. For if we consider rightly, there is to be found no rest from toil or medicine for the troubled spirit more becoming and praiseworthy in time of leisure, than this; and especially in courts, where besides the relief from tedium that music affords us all, many things are done to please the ladies, whose tender and gentle spirit is easily penetrated by harmony and filled with sweetness. Thus it is no marvel that in both ancient and modern times they have always been inclined to favor musicians, and have found refreshing spiritual food in music. . . .

"I wish to discuss another matter, which I deem of great importance and therefore think our Courtier ought by no means to omit: and this is to know how to draw and to have acquaintance with the very art of painting.

"And do not marvel that I desire this art, which to-day may seem to savor of the artisan and little to befit a gentleman; for I remember having read that the ancients, especially throughout Greece, had their boys of gentle birth study painting in school as an honorable and necessary thing, and it was admitted to the first rank of liberal arts; while by public edict they forbade that it be taught to slaves. Among the Romans too, it was held in highest honor. . . ."

[The discussion turns to defining the court lady. Giuliano de' Medici addresses the company of ladies and gentlemen:] ". . . although my lord Gaspar has said that the same rules which are set the Courtier serve also for the Lady, I am of another mind; for while some qualities are common to both and as necessary to man as to woman, there are nevertheless some others that befit woman more than man, and some are befitting man to which she ought to be wholly a stranger. The same I say of bodily exercises; but above all, methinks that in her ways, manners, words, gestures and bearing a woman ought to be very unlike a man; for just as it befits him to show a certain stout and sturdy manliness, so it is becoming in a woman to have a soft and dainty tenderness with an air of womanly sweetness in her every movement. . . .

"Now, if this precept be added to the rules that these gentlemen have taught the Courtier, I certainly think she ought to be able to profit by many of them, and to adorn herself with admirable accomplishments, as my lord Gaspar says. For I believe that many faculties of the mind are as necessary to woman as to man; likewise gentle birth, to avoid affectation, to be naturally graceful in all her doings, to be mannerly, clever, prudent, not arrogant, not envious, not slanderous, not vain, not quarrelsome, not silly, to know how to win and keep the favor of her mistress and of all others, to practice well and gracefully the exercises that befit women. I am quite of the opinion, too, that beauty is more necessary to her than to the Courtier, for in truth that woman lacks much who lacks beauty. . . .

[The Court Lady] "must have not only the good sense to discern the quality of him with whom she is speaking, but knowledge of many things, in order to entertain him graciously; and in her talk she should know how to choose those things that are adapted to the quality of him with whom she is speaking, and should be cautious lest occasionally, without intending it, she utter words that may offend him. Let her guard against wearying him by praising herself indiscreetly or by being too prolix. Let her not go about mingling serious matters with her playful or humorous discourse, or jests and jokes with her serious discourse. Let her not stupidly pretend to know that which she does not know, but modestly seek to do herself credit in that which she does know,—in all things avoiding affectation, as has been said. In this way she will be adorned with good manners, and will perform with perfect grace the bodily exercises proper to women; her discourse will be rich and full of prudence, virtue and pleasantness; and thus she will be not only loved but revered by everyone, and perhaps worthy to be placed side by side with this great Courtier as well in qualities of the mind as in those of the body. . . .

"Since I may fashion this Lady as I wish, not only am I unwilling to have her practice such vigorous and rugged manly exercises, but I would have her practice even those that are becoming to women, circumspectly and with that gentle daintiness which we have said befits her; and thus in dancing I would not see her use too active and violent movements, nor in singing or playing those abrupt and oft-repeated diminutions[1] which show more skill than sweetness; likewise the musical instruments that she uses ought, in my opinion, to be appropriate to this intent. Imagine how unlovely it would be to see a woman play drums, fifes or trumpets, or other like instruments; and this because their harshness hides and destroys that mild gentleness which so much adorns every act a woman does. Therefore when she starts to dance or make music of any kind, she ought to bring herself to it by letting herself be urged a little, and with a touch of shyness which shall show that noble shame which is the opposite of effrontery. . . .

"And to repeat in a few words part of what has been already said, I wish this Lady to have knowledge of letters, music, painting, and to know how to dance and make merry; accompanying the other precepts that have been taught the Courtier with discreet modesty and with the giving of a good impression of herself. And thus, in her talk, her laughter, her play, her jesting, in short, in everything, she will be very graceful, and will entertain appropriately, and with witticisms and pleasantries befitting her, everyone who shall come before her. . . ."

210

220

230

240

250

◆

[1]Rapid ornamentation or variation of a line of music, here implying excessive virtuosity.

Renaissance Women

As Castiglione suggests, the Renaissance provided greater opportunities for education among upper-class women than were available to medieval women. Nevertheless, women's roles and rights were carefully limited by men, who considered women their social and intellectual inferiors. Even such enlightened humanists as Alberti perpetuated old prejudices that found women "almost universally timid by nature, soft, and slow." Indeed, according to Alberti, nature had decreed "that men should bring things home and women care for them." Although Renaissance women were held in high esteem as housekeepers and mothers, they were not generally considered respectable models for male children, who, Alberti explained, should be "steered away from womanly customs and ways." Married (usually between the ages of thirteen and sixteen) to men considerably older than themselves, women often inherited large fortunes and lucrative businesses.

Renaissance women's occupations remained limited to service tasks, such as midwifery and innkeeping, but there is ample evidence that by the sixteenth century they reaped the advantages of an increasingly commercialized economy in which they might compete successfully with men. If, for centuries, women had dominated the areas of textiles, food preparation, and healthcare, many also rose to prominence in positions

Figure 16.6 Francesco Laurana, *Battista Sforza*, ca. 1473. Marble, height approx. 20 in. Museo Nazionale del Bargello, Florence. Alinari/Art Resource, New York.

of political power. Elizabeth, Queen of England, and Caterina Sforza of Milan are but two of the more spectacular examples of women whose strong will and political ingenuity shaped history. The seeds of feminism planted by Christine de Pisan (see chapter 15) flowered among increasing numbers of women writers and patrons. Battista Sforza, niece of Francesco Sforza, the powerful ruler of Milan, shared the efforts of her husband Duke Federico da Montefeltro in making Urbino a cultural and intellectual center. The Duchess of Urbino (Figure 16.6) was admired for her knowledge of Greek and Latin and for her role as patron of the arts. Women humanists, a small but visible group often bred among wealthy aristocrats, often had to choose between marriage, the convent, and the pursuit of a Liberal Arts education. Italy produced some of the most notable female humanists, including the poet Vittoria Colonna (1490–1547), whom her admirer, Michelangelo, compared to "a block of marble whose talent was hidden deep within."

Machiavelli and Power Politics

The modern notion of progress as an active process of improving the lot of the individual was born during the Renaissance. Repeatedly, Renaissance humanists asserted that society's leaders must exercise *virtù* in order to master Fate (often personified in Western art and literature as a female) and fashion their destinies in their own interests. Balanced against the ideals of human perfectibility championed by Castiglione and Pico were the realities of human greed, ignorance, and cruelty. Such technological innovations as gunpowder made warfare increasingly impersonal and devastating, while the rise of strong national rulers occasioned the worst kinds of aggression and brute force. Even the keepers of the spiritual kingdom on earth—the leaders of the Church of Rome—had become notorious for their self-indulgence and greed, as some Renaissance popes actually took mistresses, led armed attacks upon neighboring states, and lived at shocking levels of luxury.

The most acute critic of these conditions was the Florentine diplomat and statesman Niccolò Machiavelli (1469–1527). A keen political observer and a student of Roman history, Machiavelli lamented Italy's disunity in the face of continuous rivalry among the city-states. He anticipated that outside powers might try to take advantage of Italy's internal weaknesses. The threat of foreign invasion became a reality in 1494, when French armies marched into Italy, thus initiating a series of wars that left Italy divided and impoverished. Exiled from Florence upon the collapse of the republican government he had served from 1498 to 1512 and eager to win favor with the Medici now that they had returned to power, Machiavelli penned *The Prince*, a political treatise that called for the unification of Italy under a powerful and courageous leader. This notorious little book laid out the guidelines for how an aspiring ruler might gain and maintain political power.

In *The Prince*, Machiavelli argued that the need for a strong state justified the need for a strong ruler. He pictured the secular prince as one who was schooled in war and in the lessons of history. The ruler must trust no one, least of all mercenary soldiers. He must imitate the lion in his fierceness, but he must also act like a fox to outsmart his enemies. Finally, in the interest of the state, he must be ruthless, and, if necessary, he must sacrifice moral virtue. In the final analysis, the end—that is, the preservation of a strong state—justified the means of maintaining power, however cunning or violent. As indicated in the following excerpts, Machiavelli formulated the idea of the state as an entity that remains exempt from the bonds of conventional morality.

READING 3.10

From Machiavelli's *The Prince*

XII How Many Different Kinds of Soldiers There Are, and of Mercenaries

. . . a Prince must lay solid foundations since otherwise he will inevitably be destroyed. Now the main foundations of all States, whether new, old, or mixed, are good laws and good arms. But since you cannot have the former without the latter, and where you have the latter, are likely to have the former, I shall here omit all discussion on the subject of laws, and speak only of arms.

I say then that the arms wherewith a Prince defends his State are either his own subjects, or they are mercenaries, or they are auxiliaries, or they are partly one and partly another. Mercenaries and auxiliaries are at once useless and dangerous, and he who holds his State by means of mercenary troops can never be solidly or securely seated. For such troops are disunited, ambitious, insubordinate, treacherous, insolent among friends, cowardly before foes, and without fear of God or faith with man. Whenever they are attacked defeat follows; so that in peace you are plundered by them, in war by your enemies. And this because they have no tie or motive to keep them in the field beyond their paltry pay, in return for which it would be too much to expect them to give their lives. They are ready enough, therefore, to be your soldiers while you are at peace, but when war is declared they make off and disappear. I ought to have little difficulty in getting this believed, for the present ruin of Italy is due to no other cause than her having for many years trusted to mercenaries, who though heretofore they may have helped the fortunes of some one man, and made a show of strength when matched with one another, have always revealed themselves in their true colors as soon as foreign enemies appeared. . . .

1

10

20

30

XIV Of the Duty of a Prince in Respect of Military Affairs

A Prince, therefore, should have no care or thought but
for war, and for the regulations and training it requires,
and should apply himself exclusively to this as his
peculiar province; for war is the sole art looked for in one
who rules and is of such efficacy that it not merely
maintains those who are born Princes, but often enables
men to rise to that eminence from a private station;   40
while, on other hand, we often see that when Princes
devote themselves rather to pleasure than to arms, they
lose their dominions. And as neglect of this art is the
prime cause of such calamities, so to be a proficient in it
is the surest way to acquire power. . . .

XV Of the Qualities in Respect of which Princes are Praised or Blamed

It now remains for us to consider what ought to be the
conduct and bearing of a Prince in relation to his
subjects and friends. And since I know that many have
written on this subject, I fear it may be thought
presumptuous in me to write of it also; the more so,   50
because in my treatment of it I depart widely from the
views that others have taken.

But since it is my object to write what shall be useful
to whosoever understands it, it seems to me better to
follow the real truth of things than an imaginary view of
them. For many Republics and Princedoms have been
imagined that were never seen or known. It is essential,
therefore, for a Prince who would maintain his position,
to have learned how to be other than good, and to use or
not to use his goodness as necessity requires.   60

Laying aside, therefore, all fanciful notions concerning a
Prince, and considering those only that are true, I say that
all men when they are spoken of, and Princes more than
others from their being set so high, are noted for certain
of those qualities which attach either praise or blame.
Thus one is accounted liberal, another miserly . . . ; one
is generous, another greedy; one cruel, another tender-
hearted; one is faithless, another true to his word; one
effeminate and cowardly, another high-spirited and
courageous; one is courteous, another haughty; one lewd,   70
another chaste; one upright, another crafty; one firm,
another facile; one grave, another frivolous; one devout,
another unbelieving; and the like. Every one, I know, will
admit that it would be most laudable for a Prince to be
endowed with all of the above qualities that are reckoned
good; but since it is impossible for him to possess or
constantly practise them all, the conditions of human
nature not allowing it, he must be discreet enough to
know how to avoid the reproach of those vices that would
deprive him of his government, and, if possible, be on his   80
guard also against those which might not deprive him of
it; though if he cannot wholly restrain himself, he may
with less scruple indulge in the latter. But he need never
hesitate to incur the reproach of those vices without
which his authority can hardly be preserved; for if he well
consider the whole matter, he will find that there may be
a line of conduct having the appearance of virtue, to
follow which would be his ruin, and that there may be
another course having the appearance of vice, by
following which his safety and well-being are secured.   90

XVII Whether It is Better to Be Loved Than Feared

[We now consider] the question whether it is better to be
loved rather than feared, or feared rather than loved. It
might perhaps be answered that we should wish to be
both; but since love and fear can hardly exist together, if
we must choose between them, it is far safer to be
feared than loved. For of men it may generally be
affirmed that they are thankless, fickle, false, studious to
avoid danger, greedy of gain, devoted to you while you
are able to confer benefits upon them, and ready, as I
said before, while danger is distant, to shed their blood,   100
and sacrifice their property, their lives, and their children
for you; but in the hour of need they turn against you.
The Prince, therefore, who without otherwise securing
himself builds wholly on their professions is undone. For
the friendships which we buy with a price, and do not
gain by greatness and nobility of character, though they
be fairly earned are not made good, but fail us when we
have occasion to use them.

Moreover, men are less careful how they offend him
who makes himself loved than him who makes himself   110
feared. For love is held by the tie of obligation, which,
because men are a sorry breed, is broken on every whisper
of private interest; but fear is bound by the apprehension
of punishment which never relaxes its grasp.

Nevertheless a Prince should inspire fear in such a
fashion that if he do not win love he may escape hate.
For a man may very well be feared and yet not hated,
and this will be the case so long as he does not meddle
with the property or with the women of his citizens and
subjects. And if constrained to put any to death, he   120
should do so only when there is manifest cause or
reasonable justification. But, above all, he must
abstain from the property of others. For men will sooner
forget the death of their father than the loss of their
property. . . .

XVIII How Princes Should Keep Faith

Every one understands how praiseworthy it is in a Prince
to keep faith, and to live uprightly and not craftily.
Nevertheless, we see from what has taken place in our
own days that Princes who have set little store by their
world, but have known how to overreach men by their   130
cunning, have accomplished great things, and in the end
got the better of those who trusted to honest dealing.

Be it known, then, that there are two ways of
contending, one in accordance with the laws, the other
by force; the first of which is proper to men, the second
to beasts. But since the first method is often ineffectual,
it becomes necessary to resort to the second. A Prince
should, therefore, understand how to use well both the
man and the beast . . . of beasts [the Prince should
choose as his models] both the lion and the fox; for the   140
lion cannot guard himself from traps, nor the fox from
wolves. He must therefore be a fox to discern traps, and
a lion to drive off wolves.

To rely wholly on the lion is unwise; and for this reason
a prudent Prince neither can nor ought to keep his word
when to keep it is hurtful to him and the causes which
led him to pledge it are removed. If all men were good,
this would not be good advice, but since they are

dishonest and do not keep faith with you, you, in return, need not keep faith with them; and no Prince was ever at 150 a loss for plausible reasons to cloak a breach of faith. Of this numberless recent instances could be given, and it might be shown how many solemn treaties and engagements have been rendered inoperative and idle through want of faith in Princes, and that he who has best known to play the fox has had the best success.

It is necessary, indeed, to put a good disguise on this nature, and to be skillful in simulating and dissembling. But men are so simple, and governed so absolutely by their present needs, that he who wishes to deceive will 160 never fail in finding willing dupes. . . .

And you are to understand that a Prince, and most of all a new Prince, cannot observe all those rules of conduct in respect whereof men are accounted good, being often forced, in order to preserve his Princedom, to act in opposition to good faith, charity, humanity, and religion. He must therefore keep his mind to shift as the winds and tides of Fortune turn, and, as I have already said, he ought not to quit good courses if he can help it, but should know how to follow evil courses if he must. . . . 170

Moreover, in the actions of all men, and most of all Princes, where there is no tribunal to which we can appeal, we look to results. Therefore if a Prince succeeds in establishing and maintaining his authority, the means will always be judged honorable and be approved by every one. For the vulgar are always taken by appearances and by results, and the world is made up of the vulgar, the few only finding room when the many have no longer ground to stand on. . . .

———————◆———————

The advice Machiavelli gives in his handbook of power politics is based on an essentially negative view of humankind: If, by nature, human beings are "thankless," "fickle," "false," "greedy," "dishonest," and "simple" (as Machiavelli describes them), how better to govern them than by ruthless unlimited power that might keep this "sorry breed" in check? Machiavelli's treatise suggests, furthermore, that personal morality, guided by the principles of justice and benevolence, differs from the morality of the collective entity, the state. It implies, further, that the state, an impersonal phenomenon, may be declared amoral, that is, exempt from any moral judgment. In either case, Machiavelli's separation of the value-principles of governance from the principles of personal morality—of which there are all too many examples in modern political history—stunned the European community. The rules of power advertised in *The Prince* appeared to Renaissance thinkers not as idealized notions, but, rather, as expedient solutions based on a realistic analysis of contemporary political conditions. Widely circulated, *The Prince* was hailed not simply as a cynical examination of political expediency, but as an exposé of real-life politics—so much so that the word "Machiavellian" soon became synonymous with the idea of political duplicity.

Throughout *The Prince*, Machiavelli cites examples of power drawn from Roman history and contemporary politics. His political theories rested on an examination of human nature not as it should have been, but as it was. In defense of the successful use of power, for instance, one of Machiavelli's favorite models was Rodrigo Borgia (the Renaissance Pope Alexander VI), who, along with other thoroughly corrupt and decadent members of his family, exercised a ruthless military campaign to establish a papal empire in central Italy. Machiavelli provided ample evidence to justify his denunciation of the secular ruler as the divinely appointed model of moral rectitude—a medieval conception staunchly defended by Castiglione. Machiavelli's profound grasp of past and present history, which he summed up as his "knowledge of the actions of man," made him both a cynical analyst of human behavior and modern Europe's first political scientist.

SUMMARY

The effort to recover, edit, and study ancient Greek and Latin manuscripts, a movement known as classical humanism, first occurred in fourteenth-century Italy, where it marked the beginnings of the Renaissance. This revival of Greco-Roman culture was to spread throughout Western Europe over the following three hundred years. Petrarch, the Father of Humanism, provided the model for Renaissance scholarship and education. He glorified Ciceronian Latin, encouraged textual criticism, and wrote introspective and passionate sonnets that were revered and imitated for centuries to come.

The city of Florence was the unrivaled center of classical humanism for the first 150 years of the Renaissance. A thriving commercial and financial center dominated by a prosperous middle class, Florence found political and cultural leadership in such wealthy and sophisticated families as the Medici. Classical humanism helped to cultivate a sense of civic pride, a new respect for oral and written eloquence, and a set of personal values that sustained the ambitions of the rising merchant class.

Fifteenth-century humanists carried on Petrarch's quest to recover the classical past. Ficino translated the entire body of Plato's writings, while Pico's investigations in Hebrew and Arabic led him to believe that the world's great minds shared a single, universal truth. Pico's *Oration on the Dignity of Man* proclaimed the centrality of humankind and defended the unlimited freedom of the individual within the universal scheme.

Renaissance humanists cultivated the idea of the good life. Following Alberti's maxim, "A man can do anything he wants," they applied the moral precepts of the classical past to such contemporary pursuits as diplomacy, politics, and the arts. While Petrarch and his peers were concerned primarily with the recovery of classical manuscripts and the production of critical editions, Alberti, Castiglione, and Machiavelli eagerly infused scholarship with action. Allying their scrutiny of the past to an empirical study of the present, they fostered a heroic ideal of the individual that surpassed all classical models. For Alberti, wealth and authority proceeded from the exercise of *virtù*; for Castiglione, the superior breed of human being was identical with *l'uomo universale*, the well-rounded person; for Machiavelli, only a ruthless master of power politics could ensure the survival of the state. Alberti, Castiglione, and Machiavelli are representative of those thinkers who asserted the infinite capacity for self-knowledge and exalted the role of the individual in the secular world. Their views shaped the modern character of the humanistic tradition in the European West.

GLOSSARY

condottiere (plural *condottieri*) a professional soldier; a mercenary who typically served an Italian Renaissance city-state

sonnet a fourteen-line lyric poem with a fixed scheme of rhyming

SUGGESTIONS FOR READING

Aston, Margaret. *The Fifteenth Century: The Prospect of Europe*. New York: Harcourt, 1968.

Bertelli, Sergio. *The Courts of the Italian Renaissance*. New York: Oxford University Press, 1986.

Brown, Alison, ed. *Language and Images of Renaissance Italy*. New York: Oxford University Press, 1995.

Brucker, G. A. *Renaissance Florence*, rev. ed. Berkeley, Calif.: University of California Press, 1975.

Burke, Peter. *The Italian Renaissance: Culture and Society in Italy*. Princeton, N.J.: Princeton University Press, 1986.

Chamberlain, E. R. *Everyday Life in Renaissance Times*. London: Batsford, 1965.

Hale, J. R. *The Civilization of Europe in the Renaissance*. New York: Atheneum, 1994.

——. *Machiavelli and Renaissance Italy*. London: English Universities Press, 1961.

Holmes, George, ed. *Art and Politics in Renaissance Italy*. New York: Oxford University Press, 1994.

Kristeller, P. O. *Renaissance Thought: The Classic, Scholastic, and Humanistic Strains*. New York: Harper, 1961.

O'Kelly, Bernard. *The Renaissance Image of Man and the World*. Columbus, Ohio: Ohio State University Press, 1966.

Stephens, John. *The Italian Renaissance: The Origins of Intellectual and Artistic Change Before the Reformation*. New York: Longman, 1990.

17
Renaissance Artists: Disciples of Nature, Masters of Invention

The Renaissance produced a flowering in the visual arts rarely matched in the annals of world culture. Artists embraced the natural world with an enthusiasm that was equalled only by their ambition to master the lessons of classical antiquity. The result was a unique and sophisticated body of art that set the standards for most of the painting, sculpture, and architecture produced in the West until the late nineteenth century.

During the Early Renaissance, the period from roughly 1400 to 1490, Florentine artists worked side by side with literary humanists to revive the classical heritage. These artist-scientists combined their interest in Greco-Roman art with an impassioned desire to understand the natural world and imitate its visual appearance. As disciples of nature, they studied its operations and functions; as masters of invention, they devised techniques by which to represent the visible world more realistically. In the years of the High Renaissance—approximately 1490 to 1530—the spirit of individualism reached heroic proportions, as artists such as Leonardo da Vinci, Raphael, and Michelangelo integrated the new techniques of naturalistic representation with the much respected principles of classical art.

While the subject matter of Renaissance art was still largely religious, the style was more lifelike than ever. Indeed, in contrast with the generally abstract and symbolic art of the Middle Ages, Renaissance art was concrete and realistic. Most medieval art served liturgical or devotional ends; increasingly, however, wealthy patrons commissioned paintings and sculptures to embellish their homes and palaces or to commemorate secular and civic achievements. Portrait painting, a genre that glorified the individual, became popular during the Renaissance, along with other genres that described the physical and social aspects of urban life. These artistic developments reflect the needs of a culture driven by material prosperity, civic pride, and personal pleasure.

Renaissance Art and Patronage

In the commercial cities of Italy and the Netherlands, painting, sculpture, and architecture were the tangible expressions of increased affluence. In addition to the traditional medieval source of patronage—the Catholic Church—merchant princes and petty despots vied with growing numbers of middle-class patrons and urban-centered guilds whose lavish commissions brought prestige to their businesses and families. Those who supported the arts did so at least in part with an eye toward leaving their mark upon society or immortalizing themselves for posterity. Thus art became the evidence of material well-being as well as the visible extension of the ego in an age of individualism.

Active patronage enhanced the social and financial status of Renaissance artists. Such artists were first and foremost craftspeople, apprenticed to studios in which they might achieve mastery over a wide variety of techniques, including the grinding of paints, the making of brushes, and the skillful copying of images. While trained to observe firmly established artistic convention, the more innovative amongst them moved to create a new visual language. Indeed, for the first time in Western history, artists came to wield influence as humanists, scientists, and poets: A new phenomenon of the artist as hero and genius was born. The image of the artist as hero was promoted by the self-publicizing efforts of these artists, as well as by the adulation of their peers. The Italian painter, architect, and critic Giorgio Vasari (1511–1574) immortalized hundreds of Renaissance artists in his monumental biography *The Lives of the Most Excellent Painters, Architects, and Sculptors*, published in 1550. Vasari drew to legendary proportions the achievements of notable Renaissance figures, many of whom he knew personally. Consider, for instance, this terse characterization of Leonardo da Vinci (an artist whose work is featured in this chapter):

. . . He might have been a scientist if he had not been so versatile. But the instability of his character caused him to take up and abandon many things. In arithmetic, for example, he made such rapid progress during the short time he studied it that he often confounded his teacher by his questions. He also began the study of music and resolved to learn to play the lute, and as he was by nature of exalted imagination, and full of the most graceful vivacity, he sang and accompanied himself most divinely, improvising at once both verses and music. He studied not one branch of art only, but all. Admirably intelligent, and an excellent geometrician besides, Leonardo not only worked in sculpture . . . but, as an architect, designed ground plans and entire buildings; and, as an engineer, was the one who first suggested making a canal from Florence to Pisa by altering the river Arno. Leonardo also designed mills and water-driven machines. But, as he had resolved to make painting his profession, he spent most of his time drawing from life. . . .

The Early Renaissance
The Revival of the Classical Nude

Like the classical humanists, artists of the Renaissance were the self-conscious beneficiaries of ancient Greek and Roman culture. One of the most creative forces in Florentine sculpture, Donato Bardi, known as Donatello (1386–1466), traveled to Rome to study antique statuary. The works he observed there inspired his extraordinary likeness of the biblical hero David (Figure 17.1). Completed in 1432, Donatello's bronze was the first freestanding, life-sized nude sculpture since antiquity. While not an imitation of any single Greek or Roman statue, the piece reveals an indebtedness to classical models in its correct anatomical proportions and gentle *contrapposto* stance (compare the *Kritios Boy* and *Doryphorus* in chapter 6). However, the sensuousness of the youthful figure—especially apparent in the surface modeling—surpasses that of any antique statue. Indeed, in this tribute to male beauty, Donatello rejected the medieval view of the human body as the wellspring of sin and anticipated the modern Western exaltation of the body as the seat of pleasure.

The Renaissance revival of the classical nude was accompanied by a quest to understand the mechanics of the human body. Antonio Pollaiuolo (ca. 1432–1498) was among the first artists to dissect human cadavers in order to study anatomy. The results of his investigations are documented in a bronze sculpture depicting the combat between Hercules and Antaeus, a story drawn

Figure 17.1 Donatello, *David*, completed 1432. Bronze, height 5 ft. 2 in. Museo Nazionale del Bargello, Florence. Scala/Art Resource, New York.

Figure 17.2 Antonio Pollaiuolo, *Hercules and Antaeus*, ca. 1475.
Bronze, height 18 in. with base. Museo Nazionale del Bargello, Florence. Scala, Florence.

from Greco-Roman legend (Figure 17.2). This small but powerful sculpture in the round is one of many examples of the Renaissance use of classical mythology to glorify human action, rather than as an exemplum of Christian morality. The wrestling match between the two legendary strongmen of antiquity, Hercules (the most popular of all Greek heroes) and Antaeus (the son of Mother Earth), provided Pollaiuolo with the chance to display his remarkable understanding of the human physique, especially as it responds to stress. Pollaiuolo concentrates on the moment when Hercules lifts Antaeus off the ground, thus divesting him of his maternal source of strength and crushing him in a "body lock." The human capacity for tension and energy is nowhere better captured than in the straining muscles and tendons of the two athletes in combat.

Figure 17.3 Sandro Botticelli, *Birth of Venus*, after 1482. Tempera on canvas, 5 ft. 9 in. × 9 ft. ½ in. Uffizi Gallery, Florence. Scala/Art Resource, New York.

The classically inspired nude fascinated Renaissance painters as well as sculptors. In the *Birth of Venus* (Figure **17.3**) by Sandro Botticelli (1445–1510), the central image (Figure **17.4**) is an idealized portrayal of womankind based on an antique model, possibly a statue in the Medici collection (Figure **17.5**). Born of sea foam (according to the Greek poet Hesiod), Venus floats on a pearlescent scallop shell to the shore of the island of Cythera. To her right are two wind gods locked in sensuous embrace, while to her left is the welcoming figure of Pomona, the ancient Roman goddess of fruit trees and fecundity. Many elements in the painting—water, wind, flowers, trees—suggest procreation and fertility, powers associated with Venus as goddess of earthly love. But Botticelli, inspired by a contemporary neoplatonic poem honoring Aphrodite/Venus as goddess of divine love, renders Venus also as an object of ethereal beauty and spiritual love. His painting pictorializes ideas set forth at the Platonic Academy of Florence (see chapter 16), particularly the neoplatonic notion that objects of physical beauty move the soul to desire union with God, fount of all beauty and truth. Botticelli's wistful goddess assumes the double role accorded her by the neoplatonists: goddess of earthly love and goddess of divine (or Platonic) love.

Botticelli executed the *Birth of Venus* in tempera on a large canvas. He rendered the figures with a minimum of shading, so that they seem weightless, suspended in space. An undulating line animates the windblown hair, the embroidered robes, and the delicate flowers that lie on the tapestrylike surface of the canvas. Gold accents and pastel colors (including the delicious lime of the water) further remove this idyllic vision from association with the mundane world.

The Classical Revival in Early Renaissance Architecture

The art of the Early Renaissance was never a mere imitation of antique models (as was often the case with Roman copies of Greek sculpture), but rather an original effort to reinterpret Greco-Roman themes and principles. The same is true of Renaissance architecture. The revival of classical architecture was inaugurated by the architect, sculptor, and theorist Filippo Brunelleschi (1377–1446). In 1420, Brunelleschi won a civic competition for the design of the dome of Florence Cathedral. His ingeniously conceived dome, the largest since the Pantheon in Rome, consisted of two octagonal shells, each incorporating eight curved panels joined by massive ribs that soar upward from the octagonal **drum**—the section immediately beneath the dome—to

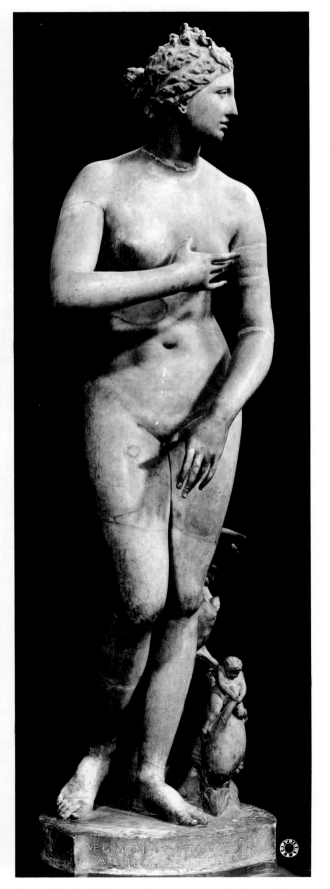

Figure 17.4 Sandro Botticelli, detail of *Birth of Venus*, Figure 17.3.

Figure 17.5 *Medici Venus*, first century C.E. Marble, height 5 ft. ¼ in. Uffizi Gallery, Florence.

Figure 17.6 Florence Cathedral. Alinari/Art Resource, New York.

converge at an elegant **lantern** through which light enters the interior (Figure 17.6). In the space between the two shells, Brunelleschi designed an interlocking system of ribs that operate like hidden flying buttresses (Figure 17.7). To raise the dome, he devised new methods of hoisting stone and new masonry techniques, all of which won him acclaim in Florence. Indeed, Brunelleschi's colleague Alberti hailed the completed dome as "a feat of engineering . . . unknown and unimaginable among the ancients."

Brunelleschi was among the first architects of the Renaissance to defend the principles of symmetry and clarity in architectural design. In the graceful little chapel he produced for the Pazzi family of Florence (Figure 17.8), he placed a dome over the central square of the inner hall and buttressed the square with two short barrel vaults. Since the exterior of this self-contained structure was later modified by the addition of a portico, it is in the interior that Brunelleschi's break with the medieval past is fully realized (Figure 17.9). Here, the repetition of geometric shapes enforces a new kind of visual clarity wherein all parts of the structure are readily accessible to the eye and to the mind. Gray stone moldings and gray Corinthian **pilasters**—shallow, flattened, rectangular columns that adhere to the wall surface—emphasize the "seams" between the individual segments of the stark white interior, producing a sense of order and harmony that is unsurpassed in Early Renaissance architecture. Whereas the medieval cathedral coaxes one's gaze heavenward, the Pazzi Chapel fixes the beholder decisively on earth.

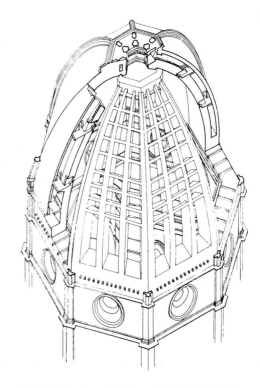

Figure 17.7 Axonometric section of the dome of Florence cathedral. Cross-section at base 11 ft. x 7 ft.

Figure 17.8 (above) Filippo Brunelleschi, Pazzi Chapel, cloister of Santa Croce, Florence, ca. 1441–1460. Scala, Florence.

Figure 17.9 (right) Filippo Brunelleschi, Pazzi Chapel, Santa Croce, Florence, ca. 1441–1460. Scala, Florence.

Brunelleschi's enthusiasm for an architecture of harmonious proportions was shared by his younger colleague, the multitalented Florentine humanist Leon Battista Alberti (see chapter 16). Alberti's scientific treatises on painting, sculpture, and architecture reveal his admiration for Roman architecture and his familiarity with the writing of Vitruvius (see chapter 6). In his *Ten Books on Architecture* (modeled after Vitruvius' *De architectura*), Alberti argued that architectural design should proceed from the square and the circle, the two most perfect geometric shapes. This proposition was the guiding precept for all of Alberti's buildings (a total of only six); it would become the definitive principle of High Renaissance composition (see Figures 17.25, 17.30, 17.31).

In the townhouse Alberti designed for the wealthy Rucellai family of Florence (Figure **17.10**)—a structure for which there were no direct antique precedents—each story is ornamented with a different classical order (see chapter 6). Rows of crisply defined arcaded windows appear on the upper stories, while square windows placed well above the street (for safety and privacy) accent the lowest level. From the Roman Colosseum (see chapter 7), Alberti borrowed the device of alternating arches and engaged columns, flattening the latter into

Figure 17.10 Leon Battista Alberti (designer) and Bernardo Rossellino (architect), Palazzo Rucellai, Florence, 1446–1451. Sapieta.

pilasters. Here the principles of clarity and proportion prevail. For the west front of Santa Maria Novella in Florence (Figure **17.11**), Alberti produced an eloquent pattern of geometric shapes ordered by a perfect square: The height of the dominantly gray and green marble facade (from the ground to the tip of the pediment) exactly equals its width. All parts are related by harmonic proportions based on numerical ratios; for instance, the upper portion is one fourth the size of the square into which the entire face of the church would fit. Huge scrolls—imitated by generations of Western architects to come—link the upper and lower divisions of the facade. At Santa Maria Novella, as in the churches he designed at Rimini and Mantua, Alberti imposed the defining features of classical architecture upon a Latin cross basilica, thus uniting Greco-Roman and Christian traditions.

Both Alberti and Brunelleschi espoused the Hellenic theory that the human form mirrored the order inherent in the universe. The human microcosm (or "lesser world") was the natural expression of the divine macrocosm (or "greater world"). Accordingly, the study of nature and the understanding and exercise of its underlying harmonies put one in touch with the macrocosm. Rational architecture, reflecting natural laws, would help to cultivate rational individuals. Just as the gentler modes in music elicited refined behavior (the Doctrine of Ethos; see chapter 6), so harmoniously proportioned buildings might produce ideal citizens.

The Renaissance Portrait

The revival of portraiture during the Renaissance was an expression of two impulses: the desire to immortalize oneself by way of one's physical appearance and the wish to publicize one's greatness in the traditional manner of Greek and Roman antiquity (see chapter 7). Like biography and autobiography—two literary genres that were revived during the Renaissance—portraiture and self-portraiture were hallmarks of a new self-consciousness. The bronze self-portrait of Alberti, a medal bearing the artist's personal emblem of a winged eye **(see** Figure 16.4), looks back to the small fourteenth-century portrait profile of King John of France (see Figure 15.15). But the former is more deliberate in its

1420	Latin translations of Muslim manuscripts on optics are studied in Florence
1421	Brunelleschi receives the first patent of monopoly for an invention (related to ship improvement)
1436	Alberti proposes the use of mathematics for obtaining graphic perspective
1545	Geronimo Cardano (Italian) publishes a new algebra text, commencing the age of modern mathematics

Figure 17.11 Leon Battista Alberti, Santa Maria Novella, Florence, completed 1470. Green and gray marble. Scala, Florence.

Figure 17.12 Jan van Eyck, *Marriage of Giovanni Arnolfini and His Bride*, 1434. Tempera and oil on panel, 32¼ × 23½ in. National Gallery, London.

effort to recreate an accurate likeness and, at the same time, more clearly imitative of Roman coins and medals.

In the art of Netherlandish masters, the portrait was a favorite genre (see also chapter 18). The full-length double portraits of Giovanni Arnolfini and Jeanne Cenami, painted by the Dutch artist Jan van Eyck (Figure 17.12), probably served to document their marriage in 1434. On the wall behind Giovanni—a wealthy Italian representative of the Medici bank in Bruges—and his bride appear the words "Johannes de Eyck fuit hic" ("Jan van Eyck was here"), while in the convex mirror that hangs below the inscription is the reflected image of the painter himself as one of the two required witnesses to the ceremony. Jan's consummate mastery of realistic detail, from the ruffles of Jeanne's headcovering to the whiskers of the terrier pup, recalls the natural realism of the Limbourg brothers (see Figure 15.13). Such realism was enhanced by the use of oil painting, a technique that Jan brought to perfection. By applying thin, translucent glazes of pigments bound with linseed oil, he achieved the impression of dense, atmospheric space and simulated the naturalistic effect of light reflecting off the surfaces of objects. For all their immediacy, however, many of Jan's minutely detailed objects revealed secondary meanings: In the Arnolfini portrait, for instance, the fruit that lies near and on the window sill of the marriage chamber alludes to the union of the First Couple in the Garden of Eden, the single candle burning in the magnificent brass chandelier symbolizes the divine presence of Christ, the dog represents fidelity, and so forth. Embedded within each ordinary and commonplace object is a sacred symbol that lends spiritual meaning to an otherwise mundane reality.

If Jan perfected the Northern Renaissance taste for hidden symbolism, he also introduced the phenomenon of the psychological portrait—the portrait that probed the temperament, character, or unique personality of the subject. In his brilliant self-image (Figure 17.13), whose level gaze and compressed lips suggest the personality of a shrewd realist, facial features are finely (almost photographically) detailed. Jan deliberately abandoned the profile portrait (see Figure 15.15) in favor of a three-quarter view that gave the figure a more aggressive spatial presence.

While Early Renaissance artists usually represented their sitters in domestic interiors, High Renaissance masters preferred to situate them in *plein-air* (outdoor) settings, as if to suggest human consonance with nature. Leonardo da Vinci's *Mona Lisa* (Figure 17.14), the world's best-known portrait, brings figure and landscape into exquisite harmony: The pyramidal shape of the sitter (probably the wife of the Florentine banker Francesco del Giocondo) is echoed in the rugged mountains; the folds of her tunic are repeated in the curves of distant roads and rivers. Soft golden tones highlight the figure

Figure 17.13 Jan van Eyck, *Man in a Turban* (*Self-Portrait?*), 1433. Tempera and oil on panel, 13⅛ × 10⅛ in. National Gallery, London.

which, like the landscape, is modeled in soft, smoky (in Italian, *sfumato*) gradations of light and shade. The setting, a rocky and ethereal wilderness, is as elusive as the sitter, whose eyes and mouth are delicately blurred to produce a facial expression that is almost impossible to decipher—a smile both melancholic and mocking. While the shaved eyebrows and plucked hairline are hallmarks of fifteenth-century female fashion, the figure resists classification by age and (in the opinion of some) by gender. Praised by Renaissance copyists for its "lifelikeness," the *Mona Lisa* has remained an object of fascination and mystery for generations of beholders.

Renaissance portraits often took the form of lifesized sculptures in the round. The marble portrait bust of Battista Sforza, a triumph of geometric abstraction and distinctive detail executed by Francesco Laurana (1430–1502), captures the beauty and self-confidence of the notable Countess of Urbino (see Figure 16.6). Laurana's portraits were often brightly painted to achieve naturalistic effects. Such is also the case with the polychrome terra-cotta likeness of Lorenzo de' Medici (see Part Opener, p.xvi), executed by the Florentine sculptor Andrea del Verrocchio (1435–1488), which reveals a spirited naturalism reminiscent of Roman portraiture (see chapter 7). Verrocchio was the Medici

Figure 17.14 Leonardo da Vinci, *Mona Lisa*, ca. 1503–1505. Oil on panel, 30¼ × 21 in. Louvre, Paris. Photo: © Studio Quattrone, Florence.

court sculptor and the close companion of Lorenzo, whose luxurious lifestyle and opulent tastes won him the title "Il Magnifico" ("the Magnificent"). Verrocchio immortalized the physical appearance of the Florentine ruler, who was also a humanist, poet, and musician. At the same time, he captured the willful vitality of the man whose *virtù* made him a legend in his time.

Renaissance sculptors revived still another antique genre: the equestrian statue. Verrocchio's monumental bronze statue of the *condottiere* Bartolommeo Colleoni (Figure 17.15), commissioned to commemorate the mercenary soldier's military victories on behalf of the city of Venice, recalls the Roman statue of Marcus Aurelius on horseback (see chapter 7) as well as the considerably smaller equestrian statue of Charlemagne (see chapter 11). However, compared with these works, Verrocchio's masterpiece displays an unprecedented degree of scientific naturalism and a close attention to anatomical detail—note the bulging muscles of Colleoni's mount. Verrocchio moreover makes his towering mercenary twist dramatically in his saddle and scowl fiercely. Such expressions of *terribilità*, or awe-inspiring power, typify the aggressive spirit that fueled the Renaissance.

Figure 17.15 Andrea del Verrocchio (completed by Alessandro Leopardi), Equestrian statue of Bartolommeo Colleoni, ca. 1481–1496. Bronze, height approx. 13 ft. Campo Santi Giovanni e Paolo, Venice. Scala/Art Resource, New York.

Early Renaissance Artist-Scientists

If Renaissance artists took formal and literary inspiration from classical antiquity, they were equally motivated by a desire to understand and record the natural world. The empirical study of the physical world—the reliance on direct observation—was the first step in their effort to recreate the "look" of nature. Medieval artists had little reason to simulate the world of the senses, a world they regarded as the imperfect reflection of the divine order (see chapters 9 and 13). For Renaissance artist-scientists, however, the visible, physical world could be mastered only if it were understood. To this end, they engaged in a program of examination, experimentation, and record keeping. They drew from live studio models, studied human and animal anatomy, and analyzed the effects of natural light on objects in space. Art became a form of rational inquiry or, as in the case of Leonardo, of scientific analysis.

For Renaissance artists, the painting constituted a window on nature: The **picture plane**, that is, the two-dimensional surface of the panel or canvas, was conceived as a transparent glass or window through which one might perceive the three-dimensional world. Various techniques aided artists in the task of recreating the illusion of reality. The technique of oil painting, refined by Jan van Eyck, was among the first of these. The application of thin oil glazes, which also became popular in Italy, produced a sense of atmospheric space rarely achieved in fresco (see Figure 15.9) or tempera (see Figure 17.3). But the more revolutionary "breakthrough" in Renaissance painting was the invention of **linear perspective**, an ingenious tool for the translation of three-dimensional space onto a two-dimensional surface. Around 1420, encouraged by research in optics stemming from humanist investigations into Arab science, Brunelleschi formulated the first laws of linear perspective. These laws described the manner by which all parallel lines in a given visual field appear to converge at a single vanishing point on the horizon (an illusion familiar to anyone who, from the rear of a train, has watched railroad tracks "merge" in the distance). Brunelleschi projected the picture plane as a cross-section through which diagonal lines (orthogonals) connected the eye of the beholder with objects along those lines and hence with the vanishing point (Figure 17.18; see also Figures 17.22, 17.39). The new perspective system, stated mathematically and geometrically by Alberti in 1435 and advanced thereafter by Leonardo and Dürer (see chapter 18), enabled artists to represent objects "in depth" at various distances from the viewer and in correct proportion to one another. Linear perspective satisfied the Renaissance craving for an exact and accurate description of the physical world. It also imposed a fixed relationship—both in time and space—

Figure 17.16 (left) Masaccio, *Trinity with the Virgin, Saint John the Evangelist, and Donors*, ca. 1426–1427. Fresco (now detached from wall), 21 ft. 10⅝ in. × 10 ft. 4¾ in. Santa Maria Novella, Florence. Photo: © Studio Quattrone, Florence.

Figure 17.17 (below) Masaccio, *Trinity with the Virgin, Saint John the Evangelist, and Donors*, showing perspective lines.

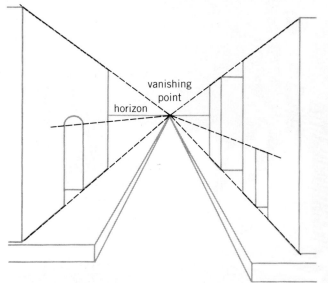

Figure 17.18 One-point perspective.

between the image and the eye of the beholder, making the latter the exclusive point of reference within the spatial field and thus, metaphorically, placing the individual at the center of the macrocosm.

The first artist to master Brunelleschi's new spatial device was the Florentine painter Tommaso Guidi, called Masaccio, or "Slovenly Tom" (1401–1428). Before his untimely death (possibly by poison) at age twenty-seven, Masaccio demonstrated his remarkable artistic talents in frescoes he painted for the churches of Florence. Masaccio's *Trinity with the Virgin, Saint John the Evangelist, and Donors* (Figure 17.16), in Santa Maria Novella, reflects the artist's mastery over the new perspective system: The lines of the painted barrel vault above the *Trinity* recede and converge at a vanishing point located at the foot of the Cross, thus corresponding precisely with the eye-level of viewers standing below the scene in the church itself (Figure 17.17). Masaccio further enhanced the illusion of real space by placing the figures of the kneeling patrons "outside of" the classical architectural forms that frame the sacred space.

The cycle of frescoes Masaccio executed for the Brancacci Chapel in Santa Maria del Carmine in Florence (Figure 17.19) represents an even more elaborate synthesis of illusionistic techniques. In *The Tribute Money* (Figure 17.20), a scene based on the Gospel story in which Jesus honors the demands of the Roman state by paying a tax or "tribute," the artist depicted Christ as he instructs the Apostle Peter to gather money from the mouth of a fish, an event seen at the left; at the right, Peter is shown delivering the coins to the Roman tax collector. Masaccio's application of one-point perspective—the orthogonals of the building on the right meet at a vanishing point just behind the head of Jesus—provides spatial unity to the three separate episodes, while tonal unity is provided by means of **aerial perspective**— the subtle blurring of details and diminution of color intensity in objects perceived at a distance. Refining the innovative techniques explored by Giotto at the Arena Chapel in Padua (see Figures 15.8, 15.9), Masaccio also made use of light and shade (*chiaroscuro*) to model his figures as though they actually stood in the light of the chapel window located to the right of the fresco.

Figure 17.19 (right) Brancacci Chapel (after restoration), Santa Maria del Carmine, Florence. Photo: © Studio Quattrone, Florence.

Figure 17.20 Masaccio, *The Tribute Money*, ca. 1425. Fresco (after restoration), 8 ft. 4 in. × 19 ft. 8 in. Brancacci Chapel, Santa Maria del Carmine, Florence. Photo: © Studio Quattrone, Florence.

Figure 17.21 (opposite) Lorenzo Ghiberti, "Gates of Paradise," 1425–1447. The east portal of the Florentine baptistry contains Lorenzo Ghiberti's immense (18 ft. 6 in. tall) gilt-bronze doors, brilliantly depicting in low relief ten episodes from the Old Testament. Scala, Florence.

Figure 17.22 (right) Lorenzo Ghiberti, *Meeting of Solomon and Sheba* (single panel of the "Gates of Paradise," Figure 17.21). Gilt-bronze relief, 31¼ × 31¼ in. Alinari/Art Resource, New York.

Eager to represent nature as precisely as possible, Masaccio worked from live models as well as from the available antique sources. From classical statuary he borrowed the graceful stance of the Roman tribune, who is shown twice in the fresco—viewed from front and back. Antique sculpture also probably inspired the Roman togas and the head of John the Evangelist (on Jesus' right). In the Brancacci Chapel frescoes, Masaccio integrated the three principal features of Italian Renaissance painting: the adaptation of classical prototypes, the empirical study of nature, and the application of the new techniques of spatial illusionism.

Masaccio was not alone in the rush to explore the new illusionism: Artists throughout Italy refined the technique of perspective **intarsia**, the inlay of various kinds of wood to achieve pictorial illusion (see Figure 16.3), and found opportunities to devise deep spatial fields in relief sculpture. The Florentine goldsmith and sculptor Lorenzo Ghiberti (1378–1455) achieved astonishingly dramatic effects by wedding the laws of linear perspective to figural grace and fine detail in the bronze panels he designed for the east doors of the Baptistry of Florence—the so-called "Gates of Paradise" (Figure 17.21). The bottom panel on the right, which depicts the biblical meeting of Solomon and Sheba (Figure 17.22), illustrates the centrally focused use of one-point perspective that profoundly influenced the next generation of artists (see Figures 17.28, 17.39).

Leonardo da Vinci as Artist-Scientist

Among all the artist-scientists of the Renaissance, Leonardo da Vinci (1452–1519) best deserves that title. A diligent investigator of natural phenomena, Leonardo examined the anatomical and organic functions of plants, animals, and human beings (Figure 17.23). He also studied the properties of wind and water and invented several hundred ingenious mechanical devices, including an armored tank and a flying machine, most of which never left the notebook stage (Figure 17.24). Between 1489 and 1518, Leonardo produced thousands of drawings accompanied by notes written in mirror-image script (devised perhaps to discourage imitators and plagiarists). This annotated record of the artist-scientist's passion to master nature includes anatomical drawings whose accuracy remained unsurpassed until 1543, when the Flemish physician Andreas Vesalius published the first medical illustrations of the human anatomy. Some of Leonardo's studies explore ideas (for example, the standardization of machine parts) that were far in advance of their time. Although Leonardo's notebooks—unpublished until 1898—had little influence upon European science, they remain a symbol of the Renaissance imagination and a timeless source of inspiration: The comic book hero Batman, according to its twentieth-century creator Bob Kane, was born when Kane first viewed Leonardo's sketches of human flight.

Figure 17.23 Leonardo da Vinci, *Embryo in the Womb*, ca. 1510. Pen and brown ink, 11¾ × 8½ in. The Royal Collection, Windsor Castle, Royal Library. © 1998 Her Majesty Queen Elizabeth II.

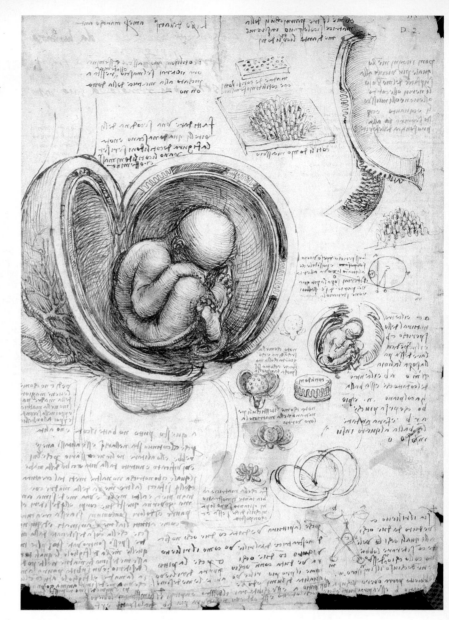

Figure 17.24 Leonardo da Vinci, *Wing Construction for a Flying Machine*, ca. 1500. Pen and brown ink. Biblioteca Ambrosiana, Milan, Codex Atlanticus, f.309v–a.

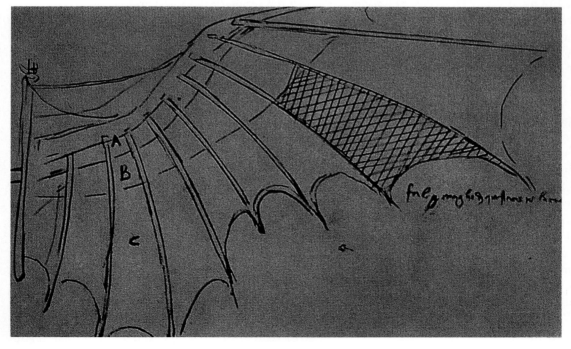

Following Alberti, Leonardo maintained that proportional principles govern both nature and art. Indeed, Leonardo's belief in a universal order led him to seek a basic correspondence between human proportions and ideal geometric shapes, as Vitruvius and his followers had advised. Leonardo's so-called "Vitruvian Man" (Figure 17.25), whose geometry haunts the compositions of High Renaissance painters and architects, is the metaphor for the Renaissance view of the microcosm as a mirror of the macrocosm. Yet, more than any other artist of his time, Leonardo exalted the importance of empirical experience for discovering the general rules of nature. Critical of abstract speculation bereft of sensory confirmation, he held that the human eye was the most dependable instrument for obtaining true knowledge of nature. When Leonardo wrote, "That painting is the most to be praised which agrees most exactly with the thing imitated," he was articulating the Renaissance

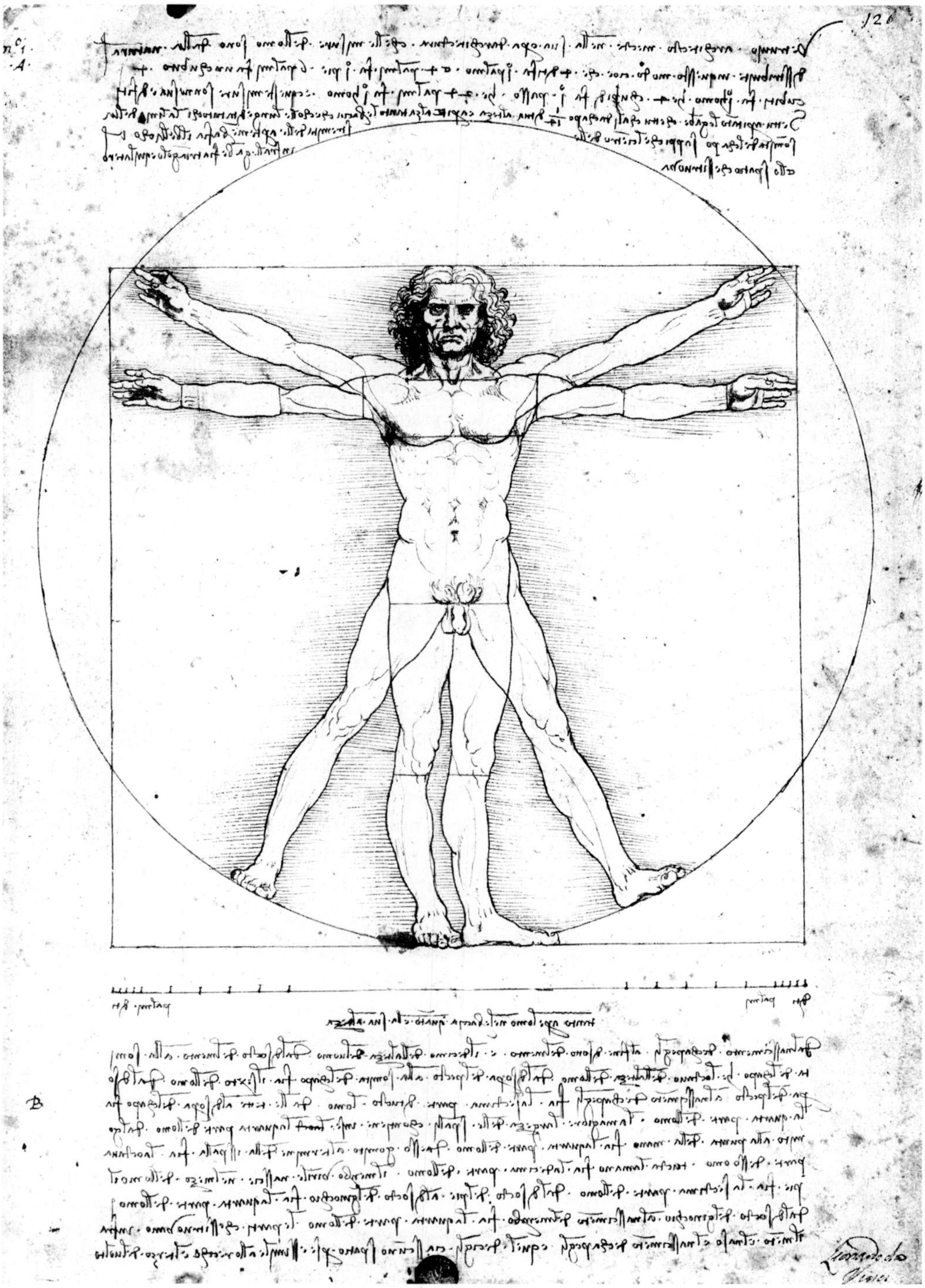

Figure 17.25 Leonardo da Vinci, *Proportional Study of a Man in the Manner of Vitruvius*, ca. 1487. Pen and ink, 13½ × 9⅝ in. Galleria dell'Accademia, Venice.

view of art as the imitation of nature. Though Leonardo never established a strict methodology for the formulation of scientific laws, his insistence on direct experience and experimentation made him the harbinger of the Scientific Revolution that would sweep through Western Europe during the next two centuries. In the following excerpts from his notebooks, Leonardo defends the superiority of sensory experience over "book learning" and argues that painting surpasses poetry as a form of human expression.

READING 3.11

From Leonardo da Vinci's *Notes*

I am fully aware that the fact of my not being a man of letters may cause certain arrogant persons to think that they may with reason censure me, alleging that I am a man ignorant of book-learning. Foolish folk! Do they not know that I might retort by saying, as did Marius to the Roman Patricians, "They who themselves go about adorned in the labor of others will not permit me my own." They will say that because of my lack of book-learning, I cannot properly express what I desire to treat of. Do they not know that my subjects require for their exposition experience rather than the words of others? And since experience has been the mistress of whoever has written well, I take her as my mistress, and to her in all points make my appeal.

I wish to work miracles. . . . And you who say that it is better to look at an anatomical demonstration than to see these drawings, you would be right, if it were possible to observe all the details shown in these drawings in a single figure, in which, with all your ability, you will not see nor acquire a knowledge of more than some few veins, while, in order to obtain an exact and complete knowledge of these, I have dissected more than ten human bodies, destroying all the various members, and removing even the very smallest particles of the flesh which surrounded these veins without causing any effusion of blood other than the imperceptible bleeding of the capillary veins. And, as one single body did not suffice for so long a time, it was necessary to proceed by stages with so many bodies as would render my knowledge complete; and this I repeated twice over in order to discover the differences. . . .

The eye, which is called the window of the soul, is the chief means whereby the understanding may most fully and abundantly appreciate the infinite works of nature; and the ear is the second inasmuch as it acquires its importance from the fact that it hears the things which the eye has seen. If you historians, or poets, or mathematicians had never seen things with your eyes you would be ill able to describe them in your writings. And if you, O poet, represent a story by depicting it with your pen, the painter with his brush will so render it as to be more easily satisfying and less tedious to understand. If you call painting "dumb poetry," then the painter may say of the poet that his art is "blind painting." Consider then which is the more grievous affliction, to be blind or be dumb! Although the poet has as wide a choice of subjects as the painter, his creations fail to afford as much

satisfaction to mankind as do paintings, for while poetry attempts with words to represent forms, actions, and scenes, the painter employs the exact images of the forms in order to reproduce these forms. Consider, then, which is more fundamental to man, the name of man or his image? The name changes with change of country; the form is unchanged except by death.

And if the poet serves the understanding by way of the ear, the painter does so by the eye which is the nobler sense. I will only cite as an instance of this how if a good painter represents the fury of a battle and a poet also describes one, and the two descriptions are shown together to the public, you will soon see which will draw most of the spectators, and where there will be most discussion, to which most praise will be given and which will satisfy the more. There is no doubt that the painting which is by far the more useful and beautiful will give the greater pleasure. Inscribe in any place the name of God and set opposite to it his image, you will see which will be held in greater reverence! . . .

If you despise painting, which is the sole imitator of all the visible works of nature, it is certain that you will be despising a subtle invention which with philosophical and ingenious speculation takes as its theme all the various kinds of forms, airs, and scenes, plants, animals, grasses and flowers, which are surrounded by light and shade. And this truly is a science and the true-born daughter of nature, since painting is the offspring of nature. But in order to speak more correctly we may call it the grandchild of nature; for all visible things derive their existence from nature, and from these same things is born painting. So therefore we may justly speak of it as the grandchild of nature and as related to God himself. . . .

————————◆————————

The High Renaissance
Leonardo and Raphael

By the end of the fifteenth century, Renaissance artists had mastered all of the fundamental techniques of visual illusionism, including linear and aerial perspective and the use of light and shade. They now began to employ these techniques in ever more heroic and monumental ways. To the techniques of scientific illusionism they wedded the basic principles of clarity, symmetry, and order, arriving at a unity of design that would typify High Renaissance art. The two artists whose paintings best represent the achievements of the High Renaissance are Leonardo da Vinci and Raphael (Raffaello Sanzio).

	1494	Leonardo devises plans to harness the waters of the Arno River
	1508	Leonardo records the results of cadaver dissections and analyzes the movements of birds in flight in unpublished manuscripts
	1513	Leonardo undertakes scientific studies of botany, geology, and hydraulic power

Figure 17.26 Leonardo da Vinci, *Last Supper*, ca. 1485–1498. Fresco: oil, tempera, and varnish on plaster, 15 ft. 1⅛ in. × 28 ft. 10½ in. Refectory, Santa Maria delle Grazie, Milan. Scala, Florence.

In his few (and largely unfinished) religious narratives, Leonardo da Vinci sought a grand design that reflected universal order. The classic example is his *Last Supper*, executed in the late 1490s to adorn the wall of the refectory of Santa Maria delle Grazie in Milan (Figure 17.26). Leonardo's experimental mixture of oil, tempera, and varnish proved non durable and despite recent efforts at restoration, much of the original fresco is lost. Nevertheless, the *Last Supper* retains its impact as one of the great religious paintings of all time. Leonardo intended that the sacred event *appear* to take place within the monastic dining room: The receding lines of the ceiling beams and side niches in the fresco create a sense of spatial depth and link the scene illusionistically with the interior of the refectory. Using clarity and harmony as organizing principles, Leonardo fixed the vanishing point at the center of the composition directly behind the head of Jesus; he further reinforced the centrality of Christ by means of a rectangular doorway and pediment. To this masterful rationalization of space, Leonardo added high drama: He divided the apostles into four groups of three who interact in response to the Master's declaration that one of them would betray him (Matthew 26:21). The tragic mood, enhanced by Christ's meditative look and submissive gesture indicating the bread and wine as symbols of the Eucharist, is punctuated by the various reactions of the apostles: astonishment, disbelief, protest, surprise, and so forth. The following excerpt from Vasari's biography of Leonardo offers a glimpse into the circumstances surrounding the creation of the *Last Supper*.

READING 3.12

From Vasari's *Lives of the Most Excellent Painters, Architects, and Sculptors*

Biography of Leonardo da Vinci

The master gave so much beauty and majesty to the heads of the Apostles that he was constrained to leave the Christ unfinished, convinced as he was that he could not render the divinity of the Redeemer. Even so, this work has always been held in the highest estimation by the Milanese and by foreigners as well. Leonardo rendered to perfection the doubts and anxieties of the Apostles, their desire to know by whom their Master is to be betrayed. All their faces show their love, terror, anger, grief, or bewilderment, unable as they are to fathom the   10 meaning of the Lord. The spectator is also struck by the determination, hatred, and treachery of Judas [fourth figure from the left]. The whole is executed with the most minute exactitude. The texture of the tablecloth seems actually made of linen.

The story goes that the prior was in a great hurry to see the picture done. He could not understand why Leonardo should sometimes remain before his work half a day together, absorbed in thought. He would have him work away, as he compelled the laborers to do who were   20 digging in his garden, and never put the pencil down. Not content with seeking to hurry Leonardo, the prior even complained to the duke, and tormented him so much that, at length, he sent for Leonardo and courteously entreated him to finish the work. Leonardo, knowing the duke to be an intelligent man, explained himself as he had never bothered to do to the prior. He made it clear that men of genius are sometimes producing most when they seem least to labor, for their minds are then occupied in the shaping of those 30 conceptions to which they afterward give form. He told the duke that two heads were yet to be done: that of the Savior, the likeness of which he could not hope to find on earth and had not yet been able to create in his imagination in perfection of celestial grace: and the other, of Judas. He said he wanted to find features fit to render the appearance of a man so depraved as to betray his benefactor, his Lord, and the Creator of the world. He said he would still search but as a last resort he could always use the head of the troublesome and impertinent 40 prior. This made the duke laugh with all his heart. The prior was utterly confounded and went away to speed the digging in his garden. Leonardo was left in peace. . . .

◆

The second of the great High Renaissance artists was the Urbino-born artist Raphael (Raffaello Sanzio; 1483–1520). Less devoted to scientific speculation than Leonardo, Raphael was first and foremost a master painter. His fashionable portraits were famous for their accuracy and incisiveness. A case in point is the portrait of Raphael's lifelong friend Baldassare Castiglione (see Figure 16.5), which captures the self-confidence and thoughtful intelligence of this celebrated Renaissance personality.

Raphael's compositions are notable for their clarity, harmony, and unity of design. In *The Alba Madonna* (Figure **17.27**), one of Raphael's many renderings of the Madonna and Child, he sets the Virgin in a landscape framed by the picturesque hills of central Italy. Using clear, bright colors and precise draftsmanship, Raphael organized the composition according to simple geometric shapes: the triangle (formed by the Virgin, Christ child, and the infant John the Baptist), the circle (the painting's basic shape and the head of the Virgin), and the trapezoid (one length of which is formed by the Virgin's outstretched leg). Despite the dignity of the composition and the nobility of the figures, the scene might be construed as a record of an ordinary woman with two children in a landscape, for Raphael has avoided obvious religious symbolism and distracting detail. In Raphael's world, all is sweetness and light. Raphael idealized his figures, especially his female saints, and often gave them sentimental facial expressions and theatrical poses—features that were taken to extremes by the artist's many imitators.

Figure 17.27 Raphael, *The Alba Madonna*, ca. 1510. Oil on wood transferred to canvas, diameter 37¼ in. © 1998 Board of Trustees, National Gallery of Art, Washington, D.C. Andrew W. Mellon Collection.

Figure 17.28 Raphael, *The School of Athens*, 1509–1511. Fresco, 26 ft. × 18 ft. Stanza della Segnatura, Vatican, Rome. Scala/Art Resource, New York.

Figure 17.29 Plan of *The School of Athens.*

1 Apollo
2 Alcibiades or Alexander
3 Socrates
4 Plato (Leonardo)
5 Aristotle
6 Minerva
7 Sodoma
8 Raphael
9 Ptolemy
10 Zoroaster (Pietro Bembo?)
11 Euclid (Bramante)
12 Diogenes
13 Heraclitus (Michelangelo)
14 Parmenides, Xenocrates, or Aristossenus
15 Francesco Maria della Rovere
16 Telauges
17 Pythagoras
18 Averhöes
19 Epicurus
20 Federigo Gonzaga
21 Zeno

In 1510 Pope Julius II, the greatest of Renaissance Church patrons, commissioned Raphael to execute a series of frescoes for the Vatican Stanza della Segnatura—the Pope's personal library and the room in which official church papers were signed. The paintings were to represent the four domains of human learning: theology, philosophy, law, and the arts. To illustrate philosophy, Raphael painted *The School of Athens* (Figure **17.28**). In this landmark fresco, the artist immortalized with unsurpassed dignity the company of the great philosophers and scientists of ancient history (Figure **17.29**). At the center of the composition appear, as if in scholarly debate, the two giants of classical philosophy: Plato, who points heavenward to indicate his view of reality as fixed in universal Forms, and Aristotle, who points to the earth to indicate that universal truth depends on the study of nature. Framed by a series of receding arches, the two philosophers stand against the bright sky, beneath the lofty vaults of a Roman basilica that resembles the newly remodeled Saint Peter's Cathedral. Between their heads lies the invisible vanishing point at which all the principal lines of sight converge. On either side of the great hall appear historical figures belonging to each of the two philosophic "camps": the Platonists (left) and the Aristotelians (right).

The School of Athens is a portrait gallery of Renaissance artists whose likenesses Raphael borrowed to depict his classical heroes. The stately, bearded Plato is an idealized portrait of Leonardo, who was visiting Rome while Raphael was at work in the Vatican. The balding Euclid, seen bending over his slate in the lower right corner of the composition, resembles a friend of Raphael, the architect Bramante. In the far right corner, Raphael himself (wearing a dark hat) appears discreetly among the Aristotelians. And in final revisions of the fresco, Raphael added to the left foreground the likeness of Michelangelo in the guise of the brooding and solitary Greek philosopher Heraclitus. *The School of Athens* is the ultimate tribute to the rebirth of classical humanism in the age of the Renaissance, for here, in a unified, imaginary space, the artists of Raphael's day are presented as the incarnations of the intellectual titans of antiquity.

In the restrained nobility of the near life-sized figures and the measured symmetry of the composition, Raphael's *School of Athens* marked the culmination of a style that had begun with Giotto and Masaccio; here, Raphael gave concrete vision to a world purged of accident and emotion. Monumental in conception and size (26 × 18 feet) and flawless in execution, *The School of Athens* advanced a set of formal principles that came to epitomize *the grand style*: spatial clarity, decorum (that is, propriety and good taste), balance, and grace (the last, especially evident in the subtle symmetries of line and color). These principles remained touchstones for Western academic art until the late nineteenth century.

Architecture of the High Renaissance: Bramante and Palladio

During the High Renaissance, the center of artistic activity shifted from Florence to Rome, as the popes undertook a campaign to restore the ancient city of Rome to its original grandeur as the capital of Christendom. When Pope Julius II commissioned Donato Bramante (1444–1514) to rebuild Saint Peter's Cathedral, the architect designed a monumentally proportioned, centrally planned church to be capped by an immense dome. Bramante's plan was much modified in the 120 years it took to complete the new Saint Peter's. But his ideal of a building organized so that all structural elements were evenly disposed around a central point took shape on a smaller scale in his Tempietto, the "little temple" that marked the site of Saint Peter's martyrdom in Rome (Figure **17.30**). Modeled on the classical *tholos*

Figure 17.30 Donato Bramante, Tempietto, San Pietro in Montorio, Rome, 1502. Height 46 ft., external diameter 29 ft. Photo: © James Morris, London.

Figure 17.31 Andrea Palladio (Andrea di Pietro Gondola), Villa Rotonda, Vicenza, Italy, completed 1569. Photo: Phyllis D. Massar, New York.

(see chapter 6), Bramante's shrine is ringed by a simple colonnade and topped by a dome elevated upon a niched drum. Although the interior affords little light and space, the exterior gives the appearance of an elegant marble reliquary, a perfect structure from which nothing can be added or subtracted without damage to the whole.

The Renaissance passion for harmonious design had an equally powerful influence on the history of domestic architecture, a circumstance for which the Italian architect Andrea Palladio (1518–1580) was especially responsible. In his *Four Books on Architecture*, published in Venice in 1570, Palladio defended symmetry and stability as the controlling elements of architectural design. He put his ideals into practice in a number of magnificent country houses he built for patrons in Northern Italy. The Villa Rotonda near Vicenza—a centrally planned, thirty-two-room country house—is a perfectly symmetrical structure featuring a central room (or rotunda) covered by a dome (Figure 17.31). All four facades of the villa are identical, and each features a projecting Ionic portico approached by a flight of steps (Figure 17.32). In its geometric clarity, its cool elegance, and its total dominance over its landscape setting, the Villa Rotonda represents the Renaissance distillation of classical principles as applied to secular architecture. With this building, Palladio established the definitive ideal in domestic housing for the wealthy and provided a model that would inspire generations of neoclassical architects in England and America (see chapter 26).

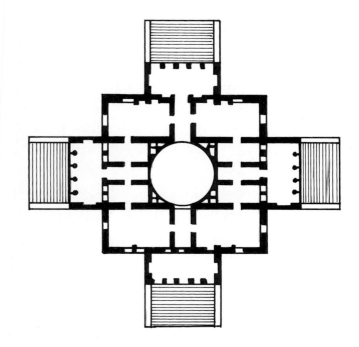

Figure 17.32 Plan of the Villa Rotonda, Vicenza, Italy.

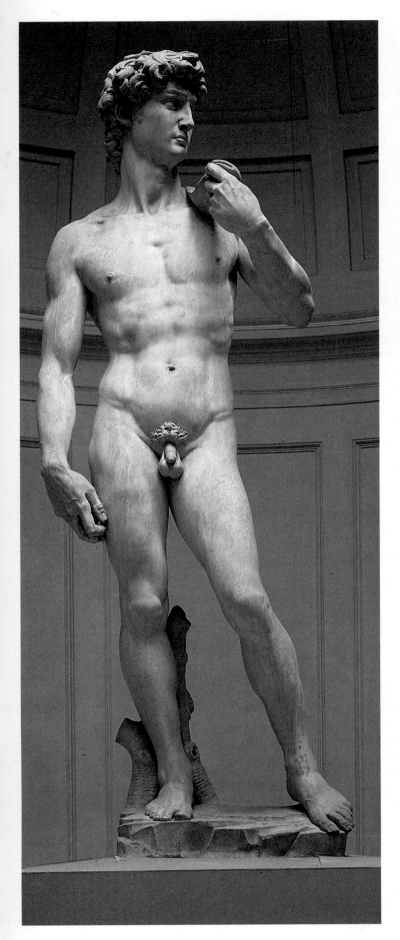

Michelangelo and Heroic Idealism

The works of the High Renaissance master Michelangelo Buonarroti (1475–1564) represent the last and most heroic phase of Renaissance art. An architect, poet, painter, and engineer, Michelangelo regarded himself first and foremost as a sculptor. He established his reputation in Florence at the age of twenty-seven, when he undertook to carve a freestanding larger-than-life statue of the biblical David from a gigantic block of marble that no other sculptor had dared to tackle (Figure **17.33**). When Michelangelo completed the statue in 1504, the rulers of Florence placed it at the entrance to the city hall as a symbol of Florentine vigilance. Compared to Donatello's lean and introspective youth (see Figure 17.1), Michelangelo's *David* is a defiant presence—the offspring of a race of giants. While indebted to classical tradition, Michelangelo deliberately violated classical proportions by making the head and hands of his figure too large for his trunk. The body of the fearless adolescent, with its swelling veins and taut muscles, is tense and brooding, powerful rather than graceful. Indeed, in this image, Michelangelo drew to heroic proportions the Renaissance ideals of *terribilità* and *virtù*.

Though Michelangelo considered himself primarily a sculptor, he spent four years fulfilling a papal commission to paint the 5,800-square-foot ceiling of the Vatican's Sistine Chapel (Figure **17.36**). The scope and monumentality of this enterprise reflect both the ambitions of Pope Julius II and the heroic aspirations of Michelangelo himself. Working from scaffolds poised some 70 feet above the floor, Michelangelo painted a vast scenario illustrating the Creation and Fall of Humankind as recorded in Genesis (1:1 through 9:27; Figure **17.34**). In the nine principal scenes, as well as in the hundreds of accompanying prophets and sibyls, he used high-keyed, clear, bright colors (restored by recent cleaning). He overthrew many traditional constraints, minimizing setting and symbolic details and maximizing the grandeur of figures that—like those he carved in stone—seem to belong to a superhuman race. In the *Creation of Adam* (Figure **17.35**), God and Man—equal in size and muscular grace—confront each other like partners in the divine plan. Adam reaches longingly toward God, seeking the moment of fulfillment, when God will charge his languid body with celestial energy. If the image depicts Creation, it is also a metaphor for the Renaissance belief in the potential divinity of humankind—the visual analogue of Pico's *Oration on the Dignity of Man* (see chapter 16).

Figure 17.33 Michelangelo, *David*, 1501–1504. Marble, height 13 ft. 5 in. Galleria dell'Accademia, Florence. Photo: © Studio Quattrone, Florence.

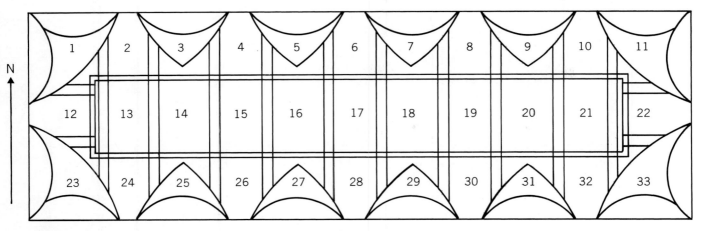

Figure 17.34 Sistine Chapel ceiling, plan of scenes (after Hibbard)

1 Death of Haman
2 Jeremiah
3 Salmon
4 Persian Sibyl
5 Roboam
6 Ezekiel
7 Ozias
8 Eritrean Sibyl
9 Zorobabel
10 Joel
11 David and Goliath

12 Jonah
13 Separation of Light from Darkness
14 Creation of Sun, Moon, Planets
15 Separation of Land from Water
16 Creation of Adam
17 Creation of Eve
18 Temptation and Expulsion
19 Sacrifice of Noah
20 The Flood
21 Drunkenness of Noah
22 Zechariah

23 Moses and the Serpent of Brass
24 Libyan Sibyl
25 Jesse
26 Daniel
27 Asa
28 Cumaean Sibyl
29 Ezekias
30 Isaiah
31 Josiah
32 Delphic Sibyl
33 Judith and Holofernes

Figure 17.35 (below) Michelangelo, *Creation of Adam*, detail of Figure 17.36. Fresco. © Nippon Television Network Corporation, Tokyo, 1998.

Figure 17.36 (overleaf) Michelangelo, Sistine Chapel ceiling (after cleaning), Vatican, Rome, 1508–1512. Fresco, 131 ft. × 141 ft.

Figure 17.37 (above) Michelangelo, dome of Saint Peter's, Vatican, Rome, ca. 1546–1564 (view from the south). Dome completed by Giacomo della Porta, 1590. Photo: © James Morris, London.

0   100 ft.

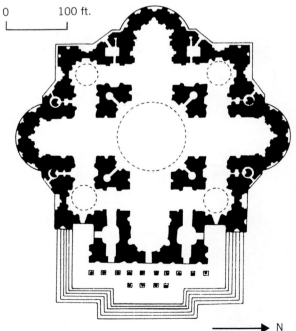

N

Figure 17.38 (right) Michelangelo, plan for the new Saint Peter's, Vatican, Rome, ca. 1537–1550.

In 1546, Michelangelo accepted the papal commission to complete the dome and east end of the new Saint Peter's Cathedral in Rome—a project that followed numerous earlier efforts to make the basilica a centrally planned, domed church. In the last twenty years of his life, Michelangelo mounted an elliptically shaped dome on a huge drum ornamented with double columns of the "colossal order" (Figures 17.37, 17.38). Rising some 450 feet from the floor of the nave to the top of its tall lantern, Michelangelo's dome was heroic in size and dramatic in contour. But its enormous double shell of brick and stone proved impractical: Cracks in the substructure appeared less than ten years after completion, and the superstructure had to be bolstered repeatedly over the centuries, most recently by means of chains. Nevertheless, the great dome inspired numerous copies, such as that of Saint Paul's Cathedral in London (see chapter 21) and the United States Capitol in Washington, D.C.

Michelangelo shared the neoplatonic belief that the soul, imprisoned in the body, yearned to return to its sacred origins. In his last works of art, as in his impassioned sonnets, he explored the conflict between flesh and spirit that had burdened many humanists, including Petrarch. The restless, brooding figures of Michelangelo's late paintings and sculptures writhe and twist, like spirits trying to free themselves of physical matter. Ever the master of invention, the aging Michelangelo moved the gravity and solemnity of High Renaissance art in the direction of mannered theatricality (see chapter 20).

The High Renaissance in Venice

The most notable artworks of the High Renaissance did not come from Florence, which suffered severe political upheavals at the end of the century but, rather, from the cities of Rome, Milan, and Venice. Venice, the Jewel of the Adriatic and a thriving center of trade, was a cluster of islands whose main streets consisted of canals lined with richly ornamented palaces. The pleasure-loving Venetians, governed by a merchant aristocracy, regularly imported costly tapestries, jewels, and other luxury goods from all parts of Asia. During the sixteenth century, Venice outshone all of the other city-states of Italy in its sumptuous architecture and its taste for pageantry, both of which are recreated in the *Procession of the Reliquary of the Cross in Piazza San Marco* (Figure 17.39) by one of Venice's leading artists, Gentile Bellini (1429? –1507). In this panoramic canvas, which employs the new system of one-point perspective to dramatize the union of civic and religious ritual, the Cathedral of Saint Mark resembles a monumental version of the ornate reliquary shrine carried in the foreground. A symbol of Venetian opulence and one of the city's most prized architectural treasures, the cathedral reflects the cross-cultural heritage of Byzantine, Islamic, and Western Christian decorative styles. The multidomed cathedral was begun during the eleventh century and ornamented over many centuries with dazzling mosaics that adorn both the interior and the exterior. As befitting this city of jeweled altarpieces, radiant mosaics, and

Figure 17.39 Gentile Bellini, *Procession of the Reliquary of the Cross in Piazza San Marco*, 1496. Oil on canvas, 12 ft. ½ in. × 24 ft. 5¼ in. Galleria dell'Accademia, Venice. © CAMERAPHOTO Arte, Venice.

sparkling lagoons, Renaissance Venice produced an art of color and light. While Florentine artists depended primarily on *line* as fundamental to design and the articulation of form, the Venetians delighted in the subjective use of *color*. In preference to fresco-painting and tempera applied on wood panels, Venetian painters favored the oil medium, by which they might build up fine color glazes on rough canvas surfaces.

The two greatest Venetian colorists were Giorgio Barbarelli, known as Giorgione (1478–1510), and Tiziano Vecelli, called Titian (ca. 1488–1547). Little is known of Giorgione's life, but his influence on his younger colleague was significant. The *Pastoral Concert* (Figure 17.40), a work that some scholars hold to be an early Titian, was probably begun by Giorgione and completed by Titian. This intriguing canvas shows two magnificently dressed Venetian courtiers—one playing a lute—in the presence of two female nudes. One woman holds a recorder, while the other pours water into a well. The precise subject of the painting is unclear, but its sensuousness—more a product of mood than of narrative content—is enhanced by textural contrasts: the satin costume of the lute player versus the golden flesh tones of bare skin, the dense foliage of the middle ground versus the thin atmosphere on the distant horizon, and so forth. In its evocation of untroubled country life, *Pastoral Concert* may be considered the visual equivalent of pastoral verse, a genre that became popular among Renaissance humanists. But the painting also introduces a new subject that would become quite fashionable in Western art: the nude in a landscape setting. During the sixteenth century, the female nude—often bearing the name of a classical goddess—became a favorite subject of patrons seeking sensuous or erotic art for private enjoyment. The most famous of such commissions, the so-called *Venus of Urbino* (Figure 17.41), was painted for the Duke of Urbino during the last stage of Titian's artistic career. Here, a curvaceous nude reclines on a bed in the curtained alcove of a typical upper-class Venetian palace. The myrtle plant in her hand, the faithful dog at her feet, and the servants who rummage in the nearby wedding chest all suggest impending marriage, while her seductive pose and arresting gaze are manifestly sexual. Titian enhanced the sensuality of the image by means of exquisitely painted surfaces: the delicate nuances of creamy skin modeled with glowing pinks, the reddish blond locks of hair, the deep burgundies of tapestries and cushions, and the cooler bluish whites of the sheets—all bathed in a pervasive golden light. Titian, who worked almost exclusively in oils, applied paint loosely, building up forms with layers of color so that contours seem to melt into each other, a technique best described as "painterly." He preferred broken and subtle tones of color to the flat, bright hues favored by such artists as Raphael. Titian's painterly style became the definitive expression of the coloristic manner in High Renaissance painting and a model for such artists as Rubens in the seventeenth century and Delacroix in the nineteenth.

Figure 17.40 Titian (begun by Giorgione), *Pastoral Concert*, ca. 1505. Oil on canvas, 3 ft. 7¼ in. × 4 ft. 6¼ in. Louvre, Paris. Photo: © R.M.N., Paris.

Figure 17.41 Titian, *Venus of Urbino*, 1538–1539. Oil on canvas, 3 ft. 11 in. × 5 ft. 5 in. Uffizi Gallery, Florence.

The Music of the Renaissance

Like Renaissance art, Renaissance music was increasingly secular in subject matter and function. However, the perception of the Renaissance as a time when secular music overtook ecclesiastical music may be due to the fact that after 1450 more secular music was committed to paper. The printing press, which was perfected in Germany in the mid-fifteenth century, encouraged the preservation and dissemination of all kinds of musical composition. With the establishment of printing presses in Venice in the late fifteenth century, printed books of lute music and part-books for individual instruments appeared in great numbers. (Most music was based on preexisting melodies, and manuscripts normally lacked tempo markings and other indications as to how a piece was to be performed.) Publishers also sold vernacular handbooks that offered instructions on how to play musical instruments. It is no surprise, then, that during the Renaissance, music was composed not only by professional musicians, but by amateurs as well. Indeed, Castiglione observed that making music was the function of all well-rounded individuals. Music was an essential ingredient at intimate gatherings, court celebrations, and public festivals. And virtuosity in performance, a hallmark of Renaissance music, was common among both amateurs and professionals. Such Renaissance princes as Lorenzo de' Medici took pleasure in

writing songs for the carnivals that traditionally preceded the Lenten season. On pageant wagons designed for holiday spectacles in Florence and other cities, masked singers, dancers, and mimes enacted mythological, religious, and contemporary tales in musical performance.

While the literary and visual evidence of classical antiquity was readily available to the humanists of the Renaissance, few musical examples had survived, and none could be accurately deciphered. For that reason, medieval tradition maintained a stronger influence in the development of music than it did in art and literature. (Not until the late sixteenth century did composers draw on Greek drama as the inspiration for a new genre: opera—discussed in chapter 20). Moreover, perhaps because performing music was believed to be within everyone's reach, musicians were not held in such high esteem as painters, sculptors, or architects of the Renaissance. Most theorists, including Leonardo da Vinci (himself a musician of some renown), considered poetry—and by extension, music—inferior to painting. Nevertheless, just as Renaissance artists pursued a more "natural-looking" art, Renaissance composers sought a more "natural-sounding" music. By the early fifteenth century, the trend toward consonant sounds encouraged the use of **intervals** of thirds in place of the traditional medieval (and ancient) intervals of fourths and fifths.

Early Renaissance Music: Dufay

While in the visual arts Italy took the lead, in music, French and Franco-Flemish composers outshone their Italian counterparts. During the fifteenth and much of the sixteenth centuries, composers from Burgundy and Flanders dominated the courts of Europe, including those of Italy. The leading Franco-Flemish composer of the fifteenth century, Guillaume Dufay (1400–1474), spent more than thirteen years of his career in Italy, during which time he set to music the verses of Petrarch and Lorenzo de' Medici (unfortunately, the latter compositions have been lost). In Dufay's more than two hundred surviving vocal and instrumental compositions, including motets, masses, and *chansons* (secular songs), he made extensive use of late medieval polyphonic techniques. At the same time, he introduced a close melodic and rhythmic kinship between all parts of a musical composition.

Just as religious subject matter inspired much of the art of Renaissance painters and sculptors, so religious music—and especially compositions for the Mass—held a prominent place in Dufay's output. However, sacred and secular themes are often indistinguishable in Dufay's works, and both are suffused by warmth of feeling. For his Mass settings, Dufay followed the common practice of using melodies borrowed from popular folk tunes. In the *Missa L'homme armé*,♪ for instance, he employed the best known of all fifteenth-century French folksongs, "The Armed Man," as the *cantus firmus* for all sections of the piece.

High Renaissance Music: Josquin

If Dufay was the leading composer of the Early Renaissance, the outstanding figure in High Renaissance music was Josquin des Prez (1440–1521). Josquin followed the example of his predecessors by serving at the courts of France and Italy, including that of the papacy. A master of masses, motets, and secular songs, he earned international recognition as "the prince of music." Like Dufay, Josquin unified each polyphonic mass around a single musical theme, but, more in the grand style of the painter Raphael, Josquin contrived complex designs in which melody and harmony were distributed symmetrically and with "geometric" clarity. He might give focus to a single musical phrase in the way that Raphael might center the Virgin and Child within a composition. And, in an effort to increase compositional balance, he might group voices into pairs, with the higher voices repeating certain phrases of the lower ones.♪ The expressive grace of Josquin's music followed from the attention he gave to the relationship between words and music. He

tailored musical lines so that they followed the natural flow of the words, a device inspired perhaps by his appreciation of the classical kinship of song and text. Josquin was among the first to practice **word painting**, the manipulation of music to convey the literal meaning of the text—as, for example, where the text describes a bird's ascent, the music might rise in pitch. Word painting characterized both the religious and secular music of the Renaissance.

In music, as in the visual arts, composers of the Renaissance valued unity of design. Josquin achieved a homogeneous musical texture by the use of **imitation**, a technique whereby a melodic fragment introduced in the first voice is repeated closely (though usually at a different pitch) in the second, third, and fourth voices, so that one overlaps the next. Simple rhythmic lines and the ingenious use of imitation contributed to the smooth and sonorous style of such motets as "Tulerunt Dominum meum."♪ A master of the integration of multiple voice lines—one of his motets has as many as twenty-four parts—Josquin wrote motets that featured a continuous flow of interwoven melodies and a graceful design comparable to that of Raphael's High Renaissance compositions.

The Madrigal

During the sixteenth century, the secular counterpart of the motet and the most popular type of vernacular song was the **madrigal**, a composition for three to six unaccompanied voices.♪ Usually polyphonic in texture and set to fine poetry, the madrigal often incorporated a large degree of vocal freedom, including the playful use of imitation and word painting. An intimate kind of musical composition, the madrigal might develop a romantic theme from a sonnet by Petrarch or give expression to a trifling and whimsical complaint. The Flemish composer Roland de Lassus (Orlando di Lasso; 1532–1594), who graced princely courts throughout Renaissance Europe, produced almost two hundred madrigals among his more than two thousand compositions. In 1550, at age eighteen, Lassus wrote one of the most delightful madrigals of the Renaissance: "Matona, mia cara" ("My lady, my beloved").♪ The piece, which describes a suitor's effort to seduce his ladyfriend, ends each stanza with a frivolous group of nonsense syllables.

> My lady, my beloved,
> Such pleasure would I choose
> To sing beneath your window
> Of love you'll never lose.
> *Dong, dong, dong, derry, derry,*
> *Dong, dong, dong, dong.*

♪ See Music Listening Selections at end of chapter.

♪ See Music Listening Selections at end of chapter.

I beg you, only hear me,
This song of sweetest news,
My love for you is boundless
Like lovebirds I enthuse.
   Dong, dong, dong, derry, derry,
    Dong, dong, dong, dong.

For I would go a-hunting
And falcons I would use
To bring you spoils a-plenty
Plump woodfowl as your dues.
   Dong, dong, dong, derry, derry,
    Dong, dong, dong, dong.

But though my words should fail me,
Lest fear my cause should lose,
E'en Petrarch could not help me
Nor Helicon's fair Muse.
   Dong, dong, dong, derry, derry,
    Dong, dong, dong, dong.

But only say you'll love me
And if you'll not refuse
I'll boldly sing of my love
Night long until the dews.
   Dong, dong, dong, derry, derry,
    Dong, dong, dong, dong.[*]

Madrigals flourished primarily in the courts of Italy and England. At the fashionable court of Queen Elizabeth I of England, such musicians as John Dowland (1563–1602) and Thomas Morley (1557–1602)[♪] composed English-language solo songs and madrigals that are still enjoyed today.

Instrumental Music of the Renaissance

Although most Renaissance music was meant to be sung, the sixteenth century made considerable advances in the development of instrumental music. Music for solo instruments was popular (the lute was still the favorite), while a wide variety of other instruments, such as shawms, cromornes, cornets, trumpets, trombones, and drums were used for accompaniment and in small instrumental ensembles (Figure **17.42**). Renaissance composers wrote music for small **organs** (popular in private homes and princely courts) and for two other types of keyboard instruments: the **clavichord** and the **harpsichord** (also called the *spinet*, the *clavecin*, and the *virginal*—the last possibly after the "Virgin Queen," Elizabeth I of England, who was an accomplished musician). Harpsichord sounds are made by quills that pluck a set of strings, while clavichord notes are produced by metal tangents that strike the

Figure 17.42 *The Music Room*, from *Der Weiss Kunig*, engraved by Hans Burgkmair, late sixteenth century. Woodcut. The J. Pierpont Morgan Library, New York. © 1990.

strings. Such instruments create bright, sharp sounds, somewhat more robust in the harpsichord. Since Renaissance instruments produce a less dynamic and smaller range of sound than do modern instruments, they demand greater attention to nuances of *timbre*—the "color" or quality of musical sound.

During the late Middle Ages, instruments occasionally took the place of one or more voice parts. It was not until the Renaissance, however, that music for instruments alone regularly appeared. Instrumental compositions developed out of dance tunes with strong rhythms and distinctive melodic lines. Indeed, the earliest model for the instrumental suite was a group of dances arranged according to contrasting rhythms. Instrumental music was characterized by the same kind of complex invention that marked the vocal compositions of Josquin, and the skillful performance of difficult instrumental passages brought acclaim to both performer and composer.

Renaissance Dance

In the Renaissance, dance played an important role in all forms of entertainment: town pageants, courtly rituals, festal displays sponsored by trade and merchant guilds, and in almost all nonecclesiastical celebrations. Folk dancing, of the kind illustrated by the Flemish painter Pieter Brueghel (see Figure 18.13), was a

[*]Translation by Susan Peach, copyright © Calmann & King 1998.
[♪] See Music Listening Selections at end of chapter.

collective experience that fostered a powerful sense of community. In contrast with folk dances, court dances stressed individual grace and poise. Renaissance dancing masters distinguished folk dance from courtly dance, a move that eventually resulted in the development of dance as a form of theatrical entertainment. In Italy, the three favorite forms of court dance were the *basse* (a slow and solemn ceremonial dance), the *saltarello* (a vigorous, three-beat dance that featured graceful leaps), and the *piva* (a dance in rapid tempo with double steps).

The Renaissance witnessed the first efforts to establish dance as an independent discipline. Guglielmo Ebreo (1439–1482), dancing master at the court of Urbino, wrote one of the first treatises on the art of dancing. He emphasized the importance of grace, the memorization of fixed steps, and the coordination of music and motion. Guglielmo also choreographed a number of lively dances or *balli*—the Italian word from which the French *ballet* derives. In Guglielmo's day, however, such dances were still performed by members of the court, rather than by professional dancers.

SUMMARY

Renaissance artists were disciples of nature in that they brought a scientific curiosity to the study of the natural world and diligently probed its operations. Donatello, Pollaiuolo, Masaccio, and Brunelleschi studied the mechanics of the human body, the effects of light on material substances, and the physical appearance of objects in three-dimensional space. At the same time, Renaissance artists were masters of invention: They perfected the technique of oil painting, formulated laws of perspective, and applied the principles of classical art to the representation of Christian and contemporary subjects. Patronized by a wealthy European middle class, they revived such this-worldly genres as portraiture and gave new attention to the nude body as an object of beauty.

The art of the High Renaissance marks the culmination of a hundred-year effort to wed the techniques of naturalistic representation to classical ideals of proportion and harmony. Leonardo, the quintessential artist-scientist, tried to reconcile empirical experience with basic principles of balance and order. The compositions of Raphael, with their monumental grace and unity of design, became standards by which Western paintings would be judged for many centuries. The multitalented Michelangelo brought a heroic idealism to the treatment of traditional Christian and classical themes. In Venice, Titian's painterly handling of the female nude represented a new and more sensuous naturalism. In architecture, the centrally planned buildings of Bramante and Palladio fulfilled the quest of such Early Renaissance architects as Brunelleschi and Alberti for an architecture of harmony, balance, and clarity.

The Renaissance produced an equally splendid flowering in music, especially among Franco-Flemish composers. Secular compositions began to outnumber religious ones. The techniques of imitation and word painting infused both religious and secular music with homogeneity and increased expressiveness. Printed sheet music helped to popularize the madrigal and other secular, vernacular song forms. Instrumental music and dance emerged as independent genres. Like their classical predecessors, Renaissance artists placed human concerns and human feelings at the center of a harmonious universe. Such optimism, combined with intellectual curiosity and increasing worldliness, fueled the early modern era in the West.

GLOSSARY

aerial perspective the means of representing distance in a painting; it relies on the imitation of the ways atmosphere affects the eye—outlines are blurred, details lost, contrasts of light and shade diminished, hues bluer, and colors less vivid; also called "atmospheric perspective"

clavichord (French, "clavier," meaning "keyboard") a stringed keyboard instrument widely used between the sixteenth and eighteenth centuries; when the player presses down on a key, a brass tangent or blade rises and strikes a string

contrapposto (Italian, "counterpoised") a position assumed by the human body in which one part is turned in opposition to another part

drum the cylindrical section immediately beneath the dome of a building

harpsichord a stringed keyboard instrument widely used between the sixteenth and eighteenth centuries; when the player presses down on a key, a quill, called a plectrum, plucks the string

imitation a technique whereby a melodic fragment introduced in the first voice of a composition is repeated closely (though usually at a different pitch) in the second, third, and fourth voices, so that one voice overlaps the next; the repetition may be exactly the same as the original, or it may differ somewhat

intarsia a type of marquetry (see chapter 23) involving the technique of wood inlay

interval the distance between the pitches of two musical tones

lantern a small, windowed tower on top of a roof or dome that allows light to enter the interior of a building

linear perspective (or **optical perspective**) a method of creating the semblance of three-dimensional space on a two-dimensional surface; it derives from two optical illusions: (1) parallel lines appear to converge as they recede toward a vanishing point on a horizon level with the viewer's eye, and (2) objects appear to shrink and move closer together as they recede from view

madrigal a vernacular song, usually composed for three to six unaccompanied voices

organ a keyboard instrument in which keyboards and pedals are used to force air into a series of pipes, causing them to sound

picture plane the two-dimensional surface of a panel or canvas

pilaster a shallow, flattened, rectangular column or pier attached to a wall surface

word painting the manipulation of music to convey a specific object, thought, or mood—that is, the content of the text

SUGGESTIONS FOR READING

Baxandall, Michael. *Painting and Experience in Fifteenth Century Italy*. New York: Oxford University Press, 1972.

Brown, H. M. *Music in the Renaissance*. Englewood Cliffs, N.J.: Prentice-Hall, 1976.

Clark, Kenneth. *Leonardo da Vinci: An Account of His Development as an Artist*. Baltimore, Md.: Penguin, 1967.

Cole, Bruce. *The Renaissance Artist at Work: From Pisano to Titian*. New York: Harper, 1993.

Kemp, Martin, and Jane Roberts. *Leonardo da Vinci: Artist, Scientist, Inventor*. New Haven: Yale University Press, 1989.

Kempers, Bram. *Painting, Power and Patronage: The Rise of the Professional Artist in Renaissance Italy*. Translated by Beverley Jackson. New York: Penguin, 1987.

Levey, Michael. *Early Renaissance*. Baltimore, Md.: Penguin, 1967.

———. *High Renaissance*. Baltimore, Md.: Penguin, 1975.

Murray, Peter, and L. Murray. *The Art of the Renaissance*. London: Thames and Hudson, 1978.

Palisca, Claude V. *Humanism in Italian Renaissance Musical Thought*. New Haven: Yale University Press, 1985.

Smith, Christine. *Architecture in the Culture of Early Humanism: Ethics, Aesthetics, and Eloquence 1400–1470*. New York: Oxford University Press, 1992.

Wittkower, Rudolf. *Architectural Principles in the Age of Humanism*. New York: St. Martin, 1988.

MUSIC LISTENING SELECTIONS

Cassette I Selection 15 Guillaume Dufay, *Missa L'homme armé* (*The Armed Man Mass*), "Kyrie I," ca. 1450.

Cassette I Selection 16 Roland de Lassus (Orlando di Lasso), Madrigal, "Matona, mia cara" ("My lady, my beloved"), 1550.

Cassette I Selection 17 Thomas Morley, Madrigal, "My bonnie lass she smileth," 1595.

Cassette I Selection 18 Josquin des Prez, Motet, "Tulerunt Dominum meum," ca. 1520.

PART

II

A BRAVE NEW WORLD

"brave new world, That has such people in it," exclaims Miranda, a character in Shakespeare's *The Tempest*, as she considers the "many goodly creatures" of the playwright's fictional island. With similar astonishment but perhaps a little less optimism, mid-sixteenth-century Europeans contemplated their brave new world—one that witnessed the fragmentation of Christendom, the onset of devastating religious wars, and the discovery of strange cultures in remote parts of the world.

By the sixteenth century, the old medieval order was crumbling. Classical humanism and the influence of Renaissance artist-scientists were spreading throughout Northern Europe. Spanish campaigns of geographic exploration now involved the colonization of the Americas. Overseas expansion led to a more accurate appreciation of world geography and the proliferation of commercial contacts with Asia and Africa. The brave new world of the sixteenth century saw the rise of a global economy and vast opportunities for material wealth. At the same time, as European nation-states tried to strengthen sovereignty and international influence, rivalry among nations intensified. The "superpowers"—Spain, under the Hapsburg ruler Philip II (1527–1598) and England under Elizabeth I (1533–1603)—contended for advantages in Atlantic shipping and trade. In order to resist the encroachment of the stronger nation-states, weaker states formed balance-of-power alliances that often invited war.

While political turmoil threatened the medieval order, sixteenth-century science also challenged age-old traditions. In 1530, the Polish astronomer Nicolas Copernicus (1473–1543) completed a treatise that opposed the earth-centered view of the universe. Contrary to the position supported by Scripture and the Church, *De revolutionibus* (*On the Revolution of the Heavenly Spheres*) contended that the planets moved around the sun. Scientific theory, geographic exploration, and commercial expansion all worked to move the West toward modernity; but it was the Protestant Reformation that most effectively destroyed the old medieval order. In the wake of Protestantism, the unity of European Christendom disappeared forever. And, as religious factionalism compounded the political rivalries among the nation-states, the future of Western civilization seemed grim indeed.

Chapter 18, "Protest and Reform: The Waning of the Old Order," treats the religious, social, and artistic upheavals of the turbulent sixteenth century. The revolt against the Catholic Church, led by Martin Luther, is framed by the broader movements of Christian humanism and the Northern Renaissance. The effort to assess one's place in a geographically expanding and spiritually fragmented world is apparent in all forms of expression—in the art of Dürer and Bosch, the satires of Erasmus, More, and Cervantes, and the essays of Montaigne. In these works, as in *Othello*, one of Shakespeare's greatest tragedies, Northern European artists and writers challenged the idealism and the optimism of their Italian counterparts.

(opposite) Pieter Brueghel the Elder, detail of *Triumph of Death*, ca. 1562–1564. Oil on panel, full image 3 ft. 10 in. × 5 ft. 3¾ in. Prado, Madrid. Photo: Arxiu MAS, Madrid.

The final chapter, "Africa, the Americas, and Cross-Cultural Encounter," examines the civilizations of Africa (especially West Africa) and the Americas in the centuries prior to their encounter with the West, as well as during the era of European expansion. The cross-cultural dimension of this chapter is enhanced by readings from the Muslim world traveller Ibn Battuta and the Spanish adventurer Hernán Cortés.

During the three-hundred-year "seam" between old and new, Westerners reassessed their relationship with the classical and medieval past, created the first global trade empires, and virtually determined the futures of Africa and the Americas. Such devices as firearms, eyeglasses, the printing press, and the clock—all products of this period—gave Europeans considerable mastery over nature. But the very people who invented these technological wonders also pursued cruel wars of religion, widespread trade in chattel slavery, and ruthless campaigns of witchburnings—activities that seem to give the lie to any optimistic theory of human progress. Nevertheless, the sixteenth century set the humanistic tradition on an irreversibly modern course.

18
Protest and Reform:
The Waning of the Old Order

The Temper of Reform

The Impact of Technology

In the transition from medieval to early modern times, technology played a crucial role. Gunpowder, the light cannon, and other military devices made warfare more impersonal and ultimately more deadly. At the same time, Western advances in navigation, shipbuilding, and maritime instrumentation brought Europe into a dominant position in world exploration and colonization. By the end of the sixteenth century, European expansion would change the map of the world.

Another kind of technology, the printing press, revolutionized the future of learning and communication. Block printing originated in China in the ninth century and movable type in the eleventh, but print technology did not reach Western Europe until the fifteenth century. By 1450, in the city of Mainz, the German goldsmith Johannes Gutenberg (ca. 1400–ca. 1468) had perfected a printing press that made it possible to fabricate books more cheaply, more rapidly, and in greater numbers than ever before. As information became a commodity for mass production, vast areas of knowledge—heretofore the exclusive domain of the monastery, the Church, and the university—became available to the public. The printing press facilitated the rise of popular education and encouraged individuals to form their own opinions by reading for themselves. Print technology proved to be the single most important

1320	paper adopted for use in Europe (having long been in use in China)
1450	the Dutch devise the first firearm small enough to be carried by a single person
1451	Nicolas of Cusa (German) uses concave lenses to amend nearsightedness
1454	Johannes Gutenberg (German) prints the Bible with movable metal type

factor in the success of the Protestant Reformation, as it brought the complaints of Church reformers to the attention of all literate folk. And, in the wake of such writers as Dante, Chaucer, Petrarch, and Boccaccio, the printing press nourished the growing interest in vernacular literature, which in turn enhanced national and individual self-consciousness.

Christian Humanism and the Northern Renaissance

The new print technology broadcast an old message of religious protest and reform. For two centuries, critics had attacked the wealth, worldliness, and unchecked corruption of the Church of Rome. During the early fifteenth century, the rekindled sparks of lay piety and anticlericalism spread throughout the Netherlands, where religious leaders launched the movement known as the *devotio moderna* ("modern devotion"). Lay Brothers and Sisters of the Common Life, as they were called, organized houses in which they studied and taught Scripture. Living in the manner of Christian monks and nuns, but taking no monastic vows, these lay Christians cultivated a devotional lifestyle that fulfilled the ideals of the apostles and the church fathers. They followed the mandate of Thomas à Kempis (1380–1471), himself a Brother of the Common Life and author of the *Imitatio Christi* (*Imitation of Christ*), to put the message of Jesus into daily practice.

The *devotio moderna* spread quickly throughout Northern Europe, harnessing the dominant strains of anticlericalism, lay piety, and mysticism, even as it coincided with the revival of classical studies in the newly established universities of Germany. Although Northern humanists, like their Italian Renaissance counterparts, encouraged learning in Greek and Latin, they were more concerned with the study and translation of Early Christian manuscripts than with the classical and largely secular texts that had preoccupied the Italian humanists. Northern humanists studied the Bible and the writings of the church fathers with the same intellectual fervor that the Italian humanists had brought to their examination of Plato and Cicero. The efforts of these Northern scholars gave rise to a rebirth (or renaissance) that focused on the late classical world and, specifically, on Christian humanism: the revival of Early Christian literature and the evangelical Christianity of the early Church.

The leading Christian humanist of the sixteenth century—often called "the Prince of Humanists"—was Desiderius Erasmus of Rotterdam (1466–1536; Figure 18.1). Schooled among the Brothers of the Common Life and learned in Latin, Greek, and Hebrew, Erasmus was a superb scholar and a prolific writer (see Reading 3.14). The first humanist to make extensive use of the printing press, he once dared a famous publisher to print his words as fast as he could write them. Erasmus was a fervent neoclassicist—he argued that almost everything worth knowing was set forth in Greek and Latin. He was also a devout Christian who advocated a return to the basic teachings of Christ. He criticized the Church and all Christians whose faith had been jaded by slavish adherence to dogma and ritual. Using four different Greek manuscripts of the Gospels, he produced a critical edition of the New Testament that corrected Jerome's mistranslations of key passages. Erasmus' New Testament became the source of most sixteenth-century German and English vernacular translations of this central text of Christian humanism.

Luther and the Protestant Reformation

During the sixteenth century, papal extravagance and immorality reached new heights, and Church reform became an urgent public issue. In the territories of Germany, loosely united under the leadership of the Holy Roman Emperor Charles V (1500–1558), the voices of protest were more strident than any elsewhere in Europe. Across Germany, the sale of indulgences for the benefit of the Church of Rome—specifically for the rebuilding of Saint Peter's Cathedral—provoked harsh criticism, especially among those who regarded the luxuries of the Roman papacy as a betrayal of apostolic ideals. As with most movements of religious reform, it fell to one individual to galvanize popular sentiment. In 1505, Martin Luther (1483–1546), the son of a rural coal miner, abandoned his legal studies to become an Augustinian monk (Figure 18.2). Thereafter, as a doctor of theology at the University of Wittenberg, Luther spoke out against the Church. His inflammatory sermons and essays offered radical remedies to what he called "the misery and wretchedness of Christendom."

Luther was convinced of the inherent sinfulness of humankind, but he took issue with the traditional medieval view—as promulgated, for instance, in *Everyman* (see chapter 12)—that salvation was earned through the performance of good works and grace received through the intermediation of the Church and its priesthood. Inspired by the words of Saint Paul, "the just shall live by faith" (Romans 1:17), Luther maintained that salvation could be gained only by faith in the validity of Christ's sacrifice. Human beings were saved by the unearned gift of God's grace, argued Luther, not by their good works on earth. The purchase of indulgences, the veneration of relics, making pilgrimages, and seeking the intercession of the saints were useless, because only the grace of God could save the Christian soul. Justified by faith alone, Christians should assume full responsibility for their own actions and intentions.

In 1517, in pointed criticism of Church abuses, Luther posted on the door of the cathedral of Wittenberg a list of ninety-five issues he intended for dispute with the leaders of the Church of Rome. The *Ninety-Five Theses*, which took the confrontational tone of the sample below, were put to press and circulated throughout Europe:

> 27 They are wrong who say that the soul flies out of Purgatory as soon as the money thrown into the chest rattles.
> 32 Those who believe that, through letters of pardon, they are made sure of their own salvation will be eternally damned along with their teachers.
> 37 Every true Christian, whether living or dead, has a share in all the benefits of Christ and of the Church, given by God, even without letters of pardon.
> 43 Christians should be taught that he who gives to a poor man, or lends to a needy man, does better than if he bought pardons.
> 62 The true treasure of the Church is the Holy Gospel of the glory and grace of God.
> 86 . . . why does not the Pope, whose riches are at this day more ample than those of the wealthiest of the wealthy, build the single Basilica of St. Peter with his own money rather than with that of poor believers? . . .*

Luther did not wish to destroy Catholicism, but rather to reform it. Gradually he extended his criticism of Church abuses to criticism of Church doctrine. For instance, because he found justification in Scripture for only two of the sacraments dispensed by the Catholic Church—Baptism and Holy Communion—he rejected

---

*J. H. Robinson, ed., *Translations and Reprints from the Original Sources of European History*, II. No. 6. Philadelphia: University of Pennsylvania Press, 1894.

Figure 18.1 Albrecht Dürer, *Erasmus of Rotterdam*, 1526. Engraving, 9¾ × 7½ in.
Reproduced by courtesy of the Trustees of the British Museum, London.

Figure 18.2 Lucas Cranach the Elder, *Portrait of Martin Luther.* Uffizi Gallery, Florence. Alinari/Art Resource, New York.

the other five. He attacked monasticism and clerical celibacy, ultimately marrying a former nun and fathering six children. Luther's boldest challenge to the old medieval order, however, was his unwillingness to accept the pope as the ultimate source of religious authority. He denied that the pope was the spiritual heir to Saint Peter and claimed that the head of the Church, like any other human being, was subject to error and correction. Christians, argued Luther, were collectively a priesthood of believers; they were "consecrated as priests by baptism." The ultimate source of authority in matters of faith and doctrine, held Luther, was Scripture, as interpreted by the individual Christian. To encourage the reading of the Bible among his followers, Luther translated the Old and New Testaments into German.

Luther's assertions were revolutionary because they defied both Church dogma and the authority of the Church of Rome. In 1520, Pope Leo X issued an edict excommunicating the outspoken reformer. Luther promptly burned the edict in the presence of his students at the University of Wittenberg. The following year, he was summoned to the city of Worms in order to appear before the Diet—the German parliamentary council. Charged with heresy, Luther stubbornly refused to recant. His confrontational temperament and down-to-earth style are captured in this excerpt from his *Address to the German Nobility,* a call for religious reform written shortly before the Diet of Worms and circulated widely in a printed edition.

READING 3.13

From Luther's *Address to the German Nobility*

It has been devised that the Pope, bishops, priests, and   1
monks are called the *spiritual estate*; princes, lords,
artificers, and peasants are the *temporal estate*. This is
an artful lie and hypocritical device, but let no one be
made afraid by it, and that for this reason: that all
Christians are truly of the spiritual estate, and there is no
difference among them, save of office alone. As St. Paul
says (1 Cor.: 12), we are all one body, though each
member does its own work, to serve the others. This is
because we have one baptism, one Gospel, one faith, and   10
are all Christians alike; for baptism, Gospel, and faith,
these alone make spiritual and Christian people.
   As for the unction by a pope or a bishop, tonsure,
ordination, consecration, and clothes differing from those
of laymen—all this may make a hypocrite or an anointed
puppet, but never a Christian or a spiritual man. Thus we
are all consecrated as priests by baptism. . . .
   And to put the matter even more plainly, if a little
company of pious Christian laymen were taken prisoners
and carried away to a desert, and had not among them a   20
priest consecrated by a bishop, and were there to agree to
elect one of them, born in wedlock or not, and were to
order him to baptise, to celebrate the mass, to absolve,
and to preach, this man would as truly be a priest, as if
all the bishops and all the popes had consecrated him.
That is why in cases of necessity every man can baptise
and absolve, which would not be possible if we were not
all priests. . . .
   [Members of the Church of Rome] alone pretend to be
considered masters of the Scriptures; although they learn   30
nothing of them all their life. They assume authority, and
juggle before us with impudent words, saying that the
Pope cannot err in matters of faith, whether he be evil or
good, albeit they cannot prove it by a single letter. That is
why the canon law contains so many heretical and
unchristian, nay unnatural, laws. . . .
   . . . And though they say that this authority was given
to St. Peter when the keys were given to him, it is plain
enough that the keys were not given to St. Peter alone,
but to the whole community. Besides, the keys were not   40
ordained for doctrine or authority, but for sin, to bind or
loose; and what they claim besides this from the keys is
mere invention. . . .
   Only consider the matter. They must needs
acknowledge that there are pious Christians among us

that have the true faith, spirit, understanding, word, and mind of Christ: why then should we reject their word and understanding, and follow a pope who has neither understanding nor spirit? Surely this were to deny our whole faith and the Christian Church. . . . 50

Therefore when need requires, and the Pope is a cause of offence to Christendom, in these cases whoever can best do so, as a faithful member of the whole body, must do what he can to procure a true free council. This no one can do so well as the temporal authorities, especially since they are fellow-Christians, fellow-priests, sharing one spirit and one power in all things, . . . Would it not be most unnatural, if a fire were to break out in a city, and every one were to keep still and let it burn on and on, whatever might be burnt, simply because they had not the mayor's 60 authority, or because the fire perchance broke out at the mayor's house? Is not every citizen bound in this case to rouse and call in the rest? How much more should this be done in the spiritual city of Christ, if a fire of offence breaks out, either at the Pope's government or wherever it may! The like happens if an enemy attacks a town. The first to rouse up the rest earns glory and thanks. Why then should not he earn glory that decries the coming of our enemies from hell and rouses and summons all Christians?

But as for their boasts of their authority, that no one 70 must oppose it, this is idle talk. No one in Christendom has any authority to do harm, or to forbid others to prevent harm being done. There is no authority in the Church but for reformation. Therefore if the Pope wished to use his power to prevent the calling of a free council, so as to prevent the reformation of the Church, we must not respect him or his power; and if he should begin to excommunicate and fulminate, we must despise this as the doings of a madman, and, trusting in God, excommunicate and repel him as best we may. . . . 80

———————————◆———————————

The Spread of Protestantism

Luther's criticism constituted an open revolt against the institution that for centuries had governed the lives of Western Christians. With the aid of the printing press, his "protestant" sermons circulated throughout Europe. Luther's defense of Christian conscience as opposed to episcopal authority worked to justify protest against all forms of dominion. In 1524, under the banner of Christian liberty, the German peasants instigated a series of bloody uprisings against the oppressive landholding aristocracy. Luther finally condemned the violence and brutality of the Peasant Revolts, but social unrest and ideological warfare had only just begun. Members of the German nobility who supported Luther used their new religious allegiance as an excuse to seize and usurp Church properties and revenues within their own domains. As the floodgates of dissent opened wide, civil wars broke out between German princes who were faithful to Rome and those who called themselves Lutheran. The wars lasted for some twenty-five years, until, by the terms of the Peace of Augsburg in 1555, it was agreed that each German prince should have the right to choose the religion to be practiced within his own domain. But religious wars resumed in the late sixteenth century and devastated German lands for almost a century.

All of Europe was affected by Luther's break with the Church. The Lutheran insistence that enlightened Christians could discover religious truth by way of Scripture led reformers everywhere to interpret the Bible for themselves. The result was the birth of many new Protestant sects, each based on its own interpretation of Scripture. In the independent city of Geneva, Switzerland, the French theologian John Calvin (1509–1564) set up a government in which elected officials, using the Bible as the supreme law, ruled the community. Calvin held that Christians were predestined from birth for either salvation or damnation, a circumstance that made good works irrelevant. The "Doctrine of Predestination" encouraged Calvinists to glorify God by living an upright life, one that required abstention from dancing, gambling, swearing, drunkenness, and from all forms of public display. For, although one's status was known only by God, Christians might manifest that they were among the "elect" by a show of moral rectitude. Finally, since Calvin taught that wealth was a sign of God's favor, Calvinists extolled the "work ethic" as consistent with the divine will.

In nearby Zürich, the humanist scholar Ulrich Zwingli (1484–1531) fathered the Anabaptist sect. Zwingli placed total emphasis on Christian conscience and the voluntary acceptance of Christ through adult baptism. He denied as sources of grace all seven of the sacraments instituted by the Church of Rome. English offshoots of the Anabaptists—the Baptists and the Quakers—would come to follow Zwingli's absolute rejection of ceremony and ritual and adopt his fundamentalist approach to Scripture.

In England, the Tudor monarch Henry VIII (1491–1547) broke with the Roman Catholic Church and established a church under his own leadership. Political expediency colored the king's motives: Henry was determined to leave England with a male heir, but when eighteen years of marriage to Catherine of Aragon produced only one heir (a female), he attempted to annul the marriage and take a new wife. The pope refused, prompting the king—formerly a staunch supporter of the Catholic Church—to break with Rome. In 1526, Henry VIII declared himself head of the Church in England. His actions led to years of dispute and warfare between Roman Catholics and Anglicans (members of the new English Church). By the mid-sixteenth century, the consequences of Luther's protests were evident: The religious unity of Western Christendom was shattered forever. Social and political upheaval had become the order of the day.

Music and the Reformation

Since the Reformation clearly dominated the religious and social history of the sixteenth century, it also touched, directly or indirectly, all forms of artistic endeavor, including music. Luther himself was a student of music, an active performer, and an admirer of Josquin des Prez. Luther's favorite music was the **chorale**, a congregational hymn that served to enhance the spirit of Protestant worship. Chorales, written in German, drew on Latin hymns and German folk tunes. They were characterized by monophonic clarity and simplicity, features that encouraged performance by untrained congregations. The most famous Lutheran chorale (the melody of which may not have originated with Luther) is "A Mighty Fortress is Our God."[§] Luther's chorales had a major influence on religious music for centuries. And although in the hands of later composers the chorale became a complex polyphonic vehicle for voices and instruments, at its inception it was performed with all voices singing the same words at the same time. It was thus an ideal medium for the communal expression of Protestant piety.

[§]This Lutheran chorale inspired Johann Sebastian Bach's Cantata No. 80, an excerpt from which may be heard on Cassette 2, as Music Listening Selection Number 4.

Northern Renaissance Art

The austerity of the Protestant reform cast its long shadow upon Church art. Protestants abandoned the traditional images of medieval piety, rejecting relics and sacred images as sources of superstition and idolatry. In Northern Europe, Protestant **iconoclasts** stripped the stained glass from Catholic churches, shattered statues, whitewashed church frescoes, and destroyed altarpieces. At the same time, however, Protestant reformers encouraged the proliferation of private devotional imagery—biblical subjects in particular.

Secular subject matter provided abundant inspiration for Northern artists. Portraiture, a favorite genre of the pre-Reformation master Jan van Eyck (see Figures 17.12, 17.13), remained popular among such sixteenth-century artists as Albrecht Dürer of Nuremberg (1471–1528), Lucas Cranach the Elder (1472–1553), and Hans Holbein the Younger (1497–1543), three of the greatest draftsmen of the Renaissance (see Figures 18.1, 18.2, 18.14). The natural world also intrigued artists: Dürer introduced landscape painting into Western art. His landscapes, often rendered with panoramic breadth, were studies to be enjoyed for themselves (Figure **18.3**), rather than as settings for sacred or secular subjects

Figure 18.3 Albrecht Dürer, *Landscape*, ca. 1495. Watercolor, approx. 12½ × 8 in. Ashmolean Museum, Oxford, U.K.

Figure 18.4 Albrecht Dürer, *The Four Horsemen of the Apocalypse*, ca. 1496. Woodcut, 15½ × 11 in. Museum of Fine Arts, Boston.

(compare Figures 17.14, 17.27, 17.40). The Flemish painter Pieter Brueghel the Elder (1525–1569) carried the tradition of the cosmic landscape to perfection in large panel paintings that describe the everyday labors of European peasants.

Dürer and Printmaking

Paralleling the invention of movable type, there developed in Northern Europe a technology for reproducing images more cheaply and in greater numbers than ever before. The two new printmaking processes were **woodcut**, the technique of cutting away all parts of a design on a wood surface except those that will be inked and transferred to paper (Figure **18.5**), and **engraving** (Figure **18.6**), the process by which lines are incised on a metal (usually copper) plate that is inked and run through a printing press. These relatively inexpensive techniques of mass-producing images made possible the proliferation of book illustrations and individual prints for private devotional use. Books with printed illustrations became cheap alternatives to the hand-illuminated manuscripts that were prohibitively expensive to all but wealthy patrons.

The unassailed leader in Northern Renaissance printmaking and one of the finest graphic artists of all time was Albrecht Dürer. Dürer earned international fame for his woodcuts and metal engravings. His mastery of the laws of linear perspective and human anatomy and his investigations into classical principles of proportions (enhanced by two trips to Italy) equaled

Figure 18.7 Albrecht Dürer, *Knight, Death, and the Devil*, 1513. Engraving, 9⅝ × 7½ in. The Metropolitan Museum of Art, New York, Harris Brisbane Dick Fund, 1943.

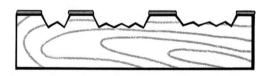

Figure 18.5 Woodcut. A relief printing process created by lines cut into the plank surface of wood. The raised portions of the block are inked and transferred by pressure to the paper by hand or with a printing press.

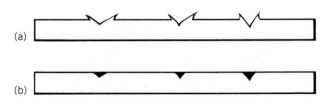

Figure 18.6 Engraving. An intaglio method of printing. The cutting tool, a *burin* or *graver*, is used to cut lines in the surface of metal plates. (a) A cross-section of an engraved plate showing burrs (ridges) produced by scratching a burin into the surface of a metal plate; (b) the burrs are removed and ink is wiped over the surface and forced into the scratches. The plate is then wiped clean, leaving ink deposits in the scratches; the ink is forced from the plate onto paper under pressure in a special press.

those of the best Italian Renaissance artist-scientists. In the genre of portraiture, Dürer was the match of Raphael but, unlike Raphael, he recorded the features of his sitters with little idealization. His portrait engraving of Erasmus (see Figure 18.1) captures the concentrated intelligence of the Prince of Humanists. Dürer included a Latin inscription confirming that the portrait was executed from life, but added modestly in Greek, "The better image is [found] in his writings."

Dürer brought to the art of his day a profoundly religious view of the world and a desire to embody the spiritual message of Scripture in art. The series of woodcuts he produced to illustrate the last book of the New Testament, The Revelation According to Saint John (also called the "Apocalypse"), reveals the extent to which Dürer achieved his purpose. Executed two decades before Luther's revolt, *The Four Horsemen of the Apocalypse*—one of fifteen woodcuts in the series— brings to life the terrifying prophecies described in Revelation 6.1–8 (Figure **18.4**). Amidst billowing clouds, Death (in the foreground), Famine (carrying a pair of scales), War (brandishing a sword), and Pestilence (drawing his bow) sweep down upon humankind; their victims fall beneath the horses' hooves, or, as with the bishop in the lower left, are devoured by infernal monsters. Dürer's image seems a grim prophecy of the coming age, in which five million people would die in religious wars.

Figure 18.8 Matthias Grünewald, *Crucifixion*, central panel of the Isenheim Altarpiece, ca. 1510–1515. Oil on panel, 8 ft. × 10 ft. 1 in. Musée Unterlinden, Colmar, France. Photo: Prestel.

Dürer was a humanist in his own right and a great admirer of both the moderate Erasmus and the zealous Luther. In one of his most memorable engravings, *Knight, Death, and the Devil*, he depicted the Christian soul in the allegorical guise of a medieval knight (Figure 18.7), a figure made famous in a treatise by Erasmus entitled *Handbook for the Militant Christian* (1504). The knight, the medieval symbol of fortitude and courage, advances against a dark and brooding landscape. Accompanied by his loyal dog, he marches forward, ignoring his fearsome companions: Death, who rides a pale horse and carries an hourglass, and the devil, a shaggy, cross-eyed, and horned demon. Here is the visual counterpart for Erasmus' message that the Christian must hold to the path of virtue, and in spite of "all of those spooks and phantoms" that come upon him, he must "look not behind." The knight's dignified bearing (probably inspired by heroic equestrian statues Dürer had seen in Italy) contrasts sharply with the bestial and cankerous features of his forbidding escorts. Dürer's engraving is remarkable for its wealth of microscopic detail. In the tradition of Jan van Eyck, but with a precision facilitated by the medium of metal engraving, Dürer records every leaf and pebble, hair and wrinkle; and yet the final effect is not a mere piling up of minutiae but, like nature itself, an astonishing amalgam of organically related substances.

The Paintings of Grünewald, Bosch, and Brueghel

Whether Catholic or Protestant, sixteenth-century Northern artists brought to religious subject matter an intensity and subjectivity that were uncharacteristic of Italian art. With the exception of Dürer, whose monumental paintings manifest a preference for unity of design and classical proportion comparable to that of Raphael, Northern Renaissance artists shared little with the Italians. In the paintings of the German artist Matthias Gothardt Neithardt, better known as

"Grünewald" (1460–1528), naturalistic detail and brutal distortion produced a highly expressive style. Grünewald's *Crucifixion* (Figure **18.8**), the central panel of the multipaneled Isenheim Altarpiece, emphasizes the physical suffering of Christ, a devotional subject that might have provided solace to the disease victims at the hospital for which this work was commissioned. In the manner of his anonymous fourteenth-century German predecessor (compare Figure 15.10), Grünewald rejects harmonious proportion and figural idealization in favor of exaggeration and painfully precise detail: The agonized body of Jesus is lengthened to emphasize its weight as it hangs from the bowed cross, the flesh putrefies with clotted blood and angry thorns, the fingers convulse and curl, while the feet—broken and bruised—contort in a spasm of pain. Grünewald reinforces the mood of lamentation by placing the scene in a darkened landscape. He exaggerates the gestures of the attending figures, including that of John the Baptist, whose oversized finger points to the prophetic Latin inscription that explains his mystical presence: "He must increase and I must decrease" (John 3:30). A comparison of this painting with, for instance, Masaccio's *Trinity* (see Figure 17.17) provides a study in contrasts between German and Italian sensibilities in the age of the Renaissance.

More difficult to interpret are the works of the extraordinary Flemish artist Hieronymus Bosch (1460–1516). Like Grünewald, Bosch was preoccupied with matters of sin and salvation. Bosch's *Death and the Miser* (Figure **18.9**), for instance, belongs to the tradition of the *memento mori* (discussed in chapter 12), which works to warn the beholder of the inevitability of death. The painting also shows the influence of popular fifteenth-century handbooks on the art of dying (the *ars moriendi*), designed to remind Christians that they must choose between sinful pleasures and the way of Christ. As Death looms on his threshold, the miser, unable to resist worldly temptations even in his last minutes of life, reaches for the bag of gold offered to him by a demon. In the foreground, Bosch depicts the miser storing gold in his money chest while clutching his rosary. Symbols of worldly power—a helmet, sword, and shield—allude to earthly follies. The depiction of such still-life objects to symbolize earthly vanity, transience, or decay would become a genre in itself among seventeenth-century Flemish artists.

Bosch's most famous work, *The Garden of Earthly Delights*—executed around 1510, the very time that

Figure 18.9 Hieronymus Bosch, *Death and the Miser*, ca. 1485–1490. Oil on oak, 36⅝ × 12⅛ in. © 1998 Board of Trustees, National Gallery of Art, Washington, D.C. Samuel H. Kress Collection.

Raphael was painting *The School of Athens*—underscores the enormous contrast between Renaissance art in Italy and in Northern Europe. Whereas Raphael celebrates the nobility and dignity of the human being, Bosch contemplates the inconstancy and degeneracy of humankind. In Bosch's **triptych** (a three-paneled painting), the Creation of Adam and Eve (left) and the Tortures of Hell (right) flank a central panel whose iconographic meaning is obscure (Figure **18.11**). Here, in an imaginary landscape, youthful nude men and women cavort in erotic pastimes, dallying affectionately with each other or with oversized flora and fauna that teeter between the fantastic and the actual. The scene, a veritable "Garden of Delights," may be an exposition on the lustful behavior of the descendants of Adam and Eve. But in this central panel, as in the scenes of Creation and Hell, Bosch has turned his back on convention—a circumstance probably related to the fact that the triptych was commissioned not by the Church but by a private patron. His imagery, the subject of endless scholarly interpretation, derives from many sources, including astrology and alchemy, both pseudosciences of some repute in Bosch's time. Astrology, the study of the influence of heavenly bodies on human affairs, and alchemy, the art of distillation (employed by apothecaries as well as by quacks who sought to transmute base metals into gold), attracted new attention when Islamic writings on both were introduced into late medieval Europe. Both, moreover, became subjects of serious study during the sixteenth century. Symbolic of the Renaissance quest to understand the operations of the material world, astrology (the ancestor of astronomy) and alchemy (precursor to chemistry) figured frequently in the works of sixteenth-century artists and writers.

In *The Garden of Earthly Delights*, egg-shaped vessels, beakers, transparent tubes, and other alchemical devices reflect Bosch's familiarity with both the equipment and the distillation process that were used in experimental transmutation. Bosch seems to have embraced alchemy—and especially the cyclical process of creation and destruction central to that pseudoscience—as a metaphor for the Christian myth of the Creation and Fall. The creatures of this garden participate in the mysteries of procreation, indulging their physical impulses with little regard for the inevitable consequences of their actions: the devastating punishments of Hell depicted in the right panel.

The fantastic demons in Bosch's Hell are products of an age that found the supernatural in natural and ordinary guises. Indeed, the witch-hunts that infested Europe (and especially Germany) during the sixteenth century were fueled by the popular belief that the devil was actively involved in human affairs. The first massive persecution of witches occurred at the end of the

fifteenth century, when two theologians published the *Malleus Maleficarum* (*Witches' Hammer*), an encyclopedia of witchcraft that described the nature of witches, their collusion with the devil, and the ways by which they were to be recognized and punished. Since women were traditionally regarded as inherently susceptible to the devil's temptations, they became the primary victims of this mass hysteria. Women—especially single, old, and eccentric women—constituted four-fifths of the witches executed between the fifteenth and early seventeenth centuries. The German artist Hans Baldung, called "Grien" (1475?–1545), was one of a number of Northern Renaissance artists who portrayed the activities of witches in painting and prints (Figure **18.10**). The witchcraft craze of this period dramatizes the prevailing gap between Christian humanism and rationalism on the one hand and barbarism and superstition on the other. Whether viewed as an instrument of post-Reformation political oppression or as the expression of the darker side of religious fanaticism, the witch-hunts of the early modern era force us to question the very notion of human progress.

Figure 18.10 Hans Baldung ("Grien"), *Witches*, 1510. *Chiaroscuro* woodcut, 15⅞ × 10¼ in. Louvre, Paris. Collection Rothschild. Photo: © R.M.N., Paris.

Figure 18.11 Hieronymus Bosch, *The Creation of Eve: The Garden of Earthly Delights: Hell* (triptych), ca. 1510–1515. Oil on wood, 7 ft. 2⅝ in. × 6 ft. 4¾ in. (center panel), 7 ft. 2⅝ in. × 3 ft. 2¼ in. (each side panel). © Prado, Madrid. Photo: Arxiu MAS, Madrid.

The realities of violence, prejudice, and immorality did not go uncriticized among sixteenth-century Northern European artists. Bosch's contemporary, Pieter Brueghel the Elder, produced numerous paintings and prints that were cloaked condemnations of human folly, immorality, and war. Brueghel's *Triumph of Death* (Figure **18.12**; see also Part Opener, p. 76), for instance, may be read as an indictment of the brutal wars that plagued sixteenth-century Europe: In a panoramic landscape that resembles the setting for a Last Judgment or a Bosch hell scene, Brueghel depicts armies of skeletons relentlessly slaughtering the living at work and at play, crushing some beneath the wheels of a death cart and subjecting others to torture and execution. Not divine judgment but human destiny rules here. Indeed, in Brueghel's hands, the late medieval Dance of Death (see chapter 15) has become a universal holocaust.

The last of the great sixteenth-century Flemish painters, Brueghel had traveled widely in Renaissance Italy; however, his paintings reflect only a passing interest in classical themes. His preoccupation with the details of rustic life, which earned him the title "Peasant Brueghel," continued the tradition of such medieval illuminators as the Limbourg brothers (see Figure 15.13). However, Brueghel's **genre paintings** (representations of the everyday life of ordinary folk) were not small-scale illustrations, but monumental records of rural activities. *The Wedding Dance* (Figure **18.13**) depicts peasant revelry in a country setting whose earthiness is reinforced by rich tones of russet, tan, and muddy green. At the very top of the panel the bride and groom sit before an improvised dais, while the villagers cavort to the music of the bagpipe (right foreground). Although Brueghel's figures are clumsy and

Figure 18.12 Pieter Brueghel the Elder, *Triumph of Death*, ca. 1562–1564. Oil on panel, 3 ft. 10 in. × 5 ft. 3¾ in. Prado, Madrid. Photo: Arxiu MAS, Madrid.

Figure 18.13 Pieter Brueghel the Elder, *The Wedding Dance*, 1566. Oil on panel, 3 ft. 11 in. × 5 ft. 2 in. Photograph © 1997 The Detroit Institute of Arts. City of Detroit Purchase. 30.374.

often ill proportioned, they share an ennobling vitality. In Brueghel's art, as in that of many other Northern Renaissance painters, we discover an unvarnished view of the individual in mundane and unheroic circumstances, in contrast with the much more idealized image of humankind found in the art of Renaissance Italy.

Northern Renaissance Literature

Erasmus and More

European literature of the sixteenth century was marked by heightened individualism and a progressive inclination to clear away the last remnants of medieval orthodoxy. It was, in many ways, a literature of protest and reform, and one whose dominant themes reflect the tension between medieval and modern ideas. European writers were especially concerned with the discrepancies between the noble ideals of classical humanism and the ignoble realities of human behavior. Religious rivalries and the horrors of war, witch-hunts, and religious persecution all seemed to contradict the optimistic view that the Renaissance had inaugurated a

more enlightened phase of human self-consciousness. Satire, a literary genre that conveys the contradictions between real and ideal situations, was especially popular during the sixteenth century. By means of satiric irony, Northern Renaissance writers held up prevailing abuses to ridicule, thus implying the need for reform.

The scholarly treatises and letters of Desiderius Erasmus won him the respect of scholars throughout Europe; but his single most popular work was *The Praise of Folly*, a satiric oration attacking a wide variety of human foibles, including greed, intellectual pomposity, and pride. *The Praise of Folly*, which went through more than two dozen editions in Erasmus' lifetime, influenced other humanists, including Erasmus' lifelong friend and colleague Thomas More (Figure 18.14), to whom it was dedicated (in Latin, *moria* means "folly"). A short excerpt from *The Praise of Folly* offers some idea of Erasmus' keen wit as applied to a typical Northern Renaissance theme: the vast gulf between human fallibility and human perfectibility. The excerpt opens with the image of the world as a stage, a favorite metaphor of sixteenth-century painters and poets—not the least of whom was William Shakespeare. Folly, the allegorical figure who is the speaker in the piece, compares life to a comedy in which the players assume various roles: In the course of the drama (she observes), one may come to play the parts of both beggar and king. The lecturer then describes each of a number of roles (or disciplines), such as medicine, law, and so on, in terms of its affinity with folly. Erasmus' most searing words were reserved for theologians and church dignitaries, but his insights expose more generally (and timelessly) the frailties of all human beings.

1540   the Swiss physician Paracelsus (Philippus van Hohenheim) pioneers the use of chemistry for medical purposes

1543   Copernicus (Polish) publishes *On the Revolution of the Heavenly Spheres*, announcing his heliocentric theory

1553   Michael Servetus (Spanish) describes the pulmonary circulation of the blood

READING 3.14

From Erasmus' *The Praise of Folly*

Now what else is the whole life of mortals but a sort of   1
comedy, in which the various actors, disguised by various
costumes and masks, walk on and play each one his
part, until the manager waves them off the stage?
Moreover, this manager frequently bids the same actor
go back in a different costume, so that he who has but
lately played the king in scarlet now acts the flunkey in
patched clothes. Thus all things are presented by
shadows; yet this play is put on in no other way. . . .

[The disciplines] that approach nearest to common   10
sense, that is, to folly, are held in highest esteem.
Theologians are starved, naturalists find cold comfort,
astrologers are mocked, and logicians are slighted. . . .
Within the profession of medicine, furthermore, so far as
any member is eminently unlearned, impudent, or
careless, he is valued the more, even in the chambers of
belted earls. For medicine, especially as now practiced
by many, is but a subdivision of the art of flattery, no
less truly than is rhetoric. Lawyers have the next place
after doctors, and I do not know but that they should   20
have first place; with great unanimity the philosophers—
not that I would say such a thing myself—are wont to
ridicule the law as an ass. Yet great matters and little
matters alike are settled by the arbitrament of these
asses. They gather goodly freeholds with broad acres,
while the theologian, after poring over chestfuls of the
great corpus of divinity, gnaws on bitter beans, at the
same time manfully waging war against lice and fleas. As
those arts are more successful which have the greatest
affinity with folly, so those people are by far the happiest   30
who enjoy the privilege of avoiding all contact with the
learned disciplines, and who follow nature as their only
guide, since she is in no respect wanting, except as a
mortal wishes to transgress the limits set for his status.
Nature hates counterfeits; and that which is innocent of
art gets along far the more prosperously.

What need we say about practitioners in the arts? Self-
love is the hallmark of them all. You will find that they
would sooner give up their paternal acres than any piece
of their poor talents. Take particularly actors, singers,   40
orators, and poets; the more unskilled one of them is,
the more insolent he will be in his self-satisfaction, the
more he will blow himself up. . . . Thus the worst art
pleases the most people, for the simple reason that the
larger part of mankind, as I said before, is subject to
folly. If, therefore, the less skilled man is more pleasing
both in his own eyes and in the wondering gaze of the
many, what reason is there that he should prefer sound
discipline and true skill? In the first place, these will
cost him a great outlay; in the second place, they will   50
make him more affected and meticulous; and finally,
they will please far fewer of his audience. . . .

———————◆———————

In England Erasmus' friend, the scholar and statesman Sir Thomas More (1478–1535), served as chancellor to King Henry VIII at the time of Henry's break with the Catholic Church. Like Erasmus, More was a Christian humanist and a man of conscience. He denounced the modern evils of acquisitive capitalism and religious fanaticism and championed religious tolerance and Christian charity. Unwilling to compromise his position as a Roman Catholic, he opposed the actions of the king and was executed for treason in 1535.

In 1516, More completed his classic political satire on European statecraft and society, a work entitled *Utopia* (Greek for "nowhere"). More's *Utopia*, the first literary description of an ideal state since Plato's *Republic*, was inspired, in part, by accounts of wondrous lands reported by sailors returning from the "New World" across the Atlantic (see chapter 19). More's fictional island ("discovered" by a fictional explorer-narrator) is a socialistic state in which goods and property are shared, war and personal vanities are held in contempt, learning is available to all citizens (except slaves), and freedom of religion is absolute. In this ideal commonwealth, natural reason, benevolence, and scorn for

Figure 18.14 Hans Holbein the Younger, *Sir Thomas More*, ca. 1530. Oil on panel, 29½ × 23¼ in. © The Frick Collection, New York. Holbein's superb portrait reveals a visionary and a man of conscience ("a man for all seasons"), who died at the hands of Henry VIII rather than compromise his religious convictions.

material wealth ensure social harmony. More's ideal society differs from Plato's in that More gives to each individual, rather than to society's guardians, full responsibility for the establishment of social justice. Like Alberti (and Calvin), More regarded work—limited in Utopia to six hours a day—as essential to moral and communal well-being. Fundamental to *Utopia* as satire is the implicit contrast More draws between his own corrupt Christian society and that of his ideal community; although More's Utopians are not Christians, they are guided by Christian principles of morality and charity. They have little use, for instance, for precious metals, jewels, and the "trifles" that drive men to war.

READING 3.15

From More's *Utopia*

[As] to their manner of living in society, the oldest man 1
of every family . . . is its governor. Wives serve their husbands, and children their parents, and always the younger serves the elder. Every city is divided into four equal parts, and in the middle of each there is a marketplace: what is brought thither, and manufactured by the several families, is carried from thence to houses appointed for that purpose, in which all things of a sort are laid by themselves; and there every father goes and takes whatsoever he or his family stand in need of, 10
without either paying for it or leaving anything in exchange. There is no reason for giving a denial to any person, since there is such plenty of everything among them; and there is no danger of a man's asking for more than he needs; they have no inducements to do this, since they are sure that they shall always be supplied. It is the fear of want that makes any of the whole race of animals either greedy or ravenous; but besides fear, there is in man a pride that makes him fancy it a particular glory to excel others in pomp and excess. But by the 20
laws of the Utopians, there is no room for this. . . .

[Since the Utopians] have no use for money among themselves, but keep it as a provision against events which seldom happen, and between which there are generally long intervening intervals, they value it no farther than it deserves, that is, in proportion to its use. So that it is plain they must prefer iron either to gold or silver; for men can no more live without iron than without fire or water, but nature has marked out no use for the other metals so essential and not easily to be 30
dispensed with. The folly of men has enhanced the value of gold and silver, because of their scarcity. Whereas, on the contrary, it is their opinion that nature, as an indulgent parent, has freely given us all the best things in great abundance, such as water and earth, but has laid up and hid from us the things that are vain and useless. . . .

. . . They eat and drink out of vessels of earth, or glass, which make an agreeable appearance though formed of

brittle materials: while they make their chamber-pots 40
and close-stools[1] of gold and silver, and that not only in their public halls, but in their private houses: of the same metals they likewise make chains and fetters for their slaves; to some [slaves], as a badge of infamy, they hang an ear-ring of gold, and [they] make others wear a chain or coronet of the same metal; and thus they take care, by all possible means, to render gold and silver of no esteem. And from hence it is that while other nations part with their gold and silver as unwillingly as if one tore out their bowels, those of Utopia would look on 50
their giving in all they possess of those [metals] but as the parting with a trifle, or as we would esteem the loss of a penny. They find pearls on their coast, and diamonds and carbuncles on their rocks; they do not look after them, but, if they find them by chance, they polish them, and with them they adorn their children, who are delighted with them, and glory in them during their childhood; but when they grow to years, and see that none but children use such baubles, they of their own accord, without being bid by their parents, lay 60
them aside; and would be as much ashamed to use them afterward as children among us, when they come to years, are of their puppets and other toys. . . .

◆

The Wit of Cervantes

While Erasmus and More wrote primarily in Latin—*Utopia* was not translated into English until 1551—other European writers favored the vernacular. The satiric novel and the essay, two new literary genres, were written in the language of everyday speech that sent defiant messages of social criticism. In Spain, Miguel de Cervantes (1547–1616) wrote *Don Quijote*, a novel that satirizes the outworn values of the Middle Ages as personified in a legendary Spanish hero. *Don Quijote* was not the first novel in world literature—the Chinese and Japanese had been writing novels since the eleventh century (see chapter 14)—but it was among the earliest Western examples of prose fiction in which a series of episodes converged on a fundamental theme. A chivalrous knight in an age of statecraft, the fifty-year-old Alonso Quixado, who changes his name to Don Quijote de la Mancha, sets out to defend the ideals glorified in medieval books of chivalry and romance. (Such ideals may have been valued by Cervantes himself, who had fought in the last Crusade against the Muslim Turks.) Seeking to right all wrongs, and misperceiving the ordinary for the sublime, the Don pursues a long series of misadventures, including an armed attack on windmills which he thinks are giants—the episode inspired the expression "to tilt at windmills." After his illusions of grandeur are exposed, the hero laments that the world is "nothing but schemes and plots."

[1] A covered chamber pot set in a stool.

READING 3.16

From Cervantes' *Don Quijote*

The great success won by our brave Don Quijote in his dreadful, unimaginable encounter with two windmills, plus other honorable events well worth remembering

Just then, they came upon thirty or forty windmills, which (as it happens) stand in the fields of Montiel, and as soon as Don Quijote saw them he said to his squire:

"Destiny guides our fortunes more favorably than we could have expected. Look there, Sancho Panza, my friend, and see those thirty or so wild giants, with whom I intend to do battle and to kill each and all of them, so with their stolen booty we can begin to enrich ourselves. This is noble, righteous warfare, for it is wonderfully useful to God to have such an evil race wiped from the face of the earth."

"What giants?" asked Sancho Panza.

"The ones you can see over there," answered his master, "with the huge arms, some of which are very nearly two leagues long."

"Now look, your grace," said Sancho, "what you see over there aren't giants, but windmills, and what seem to be arms are just their sails, that go around in the wind and turn the millstone."

"Obviously," replied Don Quijote, "you don't know much about adventures. Those are giants—and if you're frightened, take yourself away from here and say your prayers, while I go charging into savage and unequal combat with them."

Saying which, he spurred his horse, Rocinante, paying no attention to the shouts of Sancho Panza, his squire, warning him that without any question it was windmills and not giants he was going to attack. So utterly convinced was he they were giants, indeed, that he neither heard Sancho's cries nor noticed, close as he was, what they really were, but charged on, crying:

"Flee not, oh cowards and dastardly creatures, for he who attacks you is a knight alone and unaccompanied."

Just then the wind blew up a bit, and the great sails began to stir, which Don Quijote saw and cried out:

"Even should you shake more arms than the giant Briareus himself, you'll still have to deal with me."

As he said this, he entrusted himself with all his heart to his lady Dulcinea, imploring her to help and sustain him at such a critical moment, and then, with his shield held high and his spear braced in its socket, and Rocinante at a full gallop, he charged directly at the first windmill he came to, just as a sudden swift gust of wind sent its sail swinging hard around, smashing the spear to bits and sweeping up the knight and his horse, tumbling them all battered and bruised to the ground. Sancho Panza came rushing to his aid, as fast as his donkey could run, but when he got to his master found him unable to move, such a blow had he been given by the falling horse.

"God help me!" said Sancho. "Didn't I tell your grace to be careful what you did, that these were just windmills, and anyone who could ignore that had to have windmills in his head?"

"Silence, Sancho, my friend," answered Don Quijote. "Even more than other things, war is subject to perpetual change. What's more, I think the truth is that the same Frestón the magician, who stole away my room and my books, transformed these giants into windmills, in order to deprive me of the glory of vanquishing them, so bitter is his hatred of me. But in the end, his evil tricks will have little power against my good sword."

"God's will be done," answered Sancho Panza.

Then, helping his master to his feet, he got him back up on Rocinante, whose shoulder was half dislocated. After which, discussing the adventure they'd just experienced, they followed the road toward Lápice Pass, for there, said Don Quijote, they couldn't fail to find adventures of all kinds, it being a well-traveled highway. But having lost his lance, he went along very sorrowfully, as he admitted to his squire, saying:

"I remember having read that a certain Spanish knight named Diego Pérez de Vargas, having lost his sword while fighting in a lost cause, pulled a thick bough, or a stem, off an oak tree, and did such things with it, that day, clubbing down so many moors that ever afterwards they nicknamed him Machuca [Clubber], and indeed from that day on he and all his descendants bore the name Vargas y Machuca. I tell you this because, the first oak tree I come to, I plan to pull off a branch like that, one every bit as good as the huge stick I can see in my mind, and I propose to perform such deeds with it that you'll be thinking yourself blessed, having the opportunity to witness them, and being a living witness to events that might otherwise be unbelievable."

"It's in God's hands," said Sancho. "I believe everything is exactly the way your grace says it is. But maybe you could sit a little straighter, because you seem to be leaning to one side, which must be because of the great fall you took."

"True," answered Don Quijote, "and if I don't say anything about the pain it's because knights errant are never supposed to complain about a wound, even if their guts are leaking through it."

"If that's how it's supposed to be," replied Sancho, "I've got nothing to say. But Lord knows I'd rather your grace told me, any time something hurts you. Me, I've got to groan, even if it's the smallest little pain, unless that rule about knights errant not complaining includes squires, too."

Don Quijote couldn't help laughing at his squire's simplicity, and cheerfully assured him he could certainly complain any time he felt like it, voluntarily or involuntarily, since in all his reading about knighthood and chivalry he'd never once come across anything to the contrary. Sancho said he thought it was dinner-time. His master replied that, for the moment, he himself had no need of food, but Sancho should eat whenever he wanted to. Granted this permission, Sancho made himself as comfortable as he could while jogging along on his donkey and, taking out of his saddlebags what he had put in them, began eating as he rode, falling back a good bit behind his master, and from time to time tilting up his wineskin with a pleasure so intense that the fanciest barman in Málaga might have envied him. And as he rode along like this, gulping quietly away, none of the promises his master had made were on his mind, nor did he feel in the least troubled or afflicted—in fact, he was thoroughly relaxed about this adventure-hunting business, no matter how dangerous it was supposed to be. 120

In the end, they spent that night sleeping in a wood, and Don Quijote pulled a dry branch from one of the trees, to serve him, more or less, as a lance, fitting onto it the spearhead he'd taken off the broken one. Nor did Don Quijote sleep, that whole night long, meditating on his lady Dulcinea—in order to fulfill what he'd read in his books, namely, that knights always spent long nights out in the woods and other uninhabited places, not sleeping, but happily mulling over memories of their 130 ladies. Which wasn't the case for Sancho Panza: with his stomach full, and not just with chicory water, his dreams swept him away, nor would he have bothered waking up, for all the sunlight shining full on his face, or the birds singing—brightly, loudly greeting the coming of the new day—if his master hadn't called to him. He got up and, patting his wineskin, found it a lot flatter than it had been the night before, which grieved his heart, since it didn't look as if they'd be making up the shortage any time soon. Don Quijote had no interest in breakfast, 140 since, as we have said, he had been sustaining himself with delightful memories. They returned to the road leading to Lápice Pass, which they could see by about three that afternoon.

"Here," said Don Quijote as soon as he saw it, "here, brother Sancho Panza, we can get our hands up to the elbows in adventures. But let me warn you: even if you see me experiencing the greatest dangers in the world, never draw your sword to defend me, unless of course you see that those who insult me are mere rabble, people 150 of low birth, in which case you may be permitted to help me. But if they're knights, the laws of knighthood make it absolutely illegal, without exception, for you to help me, unless you yourself have been ordained a knight."

"Don't worry, your grace," answered Sancho Panza. "You'll find me completely obedient about this, especially since I'm a very peaceful man—I don't like getting myself into quarrels and fights. On the other hand, when it comes to someone laying a hand on me, I won't pay much attention to those laws, because whether 160 they're divine or human they permit any man to defend himself when anyone hurts him."

"To be sure," answered Don Quijote. "But when it comes to helping me against other knights, you must restrain your natural vigor."

"And that's what I'll do," replied Sancho. "I'll observe this rule just as carefully as I keep the Sabbath. . . ."

Rabelais and Montaigne

In the earthier spirit of the prose burlesque, the French humanist François Rabelais (1495–1553) mocked the obsolete values of European society. Rabelais drew upon his experiences as a monk, a student of law, a physician, and a specialist in human affairs to produce *Gargantua and Pantagruel,* an irreverent satire filled with

biting allusions to contemporary institutions and customs. The world of the two imaginary giants, Gargantua and Pantagruel, is a world of fraud and folly drawn to fantastic dimensions. It is blighted by the absurdities of war, the evils of law and medicine, and the failure of scholastic education. To remedy the last, Rabelais advocates an education based on experience and action, rather than upon rote memorization. In the imaginary Abbey of Thélème, the modern version of a medieval monastery, he pictures a coeducational commune in which well-bred men and women are encouraged to live as they please. *Gargantua and Pantagruel* proclaims Rabelais' ultimate faith in the ability of educated individuals to follow their best instincts for establishing a society free from religious prejudice, petty abuse, and selfish desire.

The French humanist Michel de Montaigne (1533–1592) was neither a satirist nor a reformer, but, rather, an educated aristocrat who believed in the paramount importance of cultivating good judgment. Montaigne was the father of the personal **essay,** a short piece of expository prose that examines a single subject or idea. Trained in Latin, Montaigne was one of the leading proponents of classical learning in Renaissance France. But his major contribution to the humanistic tradition was his ninety-four vernacular French essays, which he began writing at the age of thirty-seven. Addressing such subjects as virtue, friendship, old age, education, and idleness, Montaigne explored certain fundamentally humanistic ideas: that contradiction is a characteristically human trait, that self-examination is the essence of true education, that education should enable us to live more harmoniously, and that since both behavior and belief vary from culture to culture, skepticism and open-mindedness are requisite alternatives to dogmatic opinion. Like Rabelais, Montaigne defended a kind of learning that posed questions rather than provided answers. In his essay on the education of children, he criticized teachers who pour information into students' ears "as though they were pouring water into a funnel" and then demand that students repeat that information instead of exercising original thought. Montaigne's essays, an expression of reasoned inquiry into human values, constitute the literary high-water mark of the French Renaissance.

1556	Georg Agricola (German) publishes *On the Principles of Mining*
1571	Ambroise Paré (French) publishes five treatises on surgery
1587	Conrad Gesner (Swiss) completes his *Historiae Animalum,* the first zoological encyclopedia
1596	Sir John Harington (English) invents the "water closet," providing indoor toilet facilities

The Genius of Shakespeare

No assessment of the early modern era would be complete without some consideration of the literary giant of the age: William Shakespeare (1464–1616). A poet of unparalleled genius, Shakespeare emerged during the golden age of England under the rule of Elizabeth I. He produced 37 plays—comedies, tragedies, romances, and histories—as well as 154 sonnets and other poems (Figure **18.15**).

Little is known about Shakespeare's early life and formal education. He grew up in Stratford-upon-Avon in the English Midlands and moved to London sometime before 1585. In London he formed an acting company in which he was shareholder, actor, and playwright. Like fifteenth-century Florence, sixteenth-century London (and especially the Queen's court) supported a galaxy of artists, musicians, and writers who enjoyed the mutually stimulating interchange of ideas. Shakespeare's theatrical association, The Lord Chamberlain's Company (also called "the King's Men"), performed at the court of Elizabeth I and that of her successor James I. But its main activities took place in the Globe Theatre (Figure **18.16**), one of a handful of playhouses built just outside London's city limits—along with brothels and taverns, theaters were relegated to the suburbs.

While Shakespeare is best known for his plays, he also wrote some of the most beautiful sonnets ever produced in the English language. Indebted to Petrarch, Shakespeare nevertheless devised most of his own sonnets in a form that would come to be called "the English sonnet": **quatrains** (four-line stanzas) with alternate rhymes, followed by a concluding **couplet**. Shakespeare's sonnets employ—and occasionally mock—such traditional Petrarchan themes as blind devotion, the value of friendship, and love's enslaving power. Some, like Sonnet 18, reflect the typically Renaissance (and classical) concern for immortality achieved through art and love. In Sonnet 18, Shakespeare contrives an extended metaphor: Like the summer day, his beloved will fade and die. But, exclaims the poet, she will remain eternal in and through the sonnet; for, so long as the poem survives, so will the object of its inspiration. As with his plays, Shakespeare's sonnets have had an enormous influence on the development of the modern English language.

Figure 18.15 Droeshout, first Folio edition portrait of William Shakespeare, 1623. By permission of the Folger Shakespeare Library, Washington, D.C.

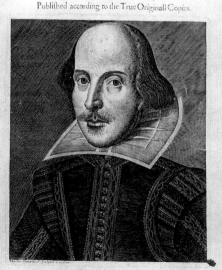

THE
GLOBE PLAYHOUSE
1599–1613
A Conjectural Reconstruction
by
C. Walter Hodges
1948

KEY

A. The "Hut", with machinery for lowering the Heavenly throne to the stage.
B. The "Heavens".
C. Top stage, sometimes used as a music gallery.
D. Upper stage.
E. Window stages.
F. Inner stage, sometimes called the "Study".
G. "Traps" leading down to the "Hell" under the stage.
H. "Gentlemen's Rooms" or "Lords' Rooms".
J. Storage lofts, dressing rooms, etc.
K. Dressing rooms.
L. Backstage area.
M. Main entrances to auditorium.
N. Doorways connecting with gallery staircase.
O. Entrance to galleries and staircases.

Gallery Staircases

Figure 18.16 Globe Playhouse, London, 1599–1613. Architectural reconstruction by C. Walter Hodges, 1948. Reproduced by courtesy of the Trustees of the British Museum, London.

READING 3.17

Shakespeare's Sonnets 18 and 116

Sonnet 18

Shall I compare thee to a summer's day?   1
Thou art more lovely and more temperate.
Rough winds do shake the darling buds of May,
And summer's lease[1] hath all too short a date.
Sometime too hot the eye[2] of heaven shines,   5
And often is his gold complexion dimm'd;
And every fair from fair sometime declines,[3]
By chance or nature's changing course untrimm'd;[4]
But thy eternal summer shall not fade
Nor lose possession of that fair thou ow'st,   10
Nor shall Death brag thou wand'rest in his shade,
When in eternal lines to time thou grow'st.[5]
　　So long as men can breathe or eyes can see,
　　So long lives this[6] and this gives life to thee.

Sonnet 116

Let me not to the marriage of true minds   1
Admit impediments. Love is not love
Which alters when it alteration finds,
Nor bends with the remover to remove.[7]
O, no, it is an ever-fixed mark,[8]   5
That looks on tempests and is never shaken;
It is the star to every wand'ring bark,
Whose worth's unknown, although his height be taken.[9]
Love's not Time's fool, though rose lips and cheeks
Within his bending sickle's compass come;   10
Love alters not with his brief hours and weeks,
But bears it out even to the edge of doom.[10]
　　If this be error, and upon me proved,
　　I never writ, nor no man ever loved.

---

[1]Allotted time.
[2]The sun.
[3]Beautiful thing from beauty.
[4]Stripped of beauty.
[5]Your fame will grow as time elapses.
[6]The sonnet itself.
[7]Changes as the beloved changes.
[8]Sea mark, an aid to navigation.
[9]Whose value is beyond estimation.
[10]Endures to the very Day of Judgment.

More famous than his sonnets, Shakespeare's plays constitute the most significant corpus of dramatic literature in the world. Indeed, secular drama was Renaissance England's most original contribution to the humanistic tradition. In the centuries following the fall of Rome, the Church condemned all forms of pagan display, including the performance of comedies and tragedies. Tragedy, in the sense that it was defined by Aristotle ("the imitation of an action" involving "some great error" made by an extraordinary man), was philosophically incompatible with the medieval worldview, which held that all events were predetermined by God. Elizabethan playwrights inaugurated an approach to drama that sprang in large part from their ability to adapt the classical and medieval literary traditions to contemporary concerns. Of these playwrights, Shakespeare was the most intellectually agile. He was familiar with the tragedies of Seneca and the comedies of Plautus, as well as with popular medieval morality plays that addressed the contest between good and evil. He was also aware of the improvisational forms of Italian comic theater known as the *commedia dell'arte*, which made use of stock or stereotypical figures.

Shakespeare's interests were enormously wide-ranging; like Machiavelli, he was an avid reader of ancient and medieval history, as well as a keen observer of his own exciting age. His history plays, including *Henry V* and *Richard III*, celebrate England's medieval past and its rise to power under the Tudors. His comedies, such as *The Taming of the Shrew, Much Ado About Nothing*, and *As You Like It*, display a wit and an exuberance unmatched in any earlier forms of that genre. But it is in such tragedies as *Hamlet, Macbeth, Othello*, and *King Lear*—the products of his mature career—that Shakespeare achieved the concentration of thought and language that have made him the greatest English playwright of all time. Shakespeare took the plots for most of his plays from classical history, medieval chronicles, and contemporary romances, but he used such stories merely as springboards for the exploration of human nature—the favorite pursuit of all Renaissance humanists. In masterful **blank verse**, he brought alive his characters, exposed their motivations, and laid bare their weaknesses and strengths. Love, sex, jealousy, greed, ambition, and self-deception are among the definitive human experiences Shakespeare examined in his plays. It may therefore be said that Shakespearean drama is the first Western literature to probe the psychological forces that motivate human action.

The Tragedy of Othello, the Moor of Venice was based on a story from a collection of tales published in Italy in the sixteenth century. The life of the handsome and distinguished Othello, an African soldier whose leadership in the Venetian wars against the Turks has brought him heroic esteem, takes a tragic turn when his ensign Iago beguiles him into thinking that his beautiful wife Desdemona has betrayed him with another man. Enraged with jealousy, Othello destroys the person he loves most in the world, his wife; and, in the unbearable grief of his error, he takes his own life as well. No brief synopsis can capture the dramatic impact of this, one of Shakespeare's most sensational plays. While Othello's jealousy is the flaw that brings about his doom, it is Iago whose unmitigated evil drives the action of the plot. Conniving Iago is the Machiavellian villain, "a demi-devil," as he is called in the play. In contrast, Desdemona is the paragon of virtue and beauty. Such characters hark back to the allegorical figures in medieval morality plays, but Shakespeare transforms these figures into complex personalities, allowing them full freedom to falter and fail through their own actions. Of these personalities, Othello is the most enigmatic. Is it jealousy that destroys him, or, rather, a corrosive combination of pride, wrath, and insecurity?

That Shakespeare made a black man the hero of one of his tragedies is significant, since his treatment of the character seems to have deliberately challenged Elizabethan stereotypes. Elizabethans used the word "Moor" to refer to all Africans. Medieval and Renaissance literature described blacks as vengeful and evil, black being the color traditionally associated with the devil. But in Shakespeare's play, the Moor is unwitting, ingenuous, and pure, while Iago, the white man who confounds him, is the personification of evil. Perhaps more significant than this irony is Shakespeare's implication that underlying the most untainted acts of heroism and the purest emotions of love is the dark possibility of misguided action that leads to self-defeat. Shakespeare's plays generally preach no explicit moral; rather, they suggest that, in a universe in which order and disorder coexist, human choices play a vital and potentially destructive part. The nihilism that darkens *The Tragedy of Othello, Macbeth*, and *Hamlet* was unthinkable before the modern era.

READING 3.18

From Shakespeare's *Tragedy of Othello, the Moor of Venice*

Characters

Othello, *the Moor*
Brabantio [a senator], *father to Desdemona*
Cassio, *an honorable lieutenant [to Othello]*
Iago [Othello's ancient], *a villain*
Roderigo, *a gull'd* gentleman [former suitor of Desdemona]*
Duke of Venice
Senators [of Venice]
Montano, *Governor of Cyprus*
Lodovico *and* Gratiano [kinsmen to Brabantio], *two noble Venetians*
Clown

Desdemona [daughter to Brabantio], *wife to Othello*
Emilia, *wife to Iago*
Bianca, *a courtezan [and mistress to Cassio]*

Gentlemen *of Cyprus*, Sailors [Messenger, Herald, Officers, Musicians, *and* Attendants]

[Scene: Venice; a sea-port in Cyprus.]

Act I, Scene I

Enter Roderigo and Iago.

RODERIGO: Tush, never tell me! I take it much unkindly   1
That thou, Iago, who hast had my purse
As if the strings were thine, shouldst know of this.
  IAGO: 'Sblood, but you'll not hear me.
If ever I did dream of such a matter,
Abhor me.
  RODERIGO: Thou tolds't me thou didst hold him in thy
    hate.
  IAGO: Despise me if I do not. Three great ones of the city,
In personal suit to make me his lieutenant,
Off-capp'd to him; and, by the faith of man,   10
I know my price, I am worth no worse a place.
But he, as loving his own pride and purposes,
Evades them with a bombast circumstance
Horribly stuff'd with epithets of war,
[And, in conclusion,]
Nonsuits my mediators; for, "Certes," says he,
"I have already chose my officer."
And what was he?
Forsooth, a great arithmetician,
One Michael Cassio, a Florentine,   20
A fellow almost damn'd in a fair wife,

That never set a squadron in the field,
Nor the division of a battle knows
More than a spinster—unless the bookish theoric,
Wherein the toged consuls can propose
As masterly as he. Mere prattle without practice
Is all his soldiership. But he, sir, had th' election;
And I, of whom his eyes had seen the proof
At Rhodes, at Cyprus, and on other grounds
Christian and heathen, must be belee'd and calm'd   30
By debitor and creditor. This counter-caster,
He, in good time, must his lieutenant be,
And I—God bless the mark!—his Moorship's ancient.
  RODERIGO: By heaven, I rather would have been his
    hangman.
  IAGO: Why, there's no remedy. 'Tis the curse of service,
Preferment goes by letter and affection,
And not by old gradation, where each second
Stood heir to th' first. Now, sir, be judge yourself
Whether I in any just term am affin'd
To love the Moor.   40
  RODERIGO: I would not follow him then.
  IAGO: O, sir content you;
I follow him to serve my turn upon him.
We cannot all be masters, nor all masters
Cannot be truly follow'd. You shall mark
Many a duteous and knee-crooking knave
That, doting on his own obsequious bondage,
Wears out his time, much like his master's ass,
For nought but provender, and, when he's old, cashier'd.
Whip me such honest knaves. Others there are
Who, trimm'd in forms and visages of duty,   50
Keep yet their hearts attending on themselves,
And, throwing but shows of service on their lords,
Do well thrive by them, and when they have lin'd their coats
Do themselves homage. These fellows have some soul;
And such a one do I profess myself. For, sir,
It is as sure as you are Roderigo,
Were I the Moor, I would not be Iago,
In following him, I follow but myself—
Heaven is my judge, not I for love and duty,
But seeming so, for my peculiar end.   60
For when my outward action doth demonstrate
The native act and figure of my heart
In compliment extern, 'tis not long after
But I will wear my heart upon my sleeve
For daws to peck at. I am not what I am.
  RODERIGO: What a full fortune does the thick-lips owe,
If he can carry 't thus!

---

*Easily duped.

I.i. Location: Venice. A street.
1 never tell me don't talk to me   **3 this** i.e., Desdemona's elopement
4 'Sblood i.e., by God's (Christ's) blood   **10 him** i.e., Othello
13 bombast circumstance wordy evasion. (*Bombast* is cotton padding.)
16 Nonsuits rejects   **19 arithmetician** i.e., a man whose military knowledge is merely theoretical, based on books of tactics
21 A...wife (Cassio does not seem to be married, but his counterpart in Shakespeare's source did have a wife.)

23 division of a battle disposition of a military unit   **24 theoric** theory
25 toged wearing the toga **propose** discuss   **28 his** i.e., Othello's
30 belee'd and calm'd left to leeward without wind, becalmed. (A sailing metaphor.)   **31 debitor and creditor** (A name for a system of bookkeeping, here used as a contemptuous nickname for Cassio.)
counter-caster i.e., bookkeeper, one who tallies with *counters* or metal discs. (Said contemptuously.)   **32 in good time** i.e., forsooth
33 ancient standard-bearer, ensign   **36 affection** favoritism
37 old gradation seniority, the traditional way   **39 term** respect **affin'd** bound
48 cashier'd dismissed from service   **50 trimm'd** accoutered, fitted out
60 peculiar particular, personal   **63 compliment extern** outward show (conforming in this case to the inner workings and intentions of the heart)
66 thick-lips (Elizabethans often applied the term "Moor" to Negroes.)
owe own

IAGO: Call up her father.
Rouse him, make after him, poison his delight,
Proclaim him in the streets; incense her kinsmen,
And, though he in a fertile climate dwell,   70
Plague him with flies. Though that his joy be joy,
Yet throw such changes of vexation on't
As it may lose some color.
    RODERIGO: Here is her father's house. I'll call aloud.
    IAGO: Do, with like timorous accent and dire yell
As when, by night and negligence, the fire
Is spied in populous cities.
    RODERIGO: What, ho, Brabantio! Signior Brabantio, ho!
    IAGO: Awake! What, ho, Brabantio! Thieves, thieves!
Look to your house, your daughter, and your bags!   80
Thieves, thieves!
Brabantio [appears] above [at a window].
    BRABANTIO: What is the reason of this terrible summons?
What is the matter there?
    RODERIGO: Signior, is all your family within?
    IAGO: Are your doors lock'd?
    BRABANTIO: Why, wherefore ask you this?
    IAGO: 'Zounds, sir, y' are robb'd. For shame, put on your
        gown!
Your heart is burst, you have lost half your soul.
Even now, now, very now, an old black ram
Is tupping your white ewe. Arise, arise!
Awake the snorting citizens with the bell,   90
Or else the devil will make a grandsire of you.
Arise, I say!
    BRABANTIO: What, have you lost your wits?
    RODERIGO: Most reverend signior, do you know my voice?
    BRABANTIO: Not I. What are you?
    RODERIGO: My name is Roderigo.
    BRABANTIO: The worser welcome.
I have charg'd thee not to haunt about my doors.
In honest plainness thou hast heard me say
My daughter is not for thee; and now, in madness,
Being full of supper and distemp'ring draughts,
Upon malicious bravery, dost thou come   100
To start my quiet.
    RODERIGO: Sir, sir, sir—
    BRABANTIO: But thou must needs be sure
My spirits and my place have in their power
To make this bitter to thee.
    RODERIGO: Patience, good sir.
    BRABANTIO: What tell'st thou me of robbing? This is Venice;
My house is not a grange.
    RODERIGO: Most grave Brabantio,
In simple and pure soul I come to you.
    IAGO: 'Zounds, sir, you are one of those that will not serve
God if the devil bid you. Because we come to do you service

and you think we are ruffians, you'll have you daughter   110
cover'd with a Barbary horse; you'll have your nephews
neigh to you; you'll have coursers for cousins and
gennets for germans.
    BRABANTIO: What profane wretch art thou?
    IAGO: I am one, sir, that comes to tell you your
daughter and the Moor are now making the beast with
two backs.
    BRABANTIO: Thou art a villain.
    IAGO: You are—a senator.
    BRABANTIO: This thou shalt answer. I know thee, Roderigo.
    RODERIGO: Sir, I will answer anything. But, I beseech you,   120
If't be your pleasure and most wise consent,
As partly I find it is, that your fair daughter,
At this odd-even and dull watch o' th' night,
Transported with no worse nor better guard
But with a knave of common hire, a gondolier,
To the gross clasps of a lascivious Moor—
If this be known to you and your allowance,
We then have done you bold and saucy wrongs;
But if you know not this, my manners tell me
We have your wrong rebuke. Do not believe   130
That, from the sense of all civility,
I thus would play and trifle with your reverence.
Your daughter, if you have not given her leave,
I say again, hath made a gross revolt,
Tying her duty, beauty, wit, and fortunes
In an extravagant and wheeling stranger
Of here and everywhere. Straight satisfy yourself.
If she be in her chamber or your house,
Let loose on me the justice of the state
For thus deluding you.
    BRABANTIO: Strike on the tinder, ho!   140
Give me a taper! Call up all my people!
This accident is not unlike my dream.
Belief of it oppresses me already.
Light, I say, light!   *Exit [above].*
    IAGO: Farewell, for I must leave you.
It seems not meet, nor wholesome to my place,
To be producted—as, if I stay, I shall—
Against the Moor. For I do know the state,
However this may gall him with some check,
Cannot with safety cast him, for he's embark'd
With such loud reason to the Cyprus wars,   150
Which even now stands in act, that, for their souls,
Another of his fathom they have none,
To lead their business; in which regard,
Though I do hate him as I do hell-pains,
Yet, for necessity of present life,
I must show out a flag and sign of love,
Which is indeed but sign. That you shall surely find him,

70–71 **though . . . flies** i.e., disrupt his seeming prosperity and happiness with
a grievous vexation (since even the best-situated life is not immune to
misery)   71 **Though . . . be joy** i.e., although he seems fortunate and happy.
(Repeats the idea of l.70.)   72 **changes of vexation** vexing changes
73 **color** appearance (of happiness)   75 **timorous** frightening
89 **tupping** copulating with. (Said of sheep.)   90 **snorting** snoring
100 **Upon malicious bravery** because of a malicious desire to defy me
101 **start** disrupt   106 **grange** isolated farmhouse

111 **nephews** i.e., grandsons   112 **coursers** powerful horses   113 **gennets**
small Spanish horses **germans** near relatives   123 **odd-even** between one
day and the next, i.e., about midnight   127 **allowance** permission
131 **from** contrary to   136 **extravagant** expatriate, wandering far from home
wheeling roving about, vagabond   137 **Straight** straightway   140 **tinder**
charred linen ignited by a spark from flint and steel, used to light torches
or *tapers*   142 **accident** occurrence, event   146 **producted** produced (as a
witness)   148 **gall** rub; oppress **check** rebuke   149 **cast** dismiss
151 **stands in act** are going on   152 **fathom** i.e., ability, depth of experience

Lead to the Sagittary the raised search,
And there will I be with him. So, farewell.   *Exit.*
*Enter [below] Brabantio [in his nightgown] with Servants and
torches.*
    BRABANTIO: It is too true an evil. Gone she is;   160
And what's to come of my despised time
Is nought but bitterness. Now, Roderigo,
Where didst thou see her?—O unhappy girl!—
With the Moor, say'st thou?—Who would be a father!—
How didst thou know 'twas she?—O, she deceives me
Past thought!—What said she to you?—Get moe tapers.
Raise all my kindred.—Are they married, think you?
    RODERIGO: Truly, I think they are.
    BRABANTIO: O heaven! How got she out? O treason of the
        blood!
Fathers, from hence trust not your daughters' minds   170
By what you see them act. Is there not charms
By which the property of youth and maidhood
May be abus'd? Have you not read, Roderigo,
Of some such thing?
    RODERIGO: Yes, sir, I have indeed.
    BRABANTIO: Call up my brother.—O, would you had had
        her!—
Some one way, some another.—Do you know
Where we may apprehend her and the Moor?
    RODERIGO: I think I can discover him, if you please
To get good guard and go along with me.
    BRABANTIO: Pray you, lead on. At every house I'll call: 180
I may command at most.—Get weapons, ho!
And raise some special officers of night.—
On, good Roderigo; I will deserve your pains.
                                                    Exeunt.

Scene II

Enter Othello, Iago, Attendants with torches.

    IAGO: Though in the trade of war I have slain men,   1
Yet do I hold it very stuff o' th' conscience
To do no contriv'd murder. I lack iniquity
Sometime to do me service. Nine or ten times
I had thought t' have yerk'd him here under the ribs.
    OTHELLO: 'Tis better as it is.
    IAGO: Nay, but he prated,
And spoke such scurvy and provoking terms
Against your honor
That, with the little godliness I have,
I did full hard forbear him. But, I pray you, sir,   10
Are you fast married? Be assur'd of this,
That the magnifico is much belov'd,

And hath in his effect a voice potential
As double as the Duke's. He will divorce you,
Or put upon you what restraint and grievance
The law, with all his might to enforce it on,
Will give him cable.
    OTHELLO: Let him do his spite.
My services which I have done the signiory
Shall out-tongue his complaints. 'Tis yet to know—
Which, when I know that boasting is an honor,   20
I shall promulgate—I fetch my life and being
From men of royal siege, and my demerits
May speak unbonneted to as proud a fortune
As this that I have reach'd. For know, Iago,
But that I love the gentle Desdemona,
I would not my unhoused free condition
Put into circumscription and confine
For the sea's worth. But, look, what lights come yond?
Enter Cassio [and certain Officers] with torches.
    IAGO: Those are the raised father and his friends.
You were best go in.
    OTHELLO: Not I; I must be found.   30
My parts, my title, and my perfect soul
Shall manifest me rightly. Is it they?
    IAGO: By Janus, I think no.
    OTHELLO: The servants of the Duke? And my lieutenant?
The goodness of the night upon you, friends!
What is the news?
    CASSIO: The Duke does greet you, general,
And he requires your haste-post-haste appearance,
Even on the instant.
    OTHELLO: What is the matter, think you?
    CASSIO: Something from Cyprus, as I may divine.
It is a business of some heat. The galleys   40
Have sent a dozen sequent messengers
This very night at one another's heels,
And many of the consuls, rais'd and met,
Are at the Duke's already. You have been hotly call'd for;
When, being not at your lodging to be found,
The Senate hath sent about three several quests
To search you out.
    OTHELLO: 'Tis well I am found by you.
I will but spend a word here in the house,
And go with you.   *[Exit.]*

[The outraged Brabantio accuses Othello of having
"enchanted" his daughter; he demands Othello's arrest and
prepares to bring his complaint before the Duke. (ed.)]

---

158 **Sagittary** (An inn where Othello and Desdemona are staying.)
s.d. nightgown dressing gown   161 **time** i.e., remainder of life
166 **moe** more   172 **property** special quality, nature
183 **deserve** show gratitude for

I.ii. **Location:** Venice. Another street.
5 **yerk'd** stabbed   10 **full hard** scarcely   12 **magnifico** Venetian grandee,
i.e., Brabantio

13 **in his effect** at his command **potential** powerful   14 **double** doubly powerful
17 **cable** i.e., scope   18 **signiory** Venetian government   19 **yet to know** not yet
widely known   22 **siege** i.e., rank. (Literally, a *seat* used by a person of
distinction.) **demerits** deserts   23 **unbonneted** without removing the hat, i.e.,
on equal terms (*Bonneted* can mean "with hat off.")
26 **unhoused** unconfined, undomesticated   31 **My . . . soul** my merits,
my position or reputation, and my unflawed conscience
33 **Janus** Roman god of beginnings   41 **sequent** successive
43 **consuls** senators   46 **several** separate

Scene III

[The Duke of Venice meets with his senators to discuss the Ottoman attack on the island of Cyprus. (ed.)]

Enter Brabantio, Othello, Cassio, Iago, Roderigo, and Officers.

DUKE: Valiant Othello, we must straight employ you   1
Against the general enemy Ottoman.
[To Brabantio.] I did not see you; welcome, gentle signior.
We lack'd your counsel and your help tonight.
   BRABANTIO: So did I yours. Good your Grace, pardon me;
Neither my place nor aught I heard of business
Hath rais'd me from my bed, nor doth the general care
Take hold on me, for my particular grief
Is of so flood-gate and o'erbearing nature
That it engluts and swallows other sorrows   10
And it is still itself.
   DUKE: Why, what's the matter?
   BRABANTIO: My daughter! O, my daughter!
   DUKE AND SENATORS: Dead?
   BRABANTIO: Ay, to me.
She is abus'd, stol'n from me, and corrupted
By spells and medicines bought of mountebanks;
For nature so preposterously to err,
Being not deficient, blind, or lame of sense,
Sans witchcraft could not.
   DUKE: Whoe'er he be that in this foul proceeding
Hath thus beguil'd your daughter of herself,
And you of her, the bloody book of law   20
You shall yourself read in the bitter letter
After your own sense—yea, though our proper son
Stood in your action.
   BRABANTIO: Humbly I thank your Grace.
Here is the man, this Moor, whom now, it seems
Your special mandate for the state-affairs
Hath hither brought.
   ALL: We are very sorry for 't.
   DUKE *[To Othello]*: What, in your own part, can you say
     to this?
   BRABANTIO: Nothing, but this is so.
   OTHELLO: Most potent, grave, and reverend signiors,
My very noble and approv'd good masters,   30
That I have ta'en away this old man's daughter,
It is most true; true, I have married her.
The very head and front of my offending
Hath this extent, no more. Rude am I in my speech,
And little bless'd with the soft phrase of peace;
For since these arms of mine had seven years' pith,
Till now some nine moons wasted, they have us'd
Their dearest action in the tented field;
And little of this great world can I speak

More than pertains to feats of broil and battle,   40
And therefore little shall I grace my cause
In speaking for myself. Yet, by your gracious patience,
I will a round unvarnish'd tale deliver
Of my whole course of love—what drugs, what charms,
What conjuration, and what mighty magic,
For such proceeding I am charg'd withal,
I won his daughter.
   BRABANTIO: A maiden never bold;
Of spirit so still and quiet that her motion
Blush'd at herself; and she, in spite of nature,
Of years, of country, credit, everything,   50
To fall in love with what she fear'd to look on!
It is a judgment maim'd and most imperfect
That will confess perfection so could err
Against all rules of nature, and must be driven
To find out practices of cunning hell
Why this should be. I therefore vouch again
That with some mixtures pow'rful o'er the blood,
Or with some dram conjur'd to this effect,
He wrought upon her.
   DUKE: To vouch this is no proof,
Without more wider and more overt test   60
Than these thin habits and poor likelihoods
Of modern seeming do prefer against him.
   FIRST SENATOR: But, Othello, speak.
Did you by indirect and forced courses
Subdue and poison this young maid's affections?
Or came it by request and such fair question
As soul to soul affordeth?
   OTHELLO: I do beseech you,
Send for the lady to the Sagittary,
And let her speak of me before her father.
If you do find me foul in her report,   70
The trust, the office I do hold of you,
Not only take away, but let your sentence
Even fall upon my life.
   DUKE: Fetch Desdemona hither.
   OTHELLO: Ancient, conduct them; you best know the
     place.
                [Exeunt Iago and Attendants.]
And, till she come, as truly as to heaven
I do confess the vices of my blood,
So justly to your grave ears I'll present
How I did thrive in this fair lady's love,
And she in mine.
   DUKE: Say it, Othello.
   OTHELLO: Her father lov'd me, oft invited me;   80
Still question'd me the story of my life,
From year to year—the battles, sieges, fortunes,

I.iii. Location: Venice. A council-chamber.
10 engluts engulfs   **13 abus'd** deceived   **16 deficient** defective
17 Sans without   **22 After . . . sense** according to your own interpretation
our proper my own   **23 Stood . . . action** were under your accusation
30 approv'd proved   **33 front** forehead, face   **34 Rude** unpolished
36 pith strength, vigor. (i.e., since I was seven.)
37 Till . . . wasted until some nine months ago (during which time Othello has evidently not been on active duty, but in Venice)

43 round plain   **48–49 her . . . herself** her very emotions prompted her to blush, to discover such feelings in herself   **50 credit** virtuous reputation
53 confess concede (that)   **55 practices** plots   **56 vouch** assert
57 blood passions   **61 habits** garments, i.e., appearances
62 modern seeming commonplace assumption **prefer** bring forth
66 question conversation   **76 blood** passions   **81 Still** continually

That I have pass'd.
I ran it through, even from my boyish days
To th' very moment that he bade me tell it,
Wherein I spoke of most disastrous chances,
Of moving accidents by flood and field,
Of hair-breadth scapes i' th' imminent deadly breach,
Of being taken by the insolent foe
And sold to slavery, of my redemption thence,   90
And portance in my travels' history,
Wherein of antres vast and deserts idle,
Rough quarries, rocks, and hills whose heads touch heaven,
It was my hint to speak—such was my process—
And of the Cannibals that each other eat,
The Anthropophagi, and men whose heads
Do grow beneath their shoulders. This to hear
Would Desdemona seriously incline;
But still the house-affairs would draw her thence,
Which ever as she could with haste dispatch   100
She'd come again, and with a greedy ear
Devour up my discourse. Which I, observing,
Took once a pliant hour, and found good means
To draw from her a prayer of earnest heart
That I would all my pilgrimage dilate,
Whereof by parcels she had something heard,
But not intentively. I did consent,
And often did beguile her of her tears,
When I did speak of some distressful stroke
That my youth suffer'd. My story being done,   110
She gave me for my pains a world of sighs.
She swore, in faith, 'twas strange, 'twas passing strange,
'Twas pitiful, 'twas wondrous pitiful.
She wish'd she had not heard it, yet she wish'd
That heaven had made her such a man. She thank'd me,
And bade me, if I had a friend that lov'd her,
I should but teach him how to tell my story,
And that would woo her. Upon this hint I spake.
She lov'd me for the dangers I had pass'd,
And I lov'd her that she did pity them.   120
This only is the witchcraft I have us'd.
Here comes the lady. Let her witness it.
Enter Desdemona, Iago, [and] Attendants.
DUKE: I think this tale would win my daughter too.
Good Brabantio,
Take up this mangled matter at the best.
Men do their broken weapons rather use
Than their bare hands.
   BRABANTIO: I pray you, hear her speak.
If she confess that she was half the wooer,
Destruction on my head if my bad blame
Light on the man! Come hither, gentle mistress.   130

Do you perceive in all this noble company
Where most you owe obedience?
   DESDEMONA: My noble father,
I do perceive here a divided duty.
To you I am bound for life and education;
My life and education both do learn me
How to respect you. You are the lord of duty;
I am hitherto your daughter. But here's my husband,
And so much duty as my mother show'd
To you, preferring you before her father,
So much I challenge that I may profess   140
Due to the Moor my lord.
   BRABANTIO: God be with you! I have done.
Please it your Grace, on to the state affairs.
I had rather to adopt a child than get it.
Come hither, Moor.
[He joins the hands of Othello and Desdemona.]
I here do give thee that with all my heart
Which, but thou hast already, with all my heart
I would keep from thee. For your sake, jewel,
I am glad at soul I have no other child;
For thy escape would teach me tyranny,
To hang clogs on them.—I have done, my lord.   150
   DUKE: Let me speak like yourself, and lay a sentence,
Which, as a grise or step, may help these lovers
[Into your favor.]
When remedies are part, the griefs are ended
By seeing the worst, which late on hopes depended.
To mourn a mischief that is past and gone
Is the next way to draw new mischief on.
What cannot be preserv'd when fortune takes,
Patience her injury a mock'ry makes.
The robb'd that smiles steals something from the thief;   160
He robs himself that spends a bootless grief.
   BRABANTIO: So let the Turk of Cyprus us beguile;
We lose it not, so long as we can smile.
He bears the sentence well that nothing bears
But the free comfort which from thence he hears,
But he bears both the sentence and the sorrow
That, to pay grief, must of poor patience borrow.
These sentences, to sugar or to gall,
Being strong on both sides, are equivocal.
But words are words. I never yet did hear   170
That the bruis'd heart was pierced through the ear.
I humbly beseech you, proceed to th' affairs of state.
   DUKE: The Turk with a most mighty preparation makes for
Cyprus. Othello, the fortitude of the place is best known to
you; and though we have there a substitute of most allow'd
sufficiency, yet opinion, a sovereign mistress of effects,
throws a more safer voice on you. You must therefore be

---

87 accidents happenings   **88 imminent . . . breach** death-threatening gap made in a fortification   **91 portance** conduct   **92 antres** caverns **idle** barren, unprofitable   **94 hint** occasion, opportunity   **96 Anthropophagi** man-eaters. (A term from Pliny's *Natural History.*)   **103 pliant** well-suiting   **105 dilate** relate in detail   **107 intentively** with full attention   **118 hint** opportunity

134 education upbringing   **135 learn** teach   **140 challenge** claim
143 get beget   **147 For your sake** on your account   **151 like yourself** i.e., as you might, in your proper temper **sentence** maxim (also at l.168)
152 grise step   **157 next** nearest   **158 What** whatever   **159 Patience . . . makes** patience laughs at the injury inflicted by fortune and thus eases the pain
161 bootless incurable   **164–167 He bears . . . borrow** i.e., a person well bears out your maxim who takes with him only the philosophic consolation it teaches him, a comfort free from sorrow; but anyone whose grief bankrupts his poor patience is left with your saying and his sorrow too. (*Bears the sentence* also plays on the meaning of *receiving judicial sentence.*)
174 fortitude strength   **175 substitute** deputy **allow'd** acknowledged
176–177 opinion . . . on you general opinion, an important determiner of affairs, chooses you as the best man

content to slubber the gloss of your new fortunes with this
more stubborn and boist'rous expedition.
    OTHELLO: The tyrant custom, most grave senators,   180
Hath made the flinty and steel couch of war
My thrice-driven bed of down. I do agnize
A natural and prompt alacrity
I find in hardness, and do undertake
These present wars against the Ottomites.
Most humbly therefore bending to your state,
I crave fit disposition for my wife,
Due reference of place and exhibition,
With such accommodation and besort
As levels with her breeding.
    DUKE: If you please,   190
Be 't her father's.
    BRABANTIO: I will not have it so.
    OTHELLO: Nor I.
    DESDEMONA: Nor I. I would not there reside,
To put my father in impatient thoughts
By being in his eye. Most gracious Duke,
To my unfolding lend your prosperous ear,
And let me find a charter in your voice
T' assist my simpleness.
    DUKE: What would you, Desdemona?
    DESDEMONA: That I did love the Moor to live with him,   200
My downright violence and storm of fortunes
May trumpet to the world. My heart's subdu'd
Even to the very quality of my lord.
I saw Othello's visage in his mind,
And to his honors and his valiant parts
Did I my soul and fortunes consecrate.
So that, dear lords, if I be left behind,
A moth of peace, and he go to war,
The rites for why I love him are bereft me,
And I a heavy interim shall support   210
By his dear absence. Let me go with him.
    OTHELLO: Let her have your voice.
Vouch with me, heaven, I therefore beg it not
To please the palate of my appetite,
Nor to comply with heat—the young affects
In me defunct—and proper satisfaction,
But to be free and bounteous to her mind.
And heaven defend your good souls, that you think
I will your serious and great business scant
When she is with me. No, when light-wing'd toys   220
Of feather'd Cupid seel with wanton dullness
My speculative and offic'd instruments,
That my disports corrupt and taint my business,
Let huswives make a skillet of my helm,
And all indign and base adversities

Make head against my estimation!
    DUKE: Be it as you shall privately determine,
Either for her stay or going. Th' affair cries haste,
And speed must answer it.
    FIRST SENATOR: You must away tonight.
    OTHELLO: With all my heart. 230
    DUKE: At nine i' th' morning here we'll meet again.
Othello, leave some officer behind,
And he shall our commission bring to you,
With such things else of quality and respect
As doth import you.
    OTHELLO: So please your Grace, my ancient;
A man he is of honesty and trust.
To his conveyance I assign my wife,
With what else needful your good Grace shall think
To be sent after me.
    DUKE: Let it be so.
Good night to everyone. *[To Brabantio.]* And, noble signior, 240
If virtue no delighted beauty lack,
Your son-in-law is far more fair than black.
    FIRST SENATOR: Adieu, brave Moor. Use Desdemona well.
    BRABANTIO: Look to her Moor, if thou hast eyes to see.
She has deceiv'd her father, and may thee.
           Exeunt [Duke, Senators, Officers, etc.].
    OTHELLO: My life upon her faith! Honest Iago,
My Desdemona must I leave to thee.
I prithee, let thy wife attend on her,
And bring them after in the best advantage.
Come, Desdemona. I have but an hour   250
Of love, of worldly matters and direction,
To spend with thee. We must obey the time.
                  Exit [with Desdemona].
    RODERIGO: Iago—
    IAGO: Why say'st thou, noble heart?
    RODERIGO: What will I do, think'st thou?
    IAGO: Why, go to bed and sleep.
    RODERIGO: I will incontinently drown myself.
    IAGO: If thou dost, I shall never love thee after. Why, thou
silly gentleman?
    RODERIGO: It is silliness to live when to live is torment; and 260
then have we a prescription to die when death is our
physician.
    IAGO: O villainous! I have look'd upon the world for four
times seven years, and, since I could distinguish betwixt a
benefit and an injury, I never found man that knew how to
love himself. Ere I would say I would drown myself for the
love of a guinea-hen, I would change my humanity with a
baboon.
    RODERIGO: What should I do? I confess it is my shame to
be so fond, but it is not in my virtue to amend it.   270

---

178 slubber soil, sully   **182 thrice-driven** thrice sifted, winnowed **agnize** know
in myself, acknowledge   **184 hardness** hardship   **186 bending . . . state**
bowing or kneeling to your authority   **188 reference. . . exhibition** provision of
place to live and allowance of money   **189 accommodation** apparel **besort**
attendance   **190 levels** equals, suits   **196 prosperous** propitious
197 charter privilege   **205 parts** qualities   **215 heat** sexual passion **young
affects** passions of youth, desires   **216 proper** personal   **221 seel** i.e., make
blind (as in falconry, by sewing up the eyes of the hawk during training)
222 speculative . . . instruments i.e., perceptive faculties used in the
performance of duty   **223 That** so that **disports** pastimes **taint** impair
225 indign unworthy, shameful

226 Make head raise an army **estimation** reputation   **235 import** concern
241 delighted capable of delighting   **249 in . . . advantage** at the most
favorable opportunity   **257 incontinently** immediately   **270 fond** infatuated
virtue strength, nature

IAGO: Virtue? A fig! 'Tis in ourselves that we are thus or thus. Our bodies are our gardens, to the which our wills are gardeners; so that if we will plant nettles or sow lettuce, set hyssop and weed up thyme, supply it with one gender of herbs or distract it with many, either to have it sterile with idleness or manur'd with industry—why, the power and corrigible authority of this lies in our wills. If the balance of our lives had not one scale of reason to poise another of sensuality, the blood and baseness of our natures would conduct us to most prepost'rous conclusions. But we have 280 reason to cool our raging motions, our carnal stings, our unbitted lusts, whereof I take this that you call love to be a sect or scion.

RODERIGO: It cannot be.

IAGO: It is merely a lust of the blood and a permission of the will. Come, be a man. Drown thyself? Drown cats and blind puppies. I have profess'd me thy friend, and I confess me knit to the deserving with cables of perdurable toughness. I could never better stead thee than now. Put money in thy purse. Follow thou the wars; defeat thy favor 290 with an usurp'd beard. I say, put money in thy purse. It cannot be long that Desdemona should continue her love to the Moor—put money in thy purse—nor he his to her. It was a violent commencement in her, and thou shalt see an answerable sequestration—put but money in thy purse. These Moors are changeable in their wills—fill thy purse with money. The food that to him now is as luscious as locusts shall be to him shortly as bitter as coloquintida. She must change for youth; when she is sated with his body, she will find the error of her choice. She must have 300 change, she must. Therefore put money in thy purse. If thou wilt needs damn thyself, do it a more delicate way than drowning. Make all the money thou canst. If sanctimony and a frail vow betwixt an erring barbarian and a super-subtle Venetian be not too hard for my wits and all the tribe of hell, thou shalt enjoy her. Therefore make money. A pox of drowning thyself! It is clean out of the way. Seek though rather to be hang'd in compassing thy joy than to be drown'd and go without her.

RODERIGO: Wilt thou be fast to my hopes, if I depend on 310 the issue?

IAGO: Thou art sure of me—go, make money. I have told thee often, and I retell thee again and again, I hate the Moor. My cause is hearted; thine hath no less reason. Let us be conjective in our revenge against him; if thou canst cuckold him, thou dost thyself a pleasure, me a sport. There are many events in the womb of time which will be deliver'd. Traverse, go, provide thy money. We will have more of this tomorrow. Adieu.

RODERIGO: Where shall we meet i' th' morning?   320

IAGO: At my lodging.

RODERIGO: I'll be with thee betimes. [Starts to leave.]

IAGO: Go to, farewell.—Do you hear, Roderigo?

RODERIGO: What say you?

IAGO: No more of drowning, do you hear?

RODERIGO: I am chang'd.

IAGO: Go to, farewell. Put money enough in your purse.

RODERIGO: I'll sell all my land.   *Exit.*

IAGO: Thus do I ever make my fool my purse;
For I mine own gain'd knowledge should profane,   330
If I would time expend with such a snipe
But for my sport and profit. I hate the Moor;
And it is thought abroad that 'twixt my sheets
H'as done my office. I know not if't be true;
But I, for mere suspicion in that kind,
Will do as if for surety. He holds me well;
The better shall my purpose work on him.
Cassio's a proper man. Let me see now:
To get his place and to plume up my will
In double knavery—How, how?—Let's see: 340
After some time, to abuse Othello's ears
That he is too familiar with his wife.
He hath a person and a smooth dispose
To be suspected, fram'd to make women false.
The Moor is of a free and open nature,
That thinks men honest that but seem to be so,
And will as tenderly be led by th' nose
As asses are.
I have 't. It is engend'red. Hell and night
Must bring this monstrous birth to the world's light.   350
                    [Exit.]

Act II, Scene I

[Montano, Governor of Cyprus, reports that the Turkish fleet has been destroyed by a tempest. The storm has also separated Othello's vessel from Cassio's, Othello is still out at sea but the rest of the party arrives safely. (ed.)]

Enter Desdemona, Iago, Roderigo, and Emilia [with Attendants].

[CASSIO:]   O, behold,   1
The riches of the ship is come on shore!   *[Kneels.]*
You men of Cyprus, let her have your knees.
Hail to thee, lady! And the grace of heaven,
Before, behind thee, and on every hand,
Enwheel thee round!   *[He rises.]*

DESDEMONA: I thank you, valiant Cassio.
What tiding can you tell me of my lord?

CASSIO: He is not yet arriv'd, nor I know I aught
But that he's well and will be shortly here.

DESDEMONA: O, but I fear—How lost you company?   10

---

274 **hyssop** a herb of the mint family **gender** kind   276 **idleness** want of cultivation   277 **corrigible authority** power to correct
278 **poise** counterbalance   281 **motions** appetites   282 **unbitted** uncontrolled
283 **sect or scion** cutting or offshoot   288 **perdurable** very durable
289 **stead** assist   290 **defeat thy favor** disguise and disfigure your face
295 **answerable sequestration** a corresponding separation or estrangement
296 **wills** carnal appetites   298 **locusts** fruit of the carob tree (see Matthew 3.4), or perhaps honeysuckle **coloquintida** colocynth or bitter apple, a purgative   303 **Make** raise, collect   304 **erring** wandering, vagabond, unsteady   310 **fast** true   314 **hearted** fixed in the heart   315 **conjunctive** united   318 **Traverse** go forward. (A military term.)

---

331 **snipe** woodcock, i.e., fool   338 **proper** handsome   339 **plume up** glorify, gratify   342 **he** i.e., Cassio   343 **dispose** manner, bearing   345 **free** frank, generous **open** unsuspicious

II.i. Location: A seaport in Cyprus. An open place near the quay.

CASSIO: The great contention of the sea and skies
Parted our fellowship.
(Within)   "A sail, a sail!" [A shot.]
                                    But hark. A sail!
SECOND GENTLEMAN: They give their greeting to the citadel.
This likewise is a friend.
CASSIO: See for the news.
                    [Exit Second Gentleman.]
Good ancient, you are welcome. [To Emilia.] Welcome
    mistress.
Let it not gall your patience, good Iago,
That I extend my manners; 'tis my breeding
That gives me this bold show of courtesy.   [Kissing her.]
IAGO: Sir, would she give you so much of her lips
As of her tongue she oft bestows on me,   20
You would have enough.
DESDEMONA: Alas, she has no speech!
IAGO: In faith, too much.
I find it still, when I have list to sleep.
Marry, before your ladyship, I grant,
She puts her tongue a little in her heart,
And chides with thinking.
EMILIA: You have little cause to say so.
IAGO: Come on, come on; you are pictures out of doors,
Bells in your parlors, wildcats in your kitchens,
Saints in your injuries, devils being offended,   30
Players in your huswifery, and huswives in your beds.
DESDEMONA: O, fie upon thee, slanderer!
IAGO: Nay, it is true, or else I am a Turk.
You rise to play, and go to bed to work.
EMILIA: You shall not write my praise.
IAGO: No, let me not.
DESDEMONA: What wouldst thou write of me, if thou
    shouldst praise me?
IAGO: O gentle lady, do not put me to 't.
For I am nothing if not critical.
DESDEMONA: Come on, assay.—There's one gone to the
    harbor?
IAGO: Ay, madam.   40
DESDEMONA: I am not merry; but I do beguile
The thing I am, by seeming otherwise.—
Come, how wouldst thou praise me?
IAGO: I am about it; but indeed my invention
Comes from my pate as birdlime does from frieze,
It plucks out brains and all. But my Muse labors,
And thus she is deliver'd:
If she be fair and wise, fairness and wit,
The one's for use, the other useth it.
DESDEMONA: Well prais'd! How if she be black and witty?   50
IAGO: If she be black, and thereto have a wit,

She'll find a white that shall her blackness fit.
DESDEMONA: Worse and worse.
EMILIA: How if fair and foolish?
IAGO: She never yet was foolish that was fair,
For even her folly help'd her to an heir.
DESDEMONA: These are old fond paradoxes to make fools
laugh i' th' alehouse. What miserable praise hast thou for
her that's foul and foolish?
IAGO: There's none so foul and foolish thereunto,   60
But does foul pranks which fair and wise ones do.
DESDEMONA: O heavy ignorance! Thou praisest the worst
best. But what praise couldst thou bestow on a deserving
woman indeed, one that, in the authority of her merit, did
justly put on the vouch of very malice itself?
IAGO: She that was ever fair, and never proud,
Had tongue at will, and yet was never loud,
Never lack'd gold, and yet went never gay,
Fled from her wish, and yet said, "Now I may,"
She that being ang'red, her revenge being nigh,   70
Bade her wrong stay, and her displeasure fly,
She that in wisdom never was so frail
To change the cod's head for the salmon's tail,
She that could think, and ne'er disclose her mind,
See suitors following, and not look behind,
She was a wight, if ever such wight were—
DESDEMONA: To do what?
IAGO: To suckle fools and chronicle small beer.
DESDEMONA: O most lame and impotent conclusion! Do
not learn of him, Emilia, though he be thy husband. How   80
say you, Cassio? Is he not a most profane and liberal
counselor?
CASSIO: He speaks home, madam. You may relish him
more in the soldier than in the scholar.
                    [Cassio and Desdemona stand together,
                                    conversing intimately.]
IAGO [Aside]: He takes her by the palm. Ay, well said,
whisper. With as little a web as this will I ensnare as great
a fly as Cassio. Ay, smile upon her, do; I will gyve thee in
thine own courtship. You say true; 'tis so, indeed. If such
tricks as these strip you out of your lieutenantry, it had
been better you had not kiss'd your three fingers so oft,   90
which now again you are most apt to play the sir in. Very
good; well kiss'd! An excellent courtesy! 'Tis so, indeed.
Yet again your fingers to your lips? Would they were clyster-
pipes for your sake!
[Trumpet within.] The Moor! I know his trumpet.
CASSIO: 'Tis truly so.
DESDEMONA: Let's meet him and receive him.
CASSIO: Lo, where he comes!
Enter Othello and Attendants.

---

17 extend show   26 with thinking i.e., in her thoughts only   28 pictures out of
doors i.e., painted surfaces, all cosmetics   29 Bells . . . kitchens i.e., making
pleasant conversation with your guests and angry shouts at your servants
30 Saints martyrs   31 huswifery housekeeping huswives hussies. (i.e., women
are "busy" in bed.)   38 critical censorious   39 assay try   45 birdlime sticky
substance used to catch small birds frieze coarse woolen cloth
49 The one's . . . it i.e., her cleverness will make use of her beauty
50 black dark complexioned

52 white a fair person (with word-play on wight a person) fit (with sexual
suggestion of mating)   56 folly (with added meaning of lechery,
wantonness) to an heir i.e., to bear a child
57 fond foolish   59 foul ugly   65 put . . . vouch compel the approval
68 gay extravagantly clothed   69 Fled . . . may avoided temptation where the
choice was hers   71 Bade . . . stay i.e., resolved to put up with her injury
patiently   73 To . . . tail i.e., to exchange something cheap and nutritious
for something expensive but worthless (? with perhaps a sexual suggestion
of exchanging wisdom for carnality)   78 suckle fools breastfeed babies
chronicle small beer i.e., keep petty household accounts   81 liberal
licentious, free-spoken   83 home i.e., without reserve   87 gyve fetter,
shackle   88 courtship courtesy, show of courtly manners   91 the sir i.e.,
the fine gentleman   93-94 clyster-pipes tubes used for enemas

OTHELLO: O my fair warrior!

DESDEMONA: My dear Othello!

OTHELLO: It gives me wonder great as my content   100
To see you here before me. O my soul's joy!
If after every tempest come such calms
May the winds blow till they have waken'd death!
And let the laboring bark climb hills of seas
Olympus-high, and duck again as low
As hell's from heaven! If it were now to die,
'Twere now to be most happy; for, I fear,
My soul hath her content so absolute
That not another comfort like to this
Succeeds in unknown fate.

DESDEMONA: The heavens forbid   110
But that our loves and comforts should increase,
Even as our days do grow!

OTHELLO: Amen to that, sweet powers!
I cannot speak enough of this content;
It stops me here; it is too much of joy.
And this, and this, the greatest discords be

[Kissing her.]

That e'er our hearts shall make!

IAGO *[Aside]*: O, you are well tun'd now!
But I'll set down the pegs that make this music,
As honest as I am.

OTHELLO: Come, let us to the castle.
News, friends! Our wars are done, the Turks are drown'd.
How does my old acquaintance of this isle?—   120
Honey, you shall be well desir'd in Cyprus;
I have found great love amongst them. O my sweet,
I prattle out of fashion, and I dote
In mine own comforts. I prithee, good Iago,
Go to the bay and disembark my coffers.
Bring thou the master to the citadel;
He is a good one, and his worthiness
Does challenge much respect. Come, Desdemona,
Once more, well met at Cyprus.

Exeunt Othello and Desdemona [and all but Iago and Roderigo].

IAGO *[To an Attendant]*: Do thou meet me presently at the   130
harbor. *[To Roderigo.]* Come hither. If thou be'st valiant—
as, they say, base men being in love have then a nobility in
their natures more than is native to them—list me. The
lieutenant tonight watches on the court of guard. First, I
must tell thee this: Desdemona is directly in love with him.

RODERIGO: With him? Why, 'tis not possible.

IAGO: Lay thy finger thus, and let thy soul be instructed.
Mark me with what violence she first lov'd the Moor, but for
bragging and telling her fantastical lies. And will she love
him still for prating? Let not thy discreet heart think it. Her   140
eye must be fed; and what delight shall she have to look on
the devil? When the blood is made dull with the act of
sport, there should be, again to inflame it and to give
satiety a fresh appetite, loveliness in favor, sympathy in
years, manners, and beauties—all which the Moor is
defective in. Now, for want of these requir'd
conveniences, her delicate tenderness will find itself
abus'd, begin to heave the gorge, disrelish and abhor the
Moor. Very nature will instruct her in it and compel her to
some second choice. Now, sir, this granted—as it is a most   150
pregnant and unforc'd position—who stands so eminent in
the degree of this fortune as Cassio does? A knave very
voluble; no further conscionable than in putting on the
mere form of civil and humane seeming, for the better
compassing of his salt and most hidden loose affection?
Why, none, why, none. A slipper and subtle knave, a finder
of occasions, that has an eye can stamp and counterfeit
advantages, though true advantage never present itself; a
devilish knave. Besides, the knave is handsome, young,
and hath all those requisites in him that folly and green   160
minds look after. A pestilent complete knave, and the
woman hath found him already.

RODERIGO: I cannot believe that in her; she's full of most
bless'd condition.

IAGO: Bless'd fig's-end! The wine she drinks is made of
grapes. If she had been bless'd, she would never have lov'd
the Moor. Bless'd pudding! Didst thou not see her paddle
with the palm of his hand! Didst not mark that?

RODERIGO: Yes, that I did; but that was but courtesy.

IAGO: Lechery, by this hand. An index and obscure   170
prologue to the history of lust and foul thoughts. They met
so near with their lips that their breaths embrac'd together.
Villainous thoughts, Roderigo! When these mutualities so
marshal the way, hard at hand comes the master and main
exercise, th' incorporate conclusion. Pish! But, sir, be you
rul'd by me. I have brought you from Venice. Watch you
tonight; for the command, I'll lay 't upon you. Cassio knows
you not. I'll not be far from you. Do you find some occasion
to anger Cassio, either by speaking too loud, or tainting his
discipline, or from what other course you please, which the   180
time shall more favorably minister.

RODERIGO: Well.

IAGO: Sir, he's rash and very sudden in choler, and
happily may strike at you. Provoke him, that he may; for
even out of that will I cause these of Cyprus to mutiny,
whose qualification shall come into no true taste again but
by the displanting of Cassio. So shall you have a shorter
journey to your desires by the means I shall then have to
prefer them; and the impediment most profitably remov'd,
without the which there were no expectation of our   190
prosperity.

---

110 **Succeeds . . . fate** i.e., can follow in the unknown future   117 **set down**
loosen (and hence untune the instrument)   121 **desir'd** welcomed
126 **master** ship's captain   128 **challenge** lay claim to, deserve   134 **court of**
guard guardhouse. (Cassio is in charge of the watch.)   137 **thus** i.e., on
your lips

147 **conveniences** compatibilities   148 **heave the gorge** experience nausea
151 **pregnant** evident, readily believable   153 **conscionable** conscientious,
conscience-bound   154 **humane** polite, courteous   155 **salt** licentious
156 **slipper** slippery   157 **an eye can stamp** an eye that can coin, create
170 **index** table of contents   173 **mutualities** exchanges, intimacies
175 **incorporate** carnal   179 **tainting** disparaging   183 **choler** wrath
184 **happily** haply, perchance   186 **qualification** appeasement **true taste**
acceptable state   189 **prefer** advance

RODERIGO: I will do this, if I can bring it to any opportunity.
IAGO: I warrant thee. Meet me by and by at the citadel.
I must fetch his necessaries ashore. Farewell.
   RODERIGO: Adieu.   *Exit.*
   IAGO: That Cassio loves her, I do well believe 't;
That she loves him, 'tis apt and of great credit.
The Moor, howbeit that I endure him not,
Is of a constant, loving, noble nature,   200
And I dare think he'll prove to Desdemona
A most dear husband. Now, I do love her too,
Not out of absolute lust, though peradventure
I stand accountant for as great a sin,
But partly led to diet my revenge,
For that I do suspect the lusty Moor
Hath leap'd into my seat; the thought whereof
Doth, like a poisonous mineral, gnaw my inwards;
And nothing can or shall content my soul
Till I am even'd with him, wife for wife,   210
Or failing so, yet that I put the Moor
At least into a jealousy so strong
That judgment cannot cure. Which thing to do,
If this poor trash of Venice, whom I trash
For his quick hunting, stand the putting on,
I'll have our Michael Cassio on the hip,
Abuse him to the Moor in the rank garb—
For I fear Cassio with my night-cap too—
Make the Moor thank me, love me, and reward me
For making him egregiously an ass   220
And practicing upon his peace and quiet
Even to madness. 'Tis here, but yet confus'd.
Knavery's plain face is never seen till us'd.   *Exit.*

Scene II

[A herald announces the public festival to celebrate the destruction of the Turkish fleet. (ed.)]

Scene III

Enter Othello, Desdemona, Cassio, and Attendants.
   OTHELLO: Good Michael, look you to the guard tonight.   1
Let's teach ourselves that honorable stop,
Not to outsport discretion.
   CASSIO: Iago hath direction what to do;
But, notwithstanding, with my personal eye
Will I look to't.
   OTHELLO: Iago is most honest.
Michael, good night. Tomorrow with your earliest
Let me have speech with you. *[To Desdemona.]* Come my
   dear love,
The purchase made, the fruits are to ensue;
That profit's yet to come 'tween me and you.—   10

Good night.
      Exit [Othello, with Desdemona and Attendants].
Enter Iago.
   CASSIO: Welcome, Iago. We must to the watch.
   IAGO: Not this hour, lieutenant; 'tis not yet ten o' th' clock.
Our general cast us thus early for the love of his
Desdemona; who let us not therefore blame. He hath not yet
made wanton the night with her, and she is sport for Jove.
   CASSIO: She's a most exquisite lady.
   IAGO: And, I'll warrant her, full of game.
   CASSIO: Indeed, she's a most fresh and delicate creature.
   IAGO: What an eye she has! Methinks it sounds a parley to 20
provocation.
   CASSIO: An inviting eye; and yet methinks right modest.
   IAGO: And when she speaks, is it not an alarum to love?
   CASSIO: She is indeed perfection.
   IAGO: Well, happiness to their sheets! Come, lieutenant, I
have a stoup of wine, and here without are a brace of Cyprus
gallants that would fain have a measure to the health of
black Othello.
   CASSIO: Not tonight, good Iago. I have very poor and
unhappy brains for drinking. I could well wish courtesy   30
would invent some other custom of entertainment.
   IAGO: O, they are our friends. But one cup! I'll drink for you.
   CASSIO: I have drunk but one cup tonight, and that was
craftily qualified too, and behold what innovation it makes
here. I am unfortunate in the infirmity, and dare not task my
weakness with any more.
   IAGO: What, man? 'Tis a night of revels. The gallants desire
it.
   CASSIO: Where are they?
   IAGO: Here at the door. I pray you, call them in.   40

   CASSIO: I'll do't; but it dislikes me.   *Exit.*
   IAGO: If I can fasten but one cup upon him,
With that which he hath drunk tonight already,
He'll be as full of quarrel and offense
As my young mistress' dog. Now, my sick fool Roderigo,
Whom love hath turn'd almost the wrong side out,
To Desdemona hath tonight carous'd
Potations pottle-deep; and he's to watch.
Three lads of Cyprus, noble swelling spirits,
That hold their honors in a wary distance,   50
The very elements of this warlike isle,
Have I tonight fluster'd with flowing cups,
And they watch too. Now, 'mongst this flock of drunkards
Am I to put our Cassio in some action
That may offend the isle.—But here they come.
*Enter Cassio, Montano, and Gentlemen [servants following
   with wine].*
If consequence do but approve my dream,
My boat sails freely, both with wind and stream.

---

194 **by and by** immediately   198 **apt** probable **credit** credibility
204 **accountant** accountable   205 **diet** feed   214 **I trash** I hold in check. (A
hunting term, meaning to put weight on a hunting dog in order to slow
him down.)   215 **For** to make more eager **stand . . . on** responds properly
when I incite him to quarrel   216 **on the hip** at my mercy, where I can
throw him. (A wrestling term.)   217 **rank garb** coarse manner, gross fashion
218 **with my night-cap** i.e., as a rival in my bed, as one who gives me
cuckold's horns   221 **practicing upon** plotting against

II.iii. **Location:** Cyprus. The citadel.   2 **stop** restraint

14 **cast** dismissed   20 **sounds a parley** calls for a conference, issues an
invitation   23 **alarum** signal calling men to arms (continuing the military
metaphor of *parley*, l.20)   26 **stoup** measure of liquor, two quarts
34 **qualified** diluted **innovation** disturbance, insurrection   35 **here** i.e., in
Cassio's head   48 **pottle-deep** to the bottom of the tankard
50 **hold . . . distance** i.e., are extremely sensitive of their honor
51 **very elements** true representatives   53 **watch** are members of the guard
56 **If . . . dream** if subsequent events will only confirm my scheme

CASSIO: 'Fore God, they have given me a rouse already.
MONTANO: Good faith, a little one; not past a pint, as I am
a soldier.   60
IAGO: Some wine, ho!

[Sings.] "And let me the canakin clink, clink;
           And let me the canakin clink.
           A soldier's a man,
           O, man's life's but a span;
           Why, then, let a soldier drink."

Some wine, boys!
CASSIO: 'Fore God, an excellent song.
IAGO: I learn'd it in England, where indeed they are most
potent in potting. Your Dane, your German, and your swag-   70
bellied Hollander—Drink, ho!—are nothing to your
English.
CASSIO: Is your Englishman so exquisite in his drinking?
IAGO: Why, he drinks you, with facility, your Dane dead
drunk, he sweats not to overthrow your Almain; he gives
your Hollander a vomit ere the next pottle can be fill'd.
CASSIO: To the health of our general!
MONTANO: I am for it, lieutenant; and I'll do you justice.
IAGO: O sweet England!

[Sings.] "King Stephen was and—a worthy peer,   80
           His breeches cost him but a crown;
           He held them sixpence all too dear,
           With that he call'd the tailor lown.

           He was a wight of high renown,
           And thou art but of low degree.
           'Tis pride that pulls the country down;
           Then take thy auld cloak about thee."

Some wine, ho!
CASSIO: 'For God, this is a more exquisite song than the
other.   90
IAGO: Will you hear 't again?
CASSIO: No; for I hold him to be unworthy of his place that
does those things. Well, God's above all; and there be souls
must be sav'd, and there be souls must not be sav'd.
IAGO: It's true, good lieutenant.
CASSIO: For mine own part—no offense to the general, nor
any man of quality—I hope to be sav'd.
IAGO: And so do I too, lieutenant.
CASSIO: Ay, but, by your leave, not before me; the
lieutenant is to be sav'd before the ancient. Let's have no   100
more of this; let's to our affairs.—God forgive us our sins!
—Gentlemen, let's look to our business. Do not think,
gentlemen, I am drunk. This is my ancient; this is my right
hand, and this is my left. I am not drunk now; I can stand
well enough, and speak well enough.
ALL: Excellent well.
CASSIO: Why, very well then; you must not think then that

I am drunk.   Exit.
[Iago suggests to Montano that Cassio is drunk and
unreliable. (ed.)]
Enter Cassio, pursuing Roderigo.
CASSIO: 'Zounds, you rogue! You rascal!
MONTANO: What's the matter, lieutenant?   110
CASSIO: A knave teach me my duty? I'll beat the knave into
a twiggen bottle.
RODERIGO: Beat me?
CASSIO: Dost though prate, rogue?
                                                  [Striking Roderigo.]
MONTANO: Nay, good lieutenant; [Staying him.] I pray you,
sir, hold your hand.
CASSIO: Let me go, sir, or I'll knock you o'er the mazzard.
MONTANO: Come, come, you're drunk.
CASSIO: Drunk?   [They fight.]
IAGO [Aside to Roderigo]: Away, I say; go out, and cry a   120
mutiny.
                                                     [Exit Roderigo.]
Nay, good lieutenant—God's will, gentlemen—
Help, ho!—Lieutenant—sir—Montano—sir—
Help, masters!—Here's a goodly watch indeed!
                                                        [Bell rings.]
Who's that which rings the bell?—Diablo, ho!
The town will rise. God's will, lieutenant, hold!
You'll be asham'd for ever.
Enter Othello and Attendants.
OTHELLO: What is the matter here?
MONTANO: 'Zounds, I bleed still;
I am hurt to th' death. He dies! [Thrusts at Cassio.]
OTHELLO: Hold for your lives!
IAGO: Hold, ho! Lieutenant—sir—Montano—gentlemen— 130
Have you forgot all sense of place and duty?
Hold! The general speaks to you. Hold, for shame!
OTHELLO: Why, how now, ho! From whence ariseth this?
Are we turn'd Turks, and to ourselves do that
Which heaven hath forbid the Ottomites?
For Christian shame, put by this barbarous brawl!
He that stirs next to carve for his own rage
Holds his soul light; he dies upon his motion.
Silence that dreadful bell. It frights the isle
From her propriety. What is the matter, masters?   140
Honest Iago, that looks dead with grieving,
Speak. Who began this? On thy love, I charge thee.
IAGO: I do not know. Friends all, but now, even now,
In quarter, and in terms like bride and groom
Devesting them for bed; and then, but now—
As if some planet had unwitted men—
Swords out, and tilting one at other's breast,
In opposition bloody. I cannot speak
Any beginning to this peevish odds;
And would in action glorious I had lost   150

---

58 **rouse** full draft of liquor   62 **canakin** small drinking vessel   75 **Almain**
German   78 **I'll . . . justice** i.e., I'll drink as much as you
83 **lown** lout, rascal   86 **pride** i.e., extravagance in dress   87 **auld** old

112 **twiggen** wicker-covered   117 **mazzard** i.e., head. (Literally, a drinking
vessel.)   125 **Diablo** the devil   126 **rise** grow riotous   135 **forbid** i.e., by
destroying their fleet, so that the Venetians need not fight them
137 **carve for** i.e., indulge, satisfy   140 **propriety** proper state or condition
144 **In quarter** in good military order, within bounds
149 **peevish odds** childish quarrel

Those legs that brought me to a part of it!
   OTHELLO: How comes it, Michael, you are thus forgot?
   CASSIO: I pray you, pardon me; I cannot speak.
   OTHELLO: Worthy Montano, you were wont to be civil;
The gravity and stillness of your youth
The world hath noted, and your name is great
In mouths of wisest censure. What's the matter
That you unlace your reputation thus,
And spend your rich opinion for the name
Of a night-brawler? Give me answer to it.   160
   MONTANO: Worthy Othello, I am hurt to danger.
Your officer, Iago, can inform you—
While I spare speech, which something now offends me—
Of all that I do know; nor know I aught
By me that's said or done amiss this night,
Unless self-charity be sometimes a vice,
And to defend ourselves it be a sin
When violence assails us.
   OTHELLO: Now, by heaven,
My blood begins my safer guides to rule,   170
And passion, having my best judgment collied,
Assays to lead the way. If I once stir,
Or do but lift his arm, the best of you
Shall sink in my rebuke. Give me to know
How this foul rout began, who set it on;
And he that is approv'd in this offense,
Though he had twinn'd with me, both at a birth,
Shall lose me. What? In a town of war,
Yet wild, the people's hearts brimful of fear,
To manage private and domestic quarrel?   180
In night, and on the court and guard of safety?
'Tis monstrous. Iago, who began 't?
   MONTANO: If partially affin'd, or leagu'd in office,
Thou dost deliver more or less than truth,
Thou art no soldier.
   IAGO: Touch me not so near.
I had rather have this tongue cut from my mouth
Than it should do offense to Michael Cassio;
Yet, I persuade myself, to speak the truth
Shall nothing wrong him. Thus it is, general.
Montano and myself being in speech,   190
There comes a fellow crying out for help,
And Cassio following him with determin'd sword
To execute upon him. Sir, this gentleman
             [Indicating Montano.]
Steps in to Cassio, and entreats his pause.
Myself the crying fellow did pursue,
Lest by his clamor—as it so fell out—
The town might fall in fright. He, swift of foot,
Outran my purpose; and I return'd the rather
For that I heard the clink and fall of swords,
And Cassio high in oath; which till tonight   200
I ne'er might say before. When I came back—

For this was brief—I found them close together,
At blow and thrust, even as again they were
When you yourself did part them.
More of this matter cannot I report.
But men are men; the best sometimes forget.
Though Cassio did some little wrong to him,
As men in rage strike those that wish them best,
Yet surely Cassio, I believe, receiv'd
From him that fled some strange indignity,   210
Which patience could not pass.
   OTHELLO: I know Iago,
Thy honesty and love doth mince this matter,
Making it light to Cassio. Cassio, I love thee;
But never more be officer of mine.
Enter Desdemona, attended.
Look, if my gentle love be not rais'd up.
I'll make thee an example.
   DESDEMONA: What is the matter, dear?
   OTHELLO: All's well now, sweeting;
Come away to bed. *[To Montano.]* Sir, for your hurts,
Myself will be your surgeon.—Lead him off.
             [Montano is led off.]
Iago, look with care about the town,   220
And silence those whom this vile brawl distracted.
Come, Desdemona. 'Tis the soldiers' life
To have their balmy slumbers wak'd with strife.
        Exit [with all but Iago and Cassio].
   IAGO: What, are you hurt, lieutenant?
   CASSIO: Ay, past all surgery.
   IAGO: Marry, God forbid!
   CASSIO: Reputation, reputation, reputation! O, I have lost
my reputation! I have lost the immortal part of myself, and
what remains is bestial. My reputation, Iago, my
reputation!   230
   IAGO: As I am an honest man, I thought you had receiv'd
some bodily wound; there is more sense in that than in
reputation. Reputation is an idle and most false
imposition; oft got without merit, and lost without
deserving. You have lost no reputation at all, unless you
repute yourself such a loser. What, man, there are ways to
recover the general again. You are but now cast in his
mood, a punishment more in policy than in malice, even so
as one would beat his offenseless dog to affright an
imperious lion. Sue to him again, and he's yours.   240
   CASSIO: I will rather sue to be despis'd than to deceive so
good a commander with so slight, so drunken, and so
indiscreet an officer. Drunk? And speak parrot? And
squabble? Swagger? Swear? And discourse fustian with
one's own shadow? O thou invisible spirit of wine, if thou
hast no name to be known by, let us call thee devil!
   IAGO: What was he that you follow'd with your sword?
What had he done to you?
   CASSIO: I know not.

---

157 censure judgment   **158 unlace** undo, degrade   **159 opinion** reputation
163 something somewhat **offends** pains   **170 blood** passion (of anger) **guides**
i.e., reason   **171 collied** darkened   **172 Assays** undertakes   **175 rout** riot
176 approv'd in found guilty of   **180 manage** undertake   **181 court and guard**
i.e., the main guardhouse or headquarters   **183 partially affin'd** made
partial by some personal relationship   **193 execute** give effect to (his
anger)   **198 rather** sooner

211 pass pass over, overlook   **234 imposition** thing artificially imposed and
of no real value   **237 recover** regain favor with   **237–238 cast in his mood**
dismissed in a moment of anger   **243 speak parrot** talk nonsense, rant
(*Discourse fustian*, l.244 has the same meaning.)

IAGO: Is 't possible? 250

CASSIO: I remember a mass of things, but nothing distinctly; a quarrel, but nothing wherefore. O God, that men should put an enemy in their mouths to steal away their brains! That we should, with joy, pleasance, revel, and applause, transform ourselves into beasts!

IAGO: Why, but you are now well enough. How came you thus recover'd?

CASSIO: It hath pleas'd the devil drunkenness to give place to the devil wrath. One unperfectness shows me another, to make me frankly despise myself. 260

IAGO: Come, you are too severe a moraler. As the time, the place, and condition of this country stands, I could heartily wish this had not befall'n; but since it is as it is, mend it for your own good.

CASSIO: I will ask him for my place again; he shall tell me I am a drunkard! Had I as many mouths as Hydra, such an answer would stop them all. To be now a sensible man, by and by a fool, and presently a beast! O strange! Ever inordinate cup is unbless'd, and the ingredient is a devil.

IAGO: Come, come, good wine is a good familiar creature, 270 if it be well us'd. Exclaim no more against it. And, good lieutenant, I think you think I love you.

CASSIO: I have well approv'd it, sir. I drunk!

IAGO: You or any man living may be drunk at a time, man. I'll tell you what you shall do. Our general's wife is now the general—I may say so in this respect, for that he hath devoted and given up himself to the contemplation, mark, and denotement of her parts and graces. Confess yourself freely to her; importune her help to put you in your place again. She is of so free, so kind, so apt, so bless'd a 280 disposition, she holds it a vice in her goodness not to do more than she is requested. This broken joint between you and her husband entreat her to splinter; and, my fortunes against any lay worth naming, this crack of your love shall grow stronger than it was before.

CASSIO: You advise me well.

IAGO: I protest, in the sincerity of love and honest kindness.

CASSIO: I think it freely; and betimes in the morning I will beseech the virtuous Desdemona to undertake for me. I am 290 desperate of my fortunes if they check me here.

IAGO: You are in the right. Good night, lieutenant; I must to the watch.

CASSIO: Good night, honest Iago. *Exit Cassio.*

IAGO: And what's he then that says I play the villain?
When this advice is free I give and honest,
Probal to thinking, and indeed the course
To win the Moor again? For 'tis most easy
Th' inclining Desdemona to subdue
In any honest suit; she's fram'd as fruitful 300
As the free elements. And then for her
To win the Moor—were 't to renounce his baptism,

All seals and symbols of redeemed sin—
His soul is so enfetter'd to her love
That she may make, unmake, do what she list,
Even as her appetite shall play the god
With his weak function. How am I then a villain
To counsel Cassio to this parallel course,
Directly to his good? Divinity of hell!
When devils will the blackest sins put on, 310
They do suggest at first with heavenly shows,
As I do now. For whiles this honest fool
Plies Desdemona to repair his fortunes,
And she for him pleads strongly to the Moor,
I'll pour his pestilence into his ear,
That she repeals him for her body's lust;
And by how much she strives to do him good,
She shall undo her credit with the Moor.
So will I turn her virtue into pitch,
And out of her own goodness make the net 320
That shall enmesh them all.
Enter Roderigo.

How now, Roderigo?

RODERIGO: I do follow here in the chase, not like a hound that hunts, but one that fills up the cry. My money is almost spent; I have been tonight exceedingly well cudgel'd; and I think the issue will be, I shall have so much experience for my pains, and so, with no money at all and a little more wit, return again to Venice.

IAGO: How poor are they that have not patience!
What wound did ever heal but by degrees?
Thou know'st we work by wit, and not by witchcraft; 330
And wit depends on dilatory time.
Does 't not go well? Cassio hath beaten thee,
And thou, by that small hurt, hast cashier'd Cassio.
Though other things grow fair against the sun,
Yet fruits that blossom first will first be ripe.
Content thyself awhile. By the mass, 'tis morning!
Pleasure and action make the hours seem short.
Retire thee; go where thou art billeted.
Away, I say! Thou shalt know more hereafter.
Nay, get thee gone. *Exit Roderigo.*

Two things are to be done. 340
My wife must move for Cassio to her mistress;
I'll set her on;
Myself the while to draw the Moor apart,
And bring him jump when he may Cassio find
Soliciting his wife. Ay, that's the way!
Dull not device by coldness and delay. *Exit.*

Act III, Scene I

[Cassio and musicians exchange words with a clown. On Iago's advice, Cassio asks Emilia to arrange a meeting with Desdemona so that he can plead his cause. (ed.)]

---

266 **Hydra** the Lernaean Hydra, a monster with many heads, slain by Hercules as the second of his twelve labors   273 **approv'd** proved   277–278 **mark, and denotement** (Both words mean observation.)   278 **parts** qualities   280 **free** generous   283 **splinter** bind with splints   284 **lay** stake, wager   291 **check** repulse   297 **Probal** probable   299 **inclining** favorably disposed **subdue** persuade   300 **fruitful** generous   301 **free elements** i.e., earth, air, fire, and water, which sustain life

---

308 **parallel** corresponding to these facts and to his best interest   309 **Divinity of hell** inverted theology of hell (which seduces the soul to its damnation)   310 **put on** further, instigate   311 **suggest** tempt   316 **repeals him** i.e., attempts to get him restored   323 **cry** pack   333 **cashier'd** dismissed from service   344 **jump** precisely

III.i. **Location: Before the chamber of Othello and Desdemona**

Scene II

[Othello sends letters of state to Venice. (ed.)]

Scene III

Enter Desdemona, Cassio, and Emilia.

    DESDEMONA: Be thou assur'd, good Cassio, I will do   1
All my abilities in thy behalf.
    EMILIA: Good madam, do. I warrant it grieves my husband
As if the case were his.
    DESDEMONA: O, that's an honest fellow. Do not doubt, Cassio,
But I will have my lord and you again
As friendly as you were.
    CASSIO: Bounteous madam,
Whatever shall become of Michael Cassio,
He's never anything but your true servant.
    DESDEMONA: I know 't; I thank you. You do love my lord;   10
You have known him long; and be you well assur'd
He shall in strangeness stand no farther off
Than in a politic distance.
    CASSIO: Ay, but, lady,
That policy may either last so long,
Or feed upon such nice and waterish diet,
Or breed itself so out of circumstance,
That, I being absent and my place supplied,
My general will forget my love and service.
    DESDEMONA: Do not doubt that; before Emilia here
I give thee warrant of thy place. Assure thee,   20
If I do vow a friendship, I'll perform it
To the last article. My lord shall never rest.
I'll watch him tame and talk him out of patience;
His bed shall seem a school, his board a shrift;
I'll intermingle everything he does
With Cassio's suit. Therefore be merry, Cassio,
For thy solicitor shall rather die
Than give thy cause away.
Enter Othello and Iago [at a distance].
    EMILIA: Madam, here comes my lord.
    CASSIO: Madam, I'll take my leave.   30
    DESDEMONA: Why, stay, and hear me speak.
    CASSIO: Madam, not now. I am very ill at ease,
Unfit for mine own purposes.
    DESDEMONA: Well, do your discretion.   *Exit Cassio.*
    IAGO: Ha! I like not that.
    OTHELLO: What dost thou say?
    IAGO: Nothing, my lord; or if—I know not what.
    OTHELLO: Was not that Cassio parted from my wife?
    IAGO: Cassio, my Lord? No, sure, I cannot think it,
That he would steal away so guilty-like,
Seeing you coming.
    OTHELLO: I do believe 'twas he.   40
    DESDEMONA: How now, my lord?

I have been talking with a suitor here,
A man that languishes in your displeasure.
    OTHELLO: Who is 't you mean?
    DESDEMONA: Why, your lieutenant, Cassio, Good my lord,
If I have any grace or power to move you,
His present reconciliation take;
For if he be not one that truly loves you,
That errs in ignorance and not in cunning,
I have no judgment in an honest face,   50
I prithee, call him back.
    OTHELLO: Went he hence now?
    DESDEMONA: Yes, faith, so humbled
That he hath left part of his grief with me
To suffer with him. Good love, call him back.
    OTHELLO: Not now, sweet Desdemona; some other time.
    DESDEMONA: But shall 't be shortly?
    OTHELLO: The sooner, sweet, for you.
    DESDEMONA: Shall 't be tonight at supper?
    OTHELLO: No, not tonight.
    DESDEMONA: Tomorrow dinner, then?
    OTHELLO: I shall not dine at home;
I meet the captains at the citadel.
    DESDEMONA: Why, then, tomorrow night, or Tuesday morn,   60
On Tuesday noon, or night, on Wednesday morn.
I prithee, name the time, but let it not
Exceed three days. In faith, he's penitent;
And yet his trespass, in our common reason—
Save that, they say, the wars must make example
Out of her best—is not almost a fault
T' incur a private check. When shall he come?
Tell me, Othello. I wonder in my soul
What you would ask me, that I should deny,
Or stand so mamm'ring on. What? Michael Cassio,   70
That came a-wooing with you, and so many a time,
When I have spoke of you dispraisingly,
Hath ta'en your part—to have so much to do
To bring him in! By'r Lady, I could do much—
    OTHELLO: Prithee, no more. Let him come when he will;
I will deny thee nothing.
    DESDEMONA: Why, this is not a boon;
'Tis as I should entreat you wear your gloves,
Or feed on nourishing dishes, or keep you warm,
Or sue to you to do a peculiar profit
To your own person. Nay, when I have a suit   80
Wherein I mean to touch your love indeed,
It shall be full of poise and difficult weight,
And fearful to be granted.
    OTHELLO: I will deny thee nothing.
Whereon, I do beseech thee, grant me this,
To leave me but a little to myself.
    DESDEMONA: Shall I deny you? No. Farewell, my lord.
    OTHELLO: Farewell, my Desdemona. I'll come to thee straight.

III.ii. Location: The citadel.

III.iii. Location: The garden of the citadel.
12 strangeness aloofness   **13 politic** required by wise policy   **15 Or . . . diet** or sustain itself at length upon a trivial and meager means of support
16 circumstance chance events   **19 doubt** fear   **23 watch him tame** tame him by keeping him from sleeping. (A term from falconry.) **out of patience** past his endurance   **24 shrift** confessional

47 present immediate   **64 common reason** everyday judgments
65–66 Save . . . best were it not that, as the saying goes, military discipline requires making an example of the very best man. (*Her* refers to *wars* as a singular concept.)   **66 not almost** scarcely   **67 a private check** even a private reprimand   **70 mamm'ring on** wavering about   **74 bring him in** restore him to favor   **79 peculiar** particular, personal   **82 poise** weight, heaviness; or equipoise, delicate balance involving hard choice

DESDEMONA: Emilia, come.—Be as your fancies teach
  you;
Whate'er you be, I am obedient.   *Exit [with Emilia].*
   OTHELLO: Excellent wretch! Perdition catch my soul   90
But I do love thee! And when I love thee not,
Chaos is come again.
   IAGO: My noble lord—
   OTHELLO: What dost thou say, Iago?
   IAGO: Did Michael Cassio, when you woo'd my lady,
Know of your love?
   OTHELLO: He did, from first to last. Why dost thou ask?
   IAGO: But for a satisfaction of my thought;
No further harm.
   OTHELLO: Why of thy thought, Iago?
   IAGO: I did not think he had been acquainted with her.
   OTHELLO: O, yes, and went between us very oft.   100
   IAGO: Indeed?
   OTHELLO: Indeed? Ay, indeed. Discern'st thou aught in
   that?
Is he not honest?
   IAGO: Honest, my lord?
   OTHELLO: Honest. Ay, honest.
   IAGO: My lord, for aught I know.
   OTHELLO: What dost thou think?
   IAGO: Think, my lord?
   OTHELLO: Think, my lord? By heaven, he echoes me,
As if there were some monster in his thought
Too hideous to be shown. Thou dost mean something.
I heard thee say even now, thou lik'st not that,
When Cassio left my wife. What didst not like?   110
And when I told thee he was of my counsel
In my whole course of wooing, thou criedst "Indeed!"
And didst contract and purse thy brow together,
As if thou then hadst shut up in thy brain
Some horrible conceit. If thou dost love me,
Show me thy thought.
   IAGO: My lord, you know I love you.
   OTHELLO: I think thou dost;
And, for I know thou 'rt full of love and honesty
And weigh'st thy words before thou giv'st them breath,
Therefore these stops of thine fright me the more;   120
For such things in a false disloyal knave
Are tricks of custom, but in a man that's just
They're close dilations, working from the heart
That passion cannot rule.
   IAGO: For Michael Cassio,
I dare be sworn I think that he is honest.
   OTHELLO: I think so too.
   IAGO: Men should be what they seem
Or those that be not, would they might seem none!
   OTHELLO: Certain, men should be what they seem.
   IAGO: Why, then, I think Cassio's an honest man.
   OTHELLO: Nay, yet there's more in this.   130
I prithee speak to me as to thy thinkings,
As thou dost ruminate, and give thy worst of thoughts
The worst of words.
   IAGO: Good my lord, pardon me.
Though I am bound to every act of duty,
I am not bound to that all slaves are free to.
Utter my thoughts? Why, say they are vile and false,
As where's that palace whereinto foul things
Sometimes intrude not? Who has a breast so pure
But some uncleanly apprehensions
Keep leets and law-days and in sessions sit   140
With meditations lawful?
   OTHELLO: Thou dost conspire against thy friend, Iago,
If thou but think'st him wrong'd, and mak'st his ear
A stranger to thy thoughts.
   IAGO: I do beseech you—
Though I perchance am vicious in my guess,
As, I confess, it is my nature's plague
To spy into abuses, and oft my jealousy
Shapes faults that are not—that your wisdom yet,
From one that so imperfectly conceits,
Would take no notice, nor build yourself a trouble   150
Out of his scattering and unsure observance.
It were not for your quiet nor your good,
Nor for my manhood, honesty, or wisdom,
To let you know my thoughts.
   OTHELLO: What dost thou mean?
   IAGO: Good name in man and woman, dear my lord,
Is the immediate jewel of their souls.
Who steals my purse steals trash; 'tis something, nothing;
'Twas mine, 'tis his, and has been slave to thousands;
But he that filches from me my good name
Robs me of that which not enriches him   160
And makes me poor indeed.
   OTHELLO: By heaven, I'll know thy thoughts.
   IAGO: You cannot, if my heart were in your hand;
Nor shall not, whilst 'tis in my custody.
   OTHELLO: Ha?
   IAGO: O, beware, my lord, of jealousy!
It is the green-ey'd monster which doth mock
The meat it feeds on. That cuckold lives in bliss
Who, certain of his fate, loves not his wronger;
But, O, what damned minutes tells her o'er
Who dotes, yet doubts, suspects, yet strongly loves!   170
   OTHELLO: O misery!
   IAGO: Poor and content is rich, and rich enough,
But riches fineless is as poor as winter
To him that ever fears he shall be poor.
Good God, the souls of all my tribe defend
From jealousy!
   OTHELLO: Why, why is this?
Think'st thou I'd make a life of jealousy,
To follow still the changes of the moon
With fresh suspicions? No! To be once in doubt
Is once to be resolv'd. Exchange me for a goat   180

---

90 **wretch** (A term of affectionate endearment.) 91 **But I do** if I do not
115 **conceit** fancy 123 **close dilations** secret or involuntary expressions
124 **passion cannot rule** i.e., are too passionately strong to be restrained

135 **that** that which **free to** i.e., free with respect to 140 **leets and
law-days** sessions of the courts 141 **With** along with **lawful** innocent
142 **thy friend** i.e., Othello 145 **vicious** wrong 147 **jealousy** suspicion of evil
149 **one** i.e., myself, Iago **conceits** judges, conjectures
168 **his wronger** i.e., his faithless wife 173 **fineless** boundless

When I shall turn the business of my soul
To such exsufflicate and blown surmises,
Matching thy inference. 'Tis not to make me jealous
To say my wife is fair, feeds well, loves company,
Is free of speech, sings, plays, and dances well;
Where virtue is, these are more virtuous.
Nor from mine own weak merits will I draw
The smallest fear or doubt of her revolt,
For she had eyes, and chose me. No, Iago,
I'll see before I doubt; when I doubt, prove;   190
And on the proof, there is no more but this—
Away at once with love or jealousy!
    IAGO: I am glad of this, for now I shall have reason
To show the love and duty that I bear you
With franker spirit. Therefore, as I am bound,
Receive it from me. I speak not yet of proof.
Look to your wife; observe her well with Cassio.
Wear your eye thus, not jealous nor secure.
I would not have your free and noble nature,
Out of self-bounty, be abus'd. Look to 't.   200
I know our country disposition well;
In Venice they do let God see the pranks
They dare not show their husbands; their best conscience
Is not to leave 't undone, but keep 't unknown.
    OTHELLO: Dost thou say so?
    IAGO: She did deceive her father, marrying you;
And when she seem'd to shake and fear your looks,
She lov'd them most.
    OTHELLO: And so she did.
    IAGO: Why, go to then!
She that, so young, could give out such a seeming
To seel her father's eyes up close as oak—   210
He thought 'twas witchcraft—but I am much to blame;
I humbly do beseech you of your pardon
For too much loving you.
    OTHELLO: I am bound to thee forever.
    IAGO: I see this hath a little dash'd your spirits.
    OTHELLO: Not a jot, not a jot.
    IAGO: I' faith, I fear it has.
I hope you will consider what is spoke
Comes from my love. But I do see y' are mov'd.
I am to pray you not to strain my speech
To grosser issues nor to larger reach
Than to suspicion.   220
    OTHELLO: I will not.
    IAGO: Should you do so, my lord,
My speech should fall into such vile success
As my thoughts aim'd not. Cassio's my worthy friend—
My lord, I see y' are mov'd.
    OTHELLO: No, not much mov'd.
I do not think but Desdemona's honest.
    IAGO: Long live she so! And long live you to think so!

    OTHELLO: And yet, how nature erring from itself—
    IAGO: Ay, there's the point! As—to be bold with you—
Not to affect many proposed matches
Of her own clime, complexion, and degree,   230
Whereto we see in all things nature tends—
Foh! One may smell in such a will most rank,
Foul disproportion, thoughts unnatural.
But pardon me; I do not in position
Distinctly speak of her; though I may fear
Her will, recoiling to her better judgment,
May fail to match you with her country forms,
And happily repent.
    OTHELLO: Farewell, farewell!
If more thou dost perceive, let me know more;
Set on thy wife to observe. Leave me, Iago.   240
    IAGO [*Going*]: My lord, I take my leave.
    OTHELLO: Why did I marry? This honest creature doubtless
Sees and knows more, much more, than he unfolds.
    IAGO [*Returning*]: My Lord, I would I might entreat your
    honor
To scan this thing no farther; leave it to time.
Although 'tis fit that Cassio have his place—
For, sure, he fills it up with great ability—
Yet, if you please to hold him off awhile,
You shall by that perceive him and his means.
Note if your lady strain his entertainment   250
With any strong or vehement importunity;
Much will be seen in that. In the mean time,
Let me be thought too busy in my fears—
As worthy cause I have to fear I am—
And hold her free, I do beseech your honor.
    OTHELLO: Fear not my government.
    IAGO: I once more take my leave.   [*Exit.*]
    OTHELLO: This fellow's of exceeding honesty,
And knows all qualities, with a learned spirit,
Of human dealings. If I do prove her haggard,   260
Though that her jesses were my dear heartstrings,
I'd whistle her off, and let her down the wind
To prey at fortune. Haply, for I am black
And have not those soft parts of conversation
That chamberers have, or for I am declin'd
Into the vale of years—yet that's not much—
She's gone. I am abus'd, and my relief
Must be to loathe her. O curse of marriage,
That we can call these delicate creatures ours,
And not their appetites! I had rather be a toad,   270
And live upon the vapor of a dungeon,
Than keep a corner in the thing I love
For others' uses. Yet, 'tis the plague of great ones;
Prerogativ'd are they less than the base.
'Tis destiny unshunnable, like death.
Even then this forked plague is fated to us

---

182 exsufflicate and blown inflated and flyblown. (*Exsufflicate* may also mean *spat out*, hence, loathsome, disgusting.) **188 doubt . . . revolt** fear of her unfaithfulness **198 not** neither **secure** free from uneasiness **200 self-bounty** inherent or natural goodness **208 go to** (An expression of impatience.) **209 seeming** false appearance **210 seel** blind. (A term from falconry.) **oak** (A close-grained wood.) **219 issues** significances **reach** meaning, scope **225 honest** chaste

229 affect prefer, desire **232 will** sensuality, appetite **233 disproportion** abnormality **234 position** argument **236 recoiling** reverting **237 fail . . . forms** undertake to compare you with Venetian norms of handsomeness **238 happily repent** haply repent her marriage **250 strain his entertainment** urge his reinstatement **255 hold her free** regard her as innocent **256 government** self-control, conduct **259 qualities** natures, types **260 haggard** a wild female hawk **261 jesses** straps fastened around the legs of a trained hawk **263 at fortune** at random **for** because **265 chamberers** gallants **274 Prerogativ'd** privileged (to have honest wives) **276 forked** (An allusion to the horns of the cuckold.)

When we do quicken. Look where she comes.
Enter Desdemona and Emilia.
If she be false, O, then heaven mocks itself!
I'll not believe 't.
    DESDEMONA: How now, my dear Othello?
Your dinner, and the generous islanders   280
By you invited, do attend your presence.
    OTHELLO: I am to blame.
    DESDEMONA: Why do you speak so faintly?
Are you not well?
    OTHELLO: I have a pain upon my forehead here.
    DESDEMONA: Faith, that's with watching; 'twill away again.
                [Offers her handkerchief.]
Let me but bind it hard, within this hour
It will be well.
    OTHELLO: Your napkin is too little.
        [He puts the handkerchief from him; and it drops.]
Let it alone. Come, I'll go in with you.
    DESDEMONA: I am very sorry that you are not well.
                  Exit [with Othello].
    EMILIA *[Picking up the handkerchief]*: I am glad I have
        found this napkin.   290
This was her first remembrance from the Moor.
My wayward husband hath a hundred times
Woo'd me to steal it; but she so loves the token,
For he conjur'd her she should ever keep it,
That she reserves it evermore about her
To kiss and talk to. I'll have the work ta'en out,
And give 't Iago. What he will do with it
Heaven knows, not I;
I nothing but to please his fantasy.
Enter Iago.
    IAGO: How now? What do you here alone?   300
    EMILIA: Do not you chide. I have a thing for you.
    IAGO: A thing for me? It is a common thing—
    EMILIA: Ha?
    IAGO: To have a foolish wife.
    EMILIA: O, is that all? What will you give me now
For that same handkerchief?
    IAGO: What handkerchief?
    EMILIA: What handkerchief?
Why, that the Moor first gave to Desdemona;
That which so often you did bid me steal.
    IAGO: Hast stol'n it from her?   310
    EMILIA: No, faith; she let it drop by negligence,
And, to th' advantage, I, being here, took 't up.
Look, here 'tis.
    IAGO: A good wench! Give it me.
    EMILIA: What will you do with 't, that you have been so
        earnest
To have me filch it?
    IAGO *[Snatching it]*: Why, what is that to you?

    EMILIA: If it be not for some purpose of import,
Give 't me again. Poor lady, she'll run mad
When she shall lack it.
    IAGO: Be not acknown of't;   320
I have use for it. Go, leave me.
                  Exit Emilia.
I will in Cassio's lodging lose this napkin,
And let him find it. Trifles light as air
Are to the jealous confirmations strong
As proofs of holy writ. This may do something.
The Moor already changes with my poison.
Dangerous conceits are, in their natures, poisons,
Which at the first are scarce found to distaste,
But with a little act upon the blood
Burn like the mines of sulphur.
Enter Othello.
                I did say so.   330
Look where he comes! Not poppy, nor mandragora,
Nor all the drowsy syrups of the world,
Shall ever medicine thee to that sweet sleep
Which thou ow'dst yesterday.
    OTHELLO: Ha, ha, false to me?
    IAGO: Why, how now, general? No more of that.
    OTHELLO: Avaunt! Be gone! Thou hast set me on the rack.
I swear 'tis better to be much abus'd
Than but to know 't a little.
    IAGO: How now, my lord?
    OTHELLO: What sense had I of her stol'n hours of lust?
I saw 't not, thought it not, it harm'd not me.   340
I slept the next night well, fed well, was free and merry;
I found not Cassio's kisses on her lips.
He that is robb'd, not wanting what is stol'n,
Let him not know 't, and he's not robb'd at all.
    IAGO: I am sorry to hear this.
    OTHELLO: I had been happy if the general camp,
Pioners and all, had tasted her sweet body,
So I had nothing known. O, now, forever
Farewell the tranquil mind! Farewell content!
Farewell the plumed troop, and the big wars   350
That makes ambition virtue! O, farewell!
Farewell the neighing steed, and the shrill trump,
The spirit-stirring drum, th' ear-piercing fife,
The royal banner, and all quality,
Pride, pomp, and circumstance of glorious war!
And, O you mortal engines, whose rude throats
Th' immortal Jove's dread clamors counterfeit,
Farewell! Othello's occupation's gone.
    IAGO: Is 't possible, my lord?
    OTHELLO: Villain, be sure thou prove my love a whore!   360
Be sure of it. Give me the ocular proof,
Or, by the worth of mine eternal soul,
Thou hadst been better have been born a dog

---

277 **quicken** receive life. (*Quicken* may also mean to swarm with maggots as the body festers, as in IV.ii.67, in which case ll.276–277 suggest that *even then*, in death, we are cuckolded by *forked* worms.) 280 **generous** noble   285 **watching** working late   287 **napkin** handkerchief 296 **work ta'en out** design of the embroidery copied   299 **fantasy** whim 302 **common thing** (with bawdy suggestion)   312 **to th' advantage** taking the opportunity

320 **Be . . . of't** do not confess knowledge of it   327 **conceits** fancies, ideas 329 **act** action, working   331 **mandragora** an opiate made of the mandrake root   341 **free** carefree   343 **wanting** missing   347 **Pioners** diggers of mines, the lowest grade of soldiers   350 **big** stately   355 **Pride** rich display **circumstance** pageantry   356 **mortal engines** i.e., cannon

Than answer my wak'd wrath!

IAGO: Is 't come to this?

OTHELLO: Make me to see 't, or, at the least, so prove it
That the probation bear no hinge nor loop
To hang a doubt on; or woe upon thy life!

IAGO: My noble lord—

OTHELLO: If thou dost slander her and torture me,
Never pray more; abandon all remorse; 370
On horror's head horrors accumulate;
Do deeds to make heaven weep, all earth amaz'd;
For nothing canst thou to damnation add
Greater than that.

IAGO: O grace! O heaven forgive me!
Are you a man? Have you a soul or sense?
God buy you; take mine office. O wretched fool,
That liv'st to make thine honesty a vice!
O monstrous world! Take note, take note, O world,
To be direct and honest is not safe.
I thank you for this profit, and from hence 380
I'll love no friend, sith love breeds such offense.

OTHELLO: Nay, stay. Thou shouldst be honest.

IAGO: I should be wise, for honesty's a fool
And loses that it works for.

OTHELLO: By the world,
I think my wife be honest and think she is not;
I think that thou art just and think thou art not.
I'll have some proof. Her name, that was as fresh
As Dian's visage, is now begrim'd and black
As mine own face. If there be cords, or knives,
Poison, or fire, or suffocating streams, 390
I'll not endure it. Would I were satisfied!

IAGO: I see, sir, you are eaten up with passion.
I do repent me that I put it to you.
You would be satisfied?

OTHELLO: Would? Nay, and I will.

IAGO: And may; but how? How satisfied, my lord?
Would you, the supervisor, grossly gape on?
Behold her topp'd?

OTHELLO: Death and damnation! O!

IAGO: It were a tedious difficulty, I think,
To bring them to that prospect; damn them then,
If ever mortal eyes do see them bolster 400
More than their own. What then? How then?
What shall I say? Where's satisfaction?
It is impossible you should see this,
Were they as prime as goats, as hot as monkeys,
As salt as wolves in pride, and fools as gross
As ignorance made drunk. But yet, I say,
If imputation and strong circumstances
Which lead directly to the door of truth
Will give you satisfaction, you might have 't.

OTHELLO: Give me a living reason she's disloyal. 410

IAGO: I do not like the office.
But sith I am ent'red in this cause so far,
Prick'd to 't by foolish honesty and love,
I will go on. I lay with Cassio lately;
And, being troubled with a raging tooth,
I could not sleep.
There are a kind of men
So loose of soul that in their sleeps will mutter
Their affairs. One of this kind is Cassio.
In sleep I heard him say, "Sweet Desdemona, 420
Let us be wary, let us hide our loves!"
And then, sir, would he gripe and wring my hand,
Cry, "O sweet creature!" and then kiss me hard,
As if he pluck'd up kisses by the roots
That grew upon my lips; then laid his leg
Over my thigh, and sigh'd, and kiss'd, and then
Cried, "Cursed fate that gave thee to the Moor!"

OTHELLO: O monstrous! Monstrous!

IAGO: Nay, this was but dream.

OTHELLO: But this denoted a foregone conclusion.
'Tis a shrewd doubt, though it be but a dream. 430

IAGO: And this may help to thicken other proofs
That do demonstrate thinly.

OTHELLO: I'll tear her all to pieces.

IAGO: Nay, but be wise. Yet we see nothing done;
She may be honest yet. Tell me but this,
Have you not sometimes seen a handkerchief
Spotted with strawberries in your wife's hand?

OTHELLO: I gave her such a one; 'twas my first gift.

IAGO: I know not that; but such a handkerchief—
I am sure it was your wife's—did I today
See Cassio wipe his beard with.

OTHELLO: If it be that— 440

IAGO: If it be that, or any that was hers,
It speaks against her with the other proofs.

OTHELLO: O, that the slave had forty thousand lives!
One is too poor, too weak for my revenge.
Now do I see 'tis true. Look here, Iago,
All my fond love thus do I blow to heaven.
'Tis gone.
Arise, black vengeance, from the hollow hell!
Yield up, O love, thy crown and hearted throne
To tyrannous hate! Swell, bosom, with thy fraught, 450
For 'tis of aspics' tongues!

IAGO: Yet be content.

OTHELLO: O, blood, blood, blood!

IAGO: Patience, I say. Your mind perhaps may change.

OTHELLO: Never, Iago. Like to the Pontic Sea,
Whose icy current and compulsive course
Nev'r feels retiring ebb, but keeps due on
To the Propontic and the Hellespont,
Even so my bloody thoughts, with violent pace,
Shall nev'r look back, nev'r ebb to humble love,
Till that a capable and wide revenge 460
Swallow them up. Now, by yond marble heaven,
[Kneels.] In the due reverence of a sacred vow

---

366 **probation** proof   370 **remorse** pity   371 **horrors accumulate** add still more horrors   376 **God buy you** i.e., goodbye   377 **vice** failing   380 **profit** profitable instruction **hence** henceforth   381 **sith** since   382 **Thou shouldst be** it appears that you are. (But Iago replies in the sense of *ought to be*.)   388 **Dian** Diana, goddess of the moon and of chastity   396 **supervisor** onlooker   399 **damn** i.e., to condemn   400–401 **If . . . own** only if some human eyes other than their own do see them lie together   404 **prime** lustful   405 **salt** wanton, sensual **pride** heat

429 **foregone conclusion** concluded experience or action   430 **shrewd doubt** suspicious circumstance   449 **hearted** fixed in the heart   450 **fraught** freight, burden   451 **aspics'** venomous serpents'   454 **Pontic Sea** Black Sea   457 **Propontic** body of water between the Bosporus and Hellespont   460 **capable** comprehensive   461 **marble** i.e., gleaming like marble

I here engage my words.
IAGO: Do not rise yet.
[Kneels.] Witness, you ever-burning lights above,
You elements that clip us round about,
Witness that here Iago doth give up
The execution of his wit, hands, heart,
To wrong'd Othello's service! Let him command,
And to obey shall be in me remorse,
What bloody business ever.   *[They rise.]*
OTHELLO: I greet thy love,   470
Not with vain thanks, but with acceptance bounteous,
And will upon the instant put thee to 't.
Within these three days let me hear thee say
That Cassio's not alive.
IAGO: My friend is dead;
'Tis done at your request. But let her live.
OTHELLO: Damn her, lewd minx! O, damn her, damn her!
Come, go with me apart. I will withdraw
To furnish me with some swift means of death
For the fair devil. Now art thou my lieutenant.
IAGO: I am your own for ever.   *Exeunt.* 480

Scene IV

[Desdemona inquires after the whereabouts of Cassio. (ed.)]

DESDEMONA: Where should I lose that handkerchief, Emilia? 1
EMILIA: I know not, madam.
DESDEMONA: Believe me, I had rather have lost my purse
Full of crusadoes; and, but my noble Moor
Is true of mind, and made of no such baseness
As jealous creatures are, it were enough
To put him to ill thinking.
EMILIA: Is he not jealous?
DESDEMONA: Who, he? I think the sun where he was born
Drew all such humors from him.
EMILIA: Look where he comes.
Enter Othello.
DESDEMONA: I will not leave him now till Cassio   10
Be call'd to him.—How is 't with you, my lord?
OTHELLO: Well, my good lady. *[Aside.]* O, hardness to
     dissemble!—
How do you, Desdemona?
DESDEMONA: Well, my good lord.
OTHELLO: Give me your hand. *[She gives her hand.]* This
     hand is moist, my lady.
DESDEMONA: It yet hath felt no age nor known no sorrow.
OTHELLO: This argues fruitfulness and liberal heart.
Hot, hot, and moist. This hand of yours requires
A sequester from liberty, fasting and prayer,
Much castigation, exercise devout;
For here's a young and sweating devil here   20
That commonly rebels. 'Tis a good hand,
A frank one.
DESDEMONA: You may, indeed, say so;

For 'twas that hand that gave away my heart.
OTHELLO: A liberal hand! The hearts of old gave hands;
But our new heraldry is hands, not hearts.
DESDEMONA: I cannot speak of this. Come now, your
     promise.
OTHELLO: What promise, chuck?
DESDEMONA: I have sent to bid Cassio come speak with you.
OTHELLO: I have a salt and sorry rheum offends me;   30
Lend me thy handkerchief.
DESDEMONA: Here, my lord.
[She gives a handkerchief.]
OTHELLO: That which I gave you.
DESDEMONA: I have it not about me.
OTHELLO: Not?
DESDEMONA: No, faith, my lord.
OTHELLO: That's a fault. That handkerchief
Did an Egyptian to my mother give;
She was a charmer, and could almost read
The thoughts of people. She told her, while she kept it,
'Twould make her amiable and subdue my father
Entirely to her love, but if she lost it   40
Or made a gift of it, my father's eye
Should hold her loathed and his spirits should hunt
After new fancies. She, dying, gave it me,
And bid me, when my fate would have me wiv'd,
To give to her. I did so; and take heed on 't;
Make it a darling like your precious eye.
To lose 't or give 't away were such perdition
As nothing else could match.
DESDEMONA: Is 't possible?
OTHELLO: 'Tis true. There's magic in the web of it.
A sibyl, that had numb'red in the world   50
The sun to course two hundred compasses,
In her prophetic fury sew'd the work;
The worms were hallow'd that did breed the silk;
And it was dy'd in mummy which the skillful
Conserv'd of maidens' hearts.
DESDEMONA: I' faith! Is t' true?
OTHELLO: Most veritable. Therefore look to 't well.
DESDEMONA: Then would to God that I had never seen 't!
OTHELLO: Ha? Wherefore?
DESDEMONA: Why do you speak so startingly and rash?
OTHELLO: Is 't lost? Is 't gone? Speak, is 't out o' th' way? 60
DESDEMONA: Heaven bless us!
OTHELLO: Say you?
DESDEMONA: It is not lost; but what an if it were?
OTHELLO: How?
DESDEMONA: I say, it is not lost.
OTHELLO: Fetch 't, let me see 't.
DESDEMONA: Why, so I can, sir, but I will not now.
This is a trick to put me from my suit.
Pray you, let Cassio be receiv'd again.
OTHELLO: Fetch me the handkerchief! My mind misgives.
DESDEMONA: Come, come;

---

465 **clip** encompass 467 **execution** exercise, action **wit** mind 469 **remorse** pity (for Othello's wrongs)

III.iv. Location: Before the citadel.
4 **crusadoes** Portuguese gold coins 9 **humors** (Refers to the four bodily fluids thought to determine temperament.) 18 **sequester** separation, sequestration

---

26 **But . . . hearts** i.e., in our decadent times the joining of hands is no longer a badge to signify the giving of hearts 30 **salt . . . rheum** distressful head cold or watering of the eyes 37 **charmer** sorceress 39 **amiable** desirable 47 **perdition** loss 51 **compasses** annual circlings. (The *sibyl*, or prophetess, was two hundred years old.) 54 **mummy** medicinal or magical preparation drained from mummified bodies 55 **Conserv'd of** prepared or preserved out of

You'll never meet a more sufficient man.   70
    OTHELLO: The handkerchief!
    [DESDEMONA: I pray, talk me of Cassio.
    OTHELLO: The handkerchief!]
    DESDEMONA: A man that all his time
Hath founded his good fortunes on your love,
Shar'd dangers with you—
    OTHELLO: The handkerchief!
    DESDEMONA: I' faith, you are to blame.
    OTHELLO: 'Zounds!   *Exit Othello.*
    EMILIA: Is not this man jealous?
    DESDEMONA: I nev'r saw this before.
Sure, there's some wonder in this handkerchief.
I am most unhappy in the loss of it.
    EMILIA: 'Tis not a year or two shows us a man.   80
They are all but stomachs, and we all but food;
They eat us hungerly, and when they are full
They belch us.
Enter Iago and Cassio.
        Look you, Cassio and my husband.
    IAGO: There is no other way; 'tis she must do 't.
And, lo, the happiness! Go, and importune her.
    DESDEMONA: How now, good Cassio? What's the news
        with you?
    CASSIO: Madam, my former suit. I do beseech you
That by your virtuous means I may again
Exist, and be a member of his love
Whom I with all the office of my heart   90
Entirely honor. I would not be delay'd.
If my offense be of such mortal kind
That nor my service past nor present sorrows,
Nor purpos'd merit in futurity,
Can ransom me into his love again,
But to know so must be my benefit;
So shall I clothe me in a forc'd content,
And shut myself up in some other course,
To fortune's alms.
    DESDEMONA: Alas, thrice-gentle Cassio,
My advocation is not now in tune.   100
My lord is not my lord; nor should I know him,
Were he in favor as in humor alter'd.
So help me every spirit sanctified,
As I have spoken for you all my best
And stood within the blank of his displeasure
For my free speech! You must awhile be patient.
What I can do I will, and more I will
Than for myself I dare. Let that suffice you.
    IAGO: Is my lord angry?
    EMILIA: He went hence but now,
And certainly in strange unquietness.   110
    IAGO: Can he be angry? I have seen the cannon,
When it hath blown his ranks into the air,

And, like the devil, from his very arm
Puff'd his own brother—and is he angry?
Something of moment then. I will go meet him.
There's matter in 't indeed, if he be angry.
    DESDEMONA: I prithee, do so.   *Exit [Iago].*
                Something, sure, of state,
Either from Venice, or some unhatch'd practice
Made demonstrable here in Cyprus to him,
Hath puddled his clear spirit; and in such cases   120
Men's natures wrangle with inferior things,
Though great ones are their object. 'Tis even so;
For let our finger ache, and it endues
Our other healthful members even to a sense
Of pain. Nay, we must think men are not gods,
Nor of them look for such observancy
As fits the bridal. Beshrew me much, Emilia,
I was, unhandsome warrior as I am,
Arraigning his unkindness with my soul;
But now I find I had suborn'd the witness,   130
And he's indicted falsely.
    EMILIA: Pray heaven it be
State matters, as you think, and no conception,
Nor no jealous toy, concerning you.
    DESDEMONA: Alas the day! I never gave him cause.
    EMILIA: But jealous souls will not be answer'd so;
They are not ever jealous for the cause,
But jealous for they're jealous. It is a monster
Begot upon itself, born on itself.
    DESDEMONA: Heaven keep that monster from Othello's
        mind!   140
    EMILIA: Lady, amen.
    DESDEMONA: I will go seek him. Cassio, walk here about.
If I do find him fit, I'll move your suit
And seek to effect it to my uttermost.
    CASSIO: I humbly thank your ladyship.
              Exit [Desdemona with Emilia].

[Cassio gives Bianca Desdemona's handkerchief. (ed.)]

Act IV, Scene I

Enter Othello and Iago.
    IAGO: Will you think so?
    OTHELLO: Think so, Iago?
    IAGO: What,   1
To kiss in private?
    OTHELLO: An unauthoriz'd kiss!
    IAGO: Or to be naked with her friend in bed
An hour or more, not meaning any harm?
    OTHELLO: Naked in bed, Iago, and not mean harm?
It is hypocrisy against the devil.

---

72 **all his time** throughout his career   80 **'Tis . . . man** i.e., you can't really know a man even in a year or two of experience (?) or, real men come along seldom (?)   81 **but** nothing but   85 **the happiness** in happy time, fortunately met   92 **mortal** fatal   93 **nor . . . nor** neither . . . nor   96 **But . . . benefit** merely to know that my case is hopeless must be all I can expect   99 **To fortune's alms** throwing myself on the mercy of fortune   100 **advocation** advocacy   102 **favor** appearance   105 **blank** white spot in the center of a target, i.e., directly in the line of fire

118 **unhatch'd practice** as yet unexecuted plot   120 **puddled** muddied   123 **endues** brings to the same condition   126 **observancy** attentiveness   127 **bridal** wedding (when a bridegroom is newly attentive to his bride)   128 **unhandsome** insufficient, unskillful   129 **with** before the bar of   134 **toy** fancy   138 **for** because   139 **Begot upon itself** generated solely from itself

IV.i. Location: Before the citadel.

They that mean virtuously, and yet do so,
The devil their virtue tempts, and they tempt heaven.
    IAGO: If they do nothing, 'tis a venial slip,
But if I give my wife a handkerchief— 10
    OTHELLO: What then?
    IAGO: Why, then, 'tis hers, my lord; and, being hers,
She may, I think, bestow 't on any man.
    OTHELLO: She is protectress of her honor too.
May she give that?
    IAGO: Her honor is an essence that's not seen;
They have it very oft that have it not.
But, for the handkerchief—
    OTHELLO: By heaven, I would most gladly have forgot it.
Thou said'st—O, it comes o'er my memory, 20
As doth the raven o'er the infectious house,
Boding to all—he had my handkerchief.
    IAGO: Ay, what of that?
    OTHELLO: That's not so good now.
    IAGO: What
If I had said I had seen him do you wrong?
Or heard him say—as knaves be such abroad,
Who having, by their own importunate suit,
Or voluntary dotage of some mistress,
Convinced or supplied them, cannot choose
But they must blab—
    OTHELLO: Hath he said anything?
    IAGO: He hath, my lord; but be you well assur'd, 30
No more than he'll unswear.
    OTHELLO: What hath he said?
    IAGO: Faith, that he did—I know not what he did.
    OTHELLO: What? What?
    IAGO: Lie—
    OTHELLO: With her?
    IAGO: With her, on her; what you will.
    OTHELLO: Lie with her? Lie on her? We say lie on her, when
they belie her. Lie with her! 'Zounds, that's fulsome.—
Handkerchief—confessions—handkerchief!—To confess,
and be hang'd for his labor—first, to be hang'd, and then
to confess.—I tremble at it. Nature would not invest
herself in such shadowing passion without some 40
instruction. It is not words that shakes me thus. Pish!
Noses, ears, and lips.—Is 't possible?—Confess—
handkerchief!—O devil!

                        Falls in a trance.

    IAGO: Work on,
My medicine, work! Thus credulous fools are caught;
And many worthy and chaste dames even thus,
All guiltless, meet reproach.—What, ho! My lord!
My lord, I say! Othello!
Enter Cassio.
              How now, Cassio?
    CASSIO: What's the matter?

    IAGO: My lord is fall'n into an epilepsy. 50
This is his second fit; he had one yesterday.
    CASSIO: Rub him about the temples.
    IAGO: [No, forbear;]
The lethargy must have his quiet course.
If not, he foams at mouth, and by and by
Breaks out to savage madness. Look he stirs.
Do you withdraw yourself a little while,
He will recover straight. When he is gone,
I would on great occasion speak with you.

                        [Exit Cassio.]

How is it, general? Have you not hurt your head?
    OTHELLO: Dost thou mock me?
    IAGO: I mock you not, by heaven. 60
Would you would bear your fortune like a man!
    OTHELLO: A horned man's a monster and a beast.
    IAGO: There's many a beast then in a populous city,
And many a civil monster.
    OTHELLO: Did he confess it?
    IAGO: Good sir, be a man.
Think every bearded fellow that's but yok'd
May draw with you. There's millions now alive
That nightly lie in those unproper beds
Which they dare swear peculiar; your case is better.
O, 'tis the spite of hell, the fiend's arch-mock, 70
To lip a wanton in a secure couch,
And to suppose her chaste! No, let me know;
And knowing what I am, I know what she shall be.
    OTHELLO: O, thou art wise. 'Tis certain.
    IAGO: Stand you awhile apart;
Confine yourself but in a patient list.
Whilst you were here o'erwhelmed with your grief—
A passion most unsuiting such a man—
Cassio came hither. I shifted him away,
And laid good 'scuses upon your ecstasy,
Bade him anon return and here speak with me, 80
The which he promis'd. Do but encave yourself
And mark the fleers, the gibes, and notable scorns,
That dwell in every region of his face;
For I will make him tell the tale anew,
Where, how, how oft, how long ago, and when
He hath, and is again to cope your wife.
I say, but mark his gesture. Marry, patience!
Or I shall say y' are all in all in spleen,
And nothing of a man.
    OTHELLO: Dost thou hear, Iago?
I will be found most cunning in my patience; 90
But—dost thou hear?—most bloody.
    IAGO: That's not amiss;
But yet keep time in all. Will you withdraw?

                        [Othello retires.]

Now will I question Cassio of Bianca,

---

17 They have it i.e., they enjoy a reputation for it   **21 raven . . . house** (Allusion to the belief that the raven hovered over a house of sickness or infection, such as one visited by the plague.)   **25 abroad** around about   **28 Convinced or supplied** seduced or gratified   **39–41 Nature . . . instruction** i.e., without some foundation in fact, nature would not have dressed herself in such an overwhelming passion that comes over me now and fills my mind with images; or, in such a lifelike fantasy as Cassio had in his dream of lying with Desdemona

53 lethargy coma   **his** its   **60 mock** (Othello takes Iago's question about hurting his head to be a mocking reference to the cuckold's horns.)   **64 civil** i.e., dwelling in a city   **66 yok'd** i.e., married   **67 draw with you** pull as you do like oxen who are yoked, i.e., share your fate as cuckold   **68 unproper** not exclusively their own   **69 peculiar** private, their own   **better** i.e., because you know the truth   **71 secure** free from suspicion   **75 in . . . list** within the bounds of patience   **79 ecstasy** trance   **81 encave** conceal   **82 fleers** sneers   **86 cope** encounter with   **88 all in all in spleen** utterly governed by passionate impulses

A huswife that by selling her desires
Buys herself bread and clothes. It is a creature
That dotes on Cassio, as 'tis the strumpet's plague
To beguile many and be beguil'd by one.
He, when he hears of her, cannot refrain
From the excess of laughter. Here he comes.
Enter Cassio.
As he shall smile, Othello shall go mad; 100
And his unbookish jealousy must conster
Poor Cassio's smiles, gestures, and light behavior
Quite in the wrong.—How do you now, lieutenant?
  CASSIO: The worser that you give me the addition
Whose want even kills me.
  IAGO: Ply Desdemona well, and you are sure on 't.
[Speaking lower.] Now, if this suit lay in Bianca's power,
How quickly should you speed!
  CASSIO *[Laughing]:*   Alas, poor caitiff!
  OTHELLO: Look, how he laughs already!
  IAGO: I never knew woman love man so. 110
  CASSIO: Alas, poor rogue! I think, i' faith, she loves me.
  OTHELLO: Now he denies it faintly, and laughs it out.
  IAGO: Do you hear, Cassio?
  OTHELLO: Now he importunes him
To tell it o'er. Go to! Well said, well said.
  IAGO: She gives it out that you shall marry her.
Do you intend it?
  CASSIO: Ha, ha, ha!
  OTHELLO: Do you triumph, Roman? Do you triumph?
  CASSIO: I marry her? What? A customer? Prithee, bear
some charity to my wit; do not think it so unwholesome. 120
Ha, ha, ha!
  OTHELLO: So, so, so, so! They laugh that win.
  IAGO: Faith, the cry goes that you shall marry her.
  CASSIO: Prithee, say true.
  IAGO: I am a very villain else.
  OTHELLO: Have you scor'd me? Well.
  CASSIO: This is the monkey's own giving out. She is
persuaded I will marry her, out of her own love and flattery,
not out of my promise.
  OTHELLO: Iago beckons me; now he begins the story. 130
  CASSIO: She was here even now; she haunts me in every
place. I was the other day talking on the seabank with
certain Venetians, and thither comes the bauble, and, by
this hand, she falls me thus about my neck—
                    [He embraces Iago.]
  OTHELLO: Crying, "O dear Cassio!" as it were; his gesture
imports it.
  CASSIO: So hangs, and lolls, and weeps upon me; so shakes,
and pulls me. Ha, ha, ha!
  OTHELLO: Now he tells how she pluck'd him to my
chamber. O, I see that nose of yours, but not that dog I 140
shall throw it to.
  CASSIO: Well, I must leave her company.
  IAGO: Before me, look where she comes.

Enter Bianca [with Othello's handkerchief].
  CASSIO: 'Tis such another fitchew! Marry, a perfum'd one.
—What do you mean by this haunting of me?
  BIANCA: Let the devil and his dam haunt you! What did
you mean by that same handkerchief you gave me even
now? I was a fine fool to take it. I must take out the work? A
likely piece of work, that you should find it in your
chamber, and know not who left it there! This is some 150
minx's token, and I must take out the work? There; give it
your hobby-horse. *[Gives him the handkerchief.]*
Wheresoever you had it, I'll take out no work on 't.
  CASSIO: How now, my sweet Bianca? How now? How now?
  OTHELLO: By heaven, that should be my handkerchief!
  BIANCA: If you'll come to supper tonight, you may; if you
will not, come when you are next prepar'd for.
                                        Exit.
  IAGO: After her, after her.
  CASSIO: Faith, I must; she'll rail in the streets else.
  IAGO: Will you sup there? 160
  CASSIO: Faith, I intend so.
  IAGO: Well, I may chance to see you, for I would very fain
speak with you.
  CASSIO: Prithee, come. Will you?
  IAGO: Go to; say no more.
                              [Exit Cassio.]
  OTHELLO *[Advancing]:* How shall I murder him, Iago?
  IAGO: Did you perceive how he laugh'd at his vice?
  OTHELLO: O Iago!
  IAGO: And did you see the handkerchief?
  OTHELLO: Was that mine? 170
  IAGO: Yours, by this hand. And to see how he prizes the
foolish woman your wife! She gave it him, and he hath giv'n
it his whore.
  OTHELLO: I would have him nine years a-killing. A fine
woman! A fair woman! A sweet woman!
  IAGO: Nay, you must forget that.
  OTHELLO: Ay, let her rot, and perish, and be damn'd
tonight; for she shall not live. No, my heart is turn'd to
stone; I strike it, and it hurts my hand. O, the world hath
not a sweeter creature! She might lie by an emperor's side 180
and command him tasks.
  IAGO: Nay, that's not your way.
  OTHELLO: Hang her! I do but say what she is. So delicate
with her needle! An admirable musician! O, she will sing
the savageness out of a bear. Of so high and plenteous wit
and invention!
  IAGO: She's the worse for all this.
  OTHELLO: O, a thousand, a thousand times! And then, of
so gentle a condition!
  IAGO: Ay, too gentle. 190
  OTHELLO: Nay, that's certain. But yet the pity of it, Iago!
O Iago, the pity of it, Iago!
  IAGO: If you are so fond over her iniquity, give her patent
to offend; for, if it touch not you, it comes near nobody.

---

94 huswife hussy **101 unbookish** uninstructed **conster** construe
104 addition title **108 caitiff** wretch **118 Roman** (The Romans were noted
for their *triumphs* or triumphal processions.) **119 customer** i.e., prostitute
122 They . . . win i.e., they that laugh last laugh best **126 scor'd me** scored
off me, beaten me, made up my reckoning **130 beckons** signals
133 bauble plaything **143 Before me** i.e., on my soul

144 fitchew polecat (because of her strong perfume; also, slang word for a
prostitute) **152 hobby-horse** harlot **182 your way** i.e., the way you should
think of her **193 fond** foolish **patent** license

OTHELLO: I will chop her into messes. Cuckold me?

IAGO: O, 'tis foul in her.

OTHELLO: With mine officer?

IAGO: That's fouler.

OTHELLO: Get me some poison, Iago; this night. I'll not expostulate with her, lest her body and beauty unprovide 200 my mind again. This night, Iago.

IAGO: Do it not with poison. Strangle her in her bed, even the bed she hath contaminated.

OTHELLO: Good, good! The justice of it pleases. Very good.

IAGO: And for Cassio, let me be his undertaker. You shall hear more by midnight.

OTHELLO: Excellent good.   [A trumpet within.]
                    What trumpet is that same?

IAGO: I warrant something from Venice.

Enter Lodovico, Desdemona, and Attendants.

'Tis Lodovico. This comes from the Duke.   210
See, your wife's with him.

LODOVICO: God save you, worthy general!

OTHELLO: With all my heart, sir.

LODOVICO: The Duke and the senators of Venice greet you.
                    [Gives him a letter.]

OTHELLO: I kiss the instrument of their pleasures.
                    [Opens the letter, and reads.]

DESDEMONA: And what's the news, good cousin Lodovico?

IAGO: I am very glad to see you, Signior;
Welcome to Cyprus.

LODOVICO: I thank you. How does Lieutenant Cassio?

IAGO: Lives, sir.

DESDEMONA: Cousin, there's fall'n between him and my
    lord   220
An unkind breach; but you shall make all well.

OTHELLO: Are you sure of that?

DESDEMONA: My lord?

OTHELLO [Reads]: "This fail you not to do, as you will—"

LODOVICO: He did not call; he's busy in the paper.
Is there division 'twixt my lord and Cassio?

DESDEMONA: A most unhappy one. I would do much
T' atone them, for the love I bear to Cassio.

OTHELLO: Fire and brimstone!

DESDEMONA: My lord?

OTHELLO: Are you wise?

DESDEMONA: What, is he angry?

LODOVICO: May be the letter mov'd him; 230
For, as I think, they do command him home,
Deputing Cassio in his government.

DESDEMONA: By my troth, I am glad on 't.

OTHELLO: Indeed?

DESDEMONA: My lord?

OTHELLO: I am glad to see you mad.

DESDEMONA: Why, sweet Othello—

OTHELLO [Striking her]: Devil!

DESDEMONA: I have not deserv'd this.

LODOVICO: My lord, this would not be believ'd in Venice,
Though I should swear I saw 't. 'Tis very much.
Make her amends; she weeps.

OTHELLO: O devil, devil!
If that the earth could teem with woman's tears,
Each drop she falls would prove a crocodile.   240
Out of my sight!

DESDEMONA: I will not stay to offend you.
                    [Going.]

LODOVICO: Truly, an obedient lady.
I do beseech your lordship, call her back.

OTHELLO: Mistress!

DESDEMONA: My lord?

OTHELLO: What would you with her, sir?

LODOVICO: Who, I, my lord?

OTHELLO: Ay, you did wish that I would make her turn.
Sir, she can turn, and turn, and yet go on
And turn again; and she can weep, sir, weep;
And she's obedient, as you say, obedient.
Very obedient.—Proceed you in your tears.—   250
Concerning this, sir—O well-painted passion!—
I am commanded home.—Get you away;
I'll send for you anon.—Sir, I obey the mandate,
And will return to Venice.—Hence, avaunt!
                    [Exit Desdemona.]
Cassio shall have my place. And, sir, tonight
I do entreat that we may sup together.
You are welcome, sir, to Cyprus.—Goats and monkeys!
                    Exit.

LODOVICO: Is this the noble Moor whom our full Senate
Call all in all sufficient? Is this the nature
Whom passion could not shake? Whose solid virtue   260
The shot of accident, nor dart of chance,
Could neither graze nor pierce?

IAGO: He is much chang'd.

LODOVICO: Are his wits safe? Is he not light of brain?

IAGO: He's that he is; I may not breathe my censure
What he might be. If what he might he is not,
I would to heaven he were!

LODOVICO: What, strike his wife?

IAGO: Faith, that was not so well; yet would I knew
That stroke would prove the worst!

LODOVICO: Is it his use?
Or did the letters work upon his blood,
And new-create this fault?

IAGO: Alas, alas!   270
It is not honesty in me to speak
What I have seen and known. You shall observe him,
And his own courses will denote him so
That I may save my speech. Do but go after,
And mark how he continues.

LODOVICO: I am sorry that I am deceiv'd in him.
                    Exeunt.

---

195 **messes** portions of food, i.e., bits   200 **unprovide** weaken, unfit
206 **be his undertaker** undertake to dispatch him   228 **atone** reconcile
232 **government** office

239 **teem** breed, be impregnated   240 **fall** lets fall **crocodile** (Crocodiles were supposed to weep hypocritical tears for their victims.)
264–266 **I may ... were** i.e., I dare not venture an opinion as to whether he's of unsound mind, as you suggest; but if he isn't, then it might be better to wish he were in fact insane, since only that could excuse his wild behavior   268 **use** custom

Scene II

Enter Othello and Emilia.

    OTHELLO: You have seen nothing then?   1
    EMILIA: Nor ever heard, nor ever did suspect.
    OTHELLO: Yes, you have seen Cassio and she together.
    EMILIA: But then I saw no harm, and then I heard
Each syllable that breath made up between them.
    OTHELLO: What, did they never whisper?
    EMILIA: Never, my lord.
    OTHELLO: Nor send you out o' th' way?
    EMILIA: Never.
    OTHELLO: To fetch her fan, her gloves, her mask, nor
    nothing?
    EMILIA: Never, my lord.
    OTHELLO: That's strange.   10
    EMILIA: I durst, my lord, to wager she is honest,
Lay down my soul at stake. If you think other,
Remove your thought; it doth abuse your bosom.
If any wretch have put this in your head,
Let heaven requite it with the serpent's curse!
For if she be not honest, chaste, and true,
There's no man happy; the purest of their wives
Is foul as slander.
    OTHELLO: Bid her come hither. Go.
                 Exit Emilia.
She says enough; yet she's a simple bawd
That cannot say as much. This is a subtle whore,   20
A closet lock and key of villainous secrets.
And yet she'll kneel and pray; I have seen her do 't.
Enter Desdemona and Emilia.
    DESDEMONA: My lord, what is your will?
    OTHELLO: Pray you, chuck, come hither.
    DESDEMONA: What is your pleasure?
    OTHELLO: Let me see your eyes;
Look in my face.
    DESDEMONA: What horrible fancy's this?
    OTHELLO *[To Emilia]*: Some of your function, mistress;
Leave procreants alone and shut the door;
Cough, or cry "hem," if anybody come.
Your mystery, your mystery! Nay, dispatch.   30
                 Exit Emilia.
    DESDEMONA *[Kneeling]*: Upon my knees, what doth your
    speech import?
I understand a fury in your words,
[But not the words.]
    OTHELLO: Why, what art thou?
    DESDEMONA: Your wife, my lord; your true
And loyal wife.
    OTHELLO: Come, swear it, damn thyself,
Lest, being like one of heaven, the devils themselves
Should fear to seize thee. Therefore be double damn'd;
Swear thou art honest.

    DESDEMONA: Heaven doth truly know it.
    OTHELLO: Heaven truly knows that thou art false as hell.
    DESDEMONA: To whom, my lord? With whom? How am I
    false?   40
    OTHELLO *[Weeping]*: Ah, Desdemon! Away, away, away!
    DESDEMONA: Alas the heavy day! Why do you weep?
Am I the motive of these tears, my lord?
If happily you my father do suspect
An instrument of this your calling back,
Lay not your blame on me. If you have lost him,
Why, I have lost him too.
    OTHELLO: Had it pleas'd heaven
To try me with affliction, had they rain'd
All kinds of sores and shames on my bare head,
Steep'd me in poverty to the very lips,   50
Given to captivity me and my utmost hopes,
I should have found in some place of my soul
A drop of patience. But, alas, to make me
A fixed figure for the time of scorn
To point his slow unmoving finger at!
Yet could I bear that too, well, very well.
But there where I have garner'd up my heart,
Where either I must live or bear no life,
The fountain from the which my current runs
Or else dries up—to be discarded thence!   60
Or keep it as a cistern for foul toads
To knot and gender in! Turn thy complexion there,
Patience, thou young and rose-lipp'd cherubin—
Ay, there look grim as hell!
    DESDEMONA: I hope my noble lord esteems me honest.
    OTHELLO: O, ay; as summer flies are in the shambles,
That quicken even with blowing. O thou weed,
Who art so lovely fair and smell'st so sweet
That the sense aches at thee, would thou hadst ne'er been
    born!
    DESDEMONA: Alas, what ignorant sin have I committed?   70
    OTHELLO: Was this fair paper, this most goodly book,
Made to write "whore" upon? What committed?
Committed? O thou public commoner!
I should make very forges of my cheeks,
That would to cinders burn up modesty,
Did I but speak thy deeds. What committed?
Heaven stops the nose at it and moon winks,
The bawdy wind that kisses all it meets
Is hush'd within the hollow mine of earth,
And will not hear 't. What committed?   80
[Impudent strumpet!]
    DESDEMONA: By heaven, you do me wrong.
    OTHELLO: Are not you a strumpet?
    DESDEMONA: No, as I am a Christian.
If to preserve this vessel for my lord
From any other foul unlawful touch
Be not to be a strumpet, I am none.
    OTHELLO: What, not a whore?

IV.ii. Location: The citadel.
15 serpent's curse the curse pronounced by God on the serpent for deceiving Eve, just as some man has done to Othello and Desdemona. (See Genesis 3.14.)   **19–20 she's . . . much** i.e., any procuress or go-between who couldn't make up as convincing a story as Emilia's would have to be pretty stupid   **21 closet lock and key** complete storeroom   **27 Some . . . function** i.e., practice your chosen profession, that of bawd (by guarding the door)   **28 procreants** mating couples   **30 mystery** trade, occupation   **36 being . . . heaven** looking like an angel

48 they i.e., heavenly powers   **54 time of scorn** i.e., scornful world
55 his its **slow unmoving finger** finger which rises slowly to the point and then stops, forever fixed and immobile in its pointing   **62 knot** i.e., couple **gender** engender **Turn . . . there** change your color, grow pale, at such a sight **63–64 Patience . . . hell** (i.e., even Patience, that rose-lipped cherub, will look grim and pale at this spectacle.)   **66 shambles** slaughterhouse **67 quicken** come to life **with blowing** i.e., with the puffing up of something rotten in which maggots are breeding   **73 commoner** prostitute
77 winks closes her eyes   **83 vessel** i.e., body

DESDEMONA: No, as I shall be sav'd.
OTHELLO: Is 't possible?
DESDEMONA: O, heaven forgive us!
OTHELLO: I cry you mercy, then.
I took you for that cunning whore of Venice
That married with Othello. *[Calling out.]* You, mistress, 90
That have the office opposite to Saint Peter,
And keep the gate of hell!
Enter Emilia.
You, you, ay, you!
We have done our course. There's money for your pains.
[Gives money.]
I pray you, turn the key and keep our counsel.
Exit.

EMILIA: Alas, what does this gentleman conceive?
How do you, madam? How do you, my good lady?
DESDEMONA: Faith, half asleep.
EMILIA: Good madam, what's the matter with my lord?
DESDEMONA: With who?
EMILIA: Why, with my lord, madam. 100
DESDEMONA: Who is thy lord?
EMILIA: He that is yours, sweet lady.
DESDEMONA: I have none. Do not talk to me, Emilia;
I cannot weep; nor answers have I none,
But what should go by water. Prithee tonight
Lay on my bed my wedding sheets, remember;
And call thy husband hither.
EMILIA: Here's a change indeed!
Exit.
DESDEMONA: 'Tis meet I should be us'd so, very meet.
How have I been behav'd, that he might stick
The small'st opinion on my least misuse?
Enter Iago and Emilia.
IAGO: What is your pleasure, madam? How is 't with you? 110
DESDEMONA: I cannot tell. Those that do teach young
babes
Do it with gentle means and easy tasks.
He might have chid me so; for, in good faith,
I am a child to chiding.
IAGO: What is the matter, lady?
EMILIA: Alas, Iago, my lord hath so bewhor'd her,
Thrown such despite and heavy terms upon her,
That true hearts cannot bear it.
DESDEMONA: Am I that name, Iago?
IAGO: What name, fair lady?
DESDEMONA: Such as she said my lord did say I was.
EMILIA: He call'd her whore. A beggar in his drink 120
Could not have laid such terms upon his callet.
IAGO: Why did he so?
DESDEMONA *[Weeping]*: I do not know; I am sure I am
none such.
IAGO: Do not weep, do not weep. Alas the day!
EMILIA: Hath she forsook so many noble matches,
Her father and her country and her friends,

To be call'd whore? Would it not make one weep?
DESDEMONA: It is my wretched fortune.
IAGO: Beshrew him for 't!
How comes this trick upon him?
DESDEMONA: Nay, heaven doth know.
EMILIA: I will be hang'd if some eternal villain, 130
Some busy and insinuating rogue,
Some cogging, cozening slave, to get some office,
Have not devis'd this slander. I will be hang'd else.
IAGO: Fie, there is no such man; it is impossible.
DESDEMONA: If any such there be, heaven pardon him!
EMILIA: A halter pardon him! And hell gnaw his bones!
Why should he call her whore? Who keeps her company?
What place? What time? What form? What likelihood?
The Moor's abus'd by some most villainous knave,
Some base notorious knave, some scurvy fellow. 140
O heaven, that such companions thou'dst unfold,
And put in every honest hand a whip
To lash the rascals naked through the world
Even from the east to th' west!
IAGO: Speak within door.
EMILIA: O, fie upon them! Some such squire he was
That turn'd your wit the seamy side without,
And made you to suspect me with the Moor.
IAGO: You are a fool; go to.
DESDEMONA: Alas, Iago,
What shall I do to win my lord again?
Good friend, go to him; for, by this light of heaven, 150
I know not how I lost him. Here I kneel. *[Kneels.]*
If e'er my will did trespass 'gainst his love,
Either in discourse of thought or actual deed,
Or that mine eyes, mine ears, or any sense
Delighted them in any other form;
Or that I do not yet, and ever did,
And ever will—though he do shake me off
To beggarly divorcement—love him dearly,
Comfort forswear me! Unkindness may do much;
And his unkindness may defeat my life, 160
But never taint my love. I cannot say "whore."
It does abhor me now I speak the word;
To do the act that might the addition earn
Not the world's mass of vanity could make me.
IAGO: I pray you, be content. 'Tis but his humor.
The business of the state does him offense,
[And he does chide with you.]
DESDEMONA: If 'twere no other—
IAGO: It is but so, I warrant.
[Trumpets within.]
Hark, how these instruments summon to supper!
The messengers of Venice stays the meat. 170
Go in, and weep not. All things shall be well.
Exeunt Desdemona and Emilia.

[Iago persuades Rodrigo to kill Cassio. (ed.)]

---

88 cry you mercy beg your pardon   **97 half asleep** i.e., dazed
104 go by water be expressed by tears   **109 opinion** censure **least misuse**
slightest misconduct   **121 callet** whore

129 trick strange behavior   **132 cogging** cheating **cozening** defrauding
138 form circumstance   **141 companions** fellows **unfold** expose
144 within door i.e., not so loud   **160 defeat** destroy   **163 addition** title
170 stays the meat are waiting to dine

Scene III

Enter Othello, Lodovico, Desdemona, Emilia, and Attendants.

LODOVICO: I do beseech you, sir, trouble yourself no
    further.   1

OTHELLO: O, pardon me; 'twill do me good to walk.

LODOVICO: Madam, good night. I humbly thank your
    ladyship.

DESDEMONA: Your honor is most welcome.

OTHELLO: Will you walk, sir?
O, Desdemona!

DESDEMONA: My lord?

OTHELLO: Get you to bed on th' instant; I will be return'd
forthwith. Dismiss your attendant there. Look 't be done.

DESDEMONA: I will, my lord.

              Exit [Othello, with Lodovico and Attendants].

EMILIA: How goes it now? He looks gentler than he did.   10

DESDEMONA: He says he will return incontinent,
And hath commanded me to go to bed,
And bade me to dismiss you.

EMILIA: Dismiss me?

DESDEMONA: It was his bidding; therefore, good Emilia,
Give me my nightly wearing, and adieu.
We must not now displease him.

EMILIA: I would you had never seen him!

DESDEMONA: So would not I. My love doth so approve him,
That even his stubbornness, his checks, his frowns—
Prithee unpin me—have grace and favor in them.   20

           [Emilia prepares Desdemona for bed.]

EMILIA: I have laid those sheets you bade me on the bed.

DESDEMONA: All's one. Good faith, how foolish are our
    minds!
If I do die before thee, prithee shroud me
In one of those same sheets.

EMILIA: Come, come, you talk.

DESDEMONA: My mother had a maid call'd Barbary.
She was in love, and he she lov'd prov'd mad
And did forsake her. She had a song of "Willow,"
An old thing 'twas, but it express'd her fortune,
And she died singing it. That song tonight
Will not go from my mind; I have much to do   30
But to go hang my head all at one side
And sing it like poor Barbary. Prithee, dispatch.

EMILIA: Shall I go fetch your nightgown?

DESDEMONA: No, unpin me here.
This Lodovico is a proper man.

EMILIA: A very handsome man.

DESDEMONA: He speaks well.

EMILIA: I know a lady in Venice would have walk'd barefoot
to Palestine for a touch of his nether lip.

DESDEMONA *[Singing]*:
"The poor soul sat sighing by a sycamore tree,
    Sing all a green willow;   40
Her hand on her bosom, her head on her knee,
    Sing willow, willow, willow.

The fresh streams ran by her, and murmur'd her moans;
    Sing willow, willow, willow;
Her salt tears fell from her, and soft'ned the stones"—
Lay by these.
[Singing.] "Sing willow, willow, willow"—
Prithee, hie thee; he'll come anon.
[Singing.] "Sing all a green willow must be my garland.
    Let nobody blame him; his scorn I approve"—   50
Nay, that's not next.—Hark! Who is 't that knocks?

EMILIA: It's the wind.

DESDEMONA *[Singing]*:
"I call'd my love false love; but what said he then?
    Sing willow, willow, willow;
If I court moe women, you'll couch with moe men"—
So, get thee gone; good night. Mine eyes do itch;
Doth that bode weeping?

EMILIA: 'Tis neither here nor there.

DESDEMONA: I have heard it said so. O, these men, these
    men!
Dost thou in conscience think—tell me, Emilia—
That there be women do abuse their husbands   60
In such gross kind?

EMILIA: There be some such, no question.

DESDEMONA: Wouldst thou do such a deed for all the world?

EMILIA: Why, would not you?

DESDEMONA: No, by this heavenly light!

EMILIA: Nor I neither by this heavenly light; I might do
    't as well i' th' dark.

DESDEMONA: Wouldst thou do such a deed for all the
    world?

EMILIA: The world's a huge thing. It is a great price
For a small vice.

DESDEMONA: Good troth, I think thou wouldst not.

EMILIA: By my troth, I think I should; and undo 't when I
had done. Marry, I would not do such a thing for a joint-   70
ring, nor for measures of lawn, nor for gowns, petticoats,
nor caps, nor any petty exhibition; but, for all the whole
world—'ud's pity, who would not make her husband a
cuckold to make him a monarch? I should venture
purgatory for 't.

DESDEMONA: Beshrew me if I would do such a wrong for the
whole world.

EMILIA: Why, the wrong is but a wrong i' th' world; and
having the world for your labor, 'tis a wrong in your own
world, and you might quickly make it right.   80

DESDEMONA: I do not think there is any such woman.

EMILIA: Yes, a dozen; and as many to th' vantage as
    would store the world they play'd for.
But I do think it is their husbands' faults
If wives do fall. Say that they slack their duties,
And pour our treasures into foreign laps,
Or else break out in peevish jealousies,
Throwing restraint upon us? Or say they strike us,
Or scant our former having in despite?
Why, we have galls, and though we have some grace,

IV.iii *Location:* The citadel.
11 incontinent immediately   **19 stubbornness** roughness **checks** rebukes
26 mad wild, i.e., faithless   **30–31 I . . . hang** I can scarcely keep myself from
hanging

---

48 hie thee hurry   **70–71 joint-ring** a ring made in separate halves
71 lawn fine linen   **72 exhibition** gift   **73 'ud's** i.e., God's   **82 to th' vantage** in
addition, to boot **store** populate   **85 pour . . . laps** i.e., are unfaithful, give
what is rightfully ours (semen) to other women   **88 scant . . . despite** reduce
our allowance to spite us   **89 have galls** i.e., are capable of resenting injury
and insult

Yet have we some revenge. Let husbands know 90
Their wives have sense like them. They see, and smell,
And have their palates both for sweet and sour,
As husbands have. What is it that they do
When they change us for others? Is it sport?
I think it is. And doth affection breed it?
I think it doth. Is 't frailty that thus errs?
It is so too. And have not we affections,
Desires for sport, and frailty, as men have?
Then let them use us well; else let them know,
The ills we do, their ills instruct us so. 100
   DESDEMONA: Good night, good night. God me such uses
     send,
Not to pick bad from bad, but by bad mend!

                       Exeunt.

Act V, Scene I

Enter Iago and Roderigo.
   IAGO: Here stand behind this bulk; straight will he come. 1
Wear thy good rapier bare, and put it home.
Quick, quick! Fear nothing; I'll be at thy elbow.
It makes us, or it mars us; think on that,
And fix most firm thy resolution.
   RODERIGO: Be near at hand; I may miscarry in 't.
   IAGO: Here, at the hand. Be bold, and take thy stand.
     [Iago stands aside. Roderigo conceals himself.]
   RODERIGO: I have no great devotion to the deed;
And yet he hath given me satisfying reasons.
'Tis but a man gone. Forth, my sword! He dies. 10
                  [Draws.]
   IAGO: I have rubb'd this young quat almost to the sense,
And he grows angry. Now, whether he kill Cassio,
Or Cassio him, or each do kill the other,
Every way makes my gain. Live Roderigo,
He calls me to a restitution large
Of gold and jewels that I bobb'd from him
As gifts to Desdemona.
It must not be. If Cassio do remain,
He hath a daily beauty in his life
That makes me ugly; and besides, the Moor 20
May unfold me to him; there stand I in much peril.
No, he must die. Be 't so. I hear him coming.
Enter Cassio.
   RODERIGO *[Coming forth]*: I know his gait, 'tis he.—Villain,
    thou diest!

         [Makes a pass at Cassio.]
   CASSIO: That thrust had been mine enemy indeed,
But that my coat is better than thou know'st.
I will make proof of thine.
        [Draws, and wounds Roderigo.]
   RODERIGO: O, I am slain!   *[Falls.]*
   [Iago from behind wounds Cassio in the leg, and exits.]
   CASSIO: I am maim'd forever. Help, ho! Murder! Murder!
Enter Othello.
   OTHELLO: The voice of Cassio! Iago keeps his word.

   RODERIGO: O, villain that I am!
   OTHELLO: It is even so.
   CASSIO: O, help, ho! Light! A surgeon! 30
   OTHELLO: 'Tis he. O brave Iago, honest and just,
That hast such noble sense of thy friend's wrong!
Thou teachest me. Minion, your dear lies dead,
And your unblest fate hies. Strumpet, I come.
Forth of my heart those charms, thine eyes, are blotted;
Thy bed, lust-stain'd, shall with lust's blood be spotted.
               Exit Othello.
Enter Lodovico and Gratiano.
   CASSIO: What, ho! No watch? No passage? Murder!
    Murder!
   GRATIANO: 'Tis some mischance; the voice is very direful.
   CASSIO: O, help!
   LODOVICO: Hark! 40
   RODERIGO: O wretched villain!
   LODOVICO: Two or three groan. 'Tis heavy night;
These may be counterfeits. Let's think 't unsafe
To come in to the cry without more help.
      [They remain near the entrance.]
   RODERIGO: Nobody come? Then shall I bleed to death.
Enter Iago [in his shirtsleeves, with a light].
   LODOVICO: Hark!
   GRATIANO: Here's one comes in his shirt, with light and
    weapons.
   IAGO: Who's there? Whose noise is this that cries on
    murder?
   LODOVICO: We do not know.
   IAGO: Did not you hear a cry?
   CASSIO: Here, here! For heaven sake, help me!
   IAGO: What's the matter? 50
        [He moves toward Cassio.]
   GRATIANO *[To Lodovico]*: This is Othello's ancient, as I take it.
   LODOVICO *[To Gratiano]*: The same indeed; a very valiant
    fellow.
   IAGO: What are you here that cry so grievously?
   CASSIO: Iago? O, I am spoil'd, undone by villains!
Give me some help.
   IAGO: O me, lieutenant! What villains have done this?
   CASSIO: I think that one of them is hereabout,
And cannot make away.
   IAGO: O treacherous villains!
[To Lodovico and Gratiano.] What are you there? Come in,
    and give some help. *[They advance.]*
   RODERIGO: O, help me there! 60
   CASSIO: That's one of them.
   IAGO: O murd'rous slave! O villain!
        [Stabs Roderigo.]
   RODERIGO: O damn'd Iago! O inhuman dog!
   IAGO: Kill men i' th' dark?—Where be these bloody
    thieves?—
How silent is this town!—Ho! Murder, murder!—
[To Lodovico and Gratiano.] What may you be? Are you of
    good or evil?

---

91 sense   physical sense   101 uses habit, practice   102 Not ... mend i.e.,
not to learn bad conduct from others' badness (as Emilia has suggested
women learn from men), but to mend my ways by perceiving what
badness is, making spiritual benefit out of evil and adversity

V.i. Location: A street in Cyprus.   1 bulk framework projecting from the front of
a shop   11 quat pimple, pustule to the sense to the quick   16 bobb'd filched
cunningly 25 coat garment of mail (under his outer clothing)

33 Minion hussy (i.e., Desdemona)   34 hies hastens on
37 passage people passing   42 heavy thick, dark
48 cries on cries out   58 make get   59 What who (Also at l.65.)

LODOVICO: As you shall prove us, praise us.
IAGO: Signior Lodovico?
LODOVICO: He, sir.
IAGO: I cry you mercy. Here's Cassio hurt by villains.
GRATIANO: Cassio?   70
IAGO: How is 't, brother?
CASSIO: My leg is cut in two.
IAGO: Marry, heaven forbid!
Light gentlemen! I'll bind it with my shirt.
[He hands them the light, and tends to Cassio's wound.]
[Iago tries to implicate Bianca in the stabbing of Roderigo. (ed.)]
EMILIA: 'Las, what's the matter? What's the matter,
    husband?
IAGO: Cassio hath here been set on in the dark
By Roderigo and fellows that are scap'd.
He's almost slain, and Roderigo dead.
EMILIA: Alas, good gentleman! Alas, good Cassio!
IAGO: This is the fruits of whoring. Prithee, Emilia,
Go know of Cassio where he supp'd tonight.   80
[To Bianca.] What, do you shake at that?
BIANCA: He supp'd at my house; but I therefore shake not.
IAGO: O, did he so? I charge you go with me.
EMILIA: O, fie upon thee, strumpet!
BIANCA: I am no strumpet, but of life as honest
As you that thus abuse me.
EMILIA: As I? Foh! Fie upon thee!
IAGO: Kind gentlemen, let's go see poor Cassio dress'd.
Come mistress, you must tell 's another tale.
Emilia, run you to the citadel.
And tell my lord and lady what hath happ'd.—   90
Will you go on afore? *[Aside.]* This is the night
That either makes me or fordoes me quite.   *Exeunt.*

Scene II

Enter Othello [with a light], and Desdemona in her bed.
OTHELLO: It is the cause, it is the cause, my soul.   1
Let me not name it to you, you chaste stars!
It is the cause. Yet I'll not shed her blood,
Nor scar that whiter skin of hers than snow,
And smooth as monumental alabaster.
Yet she must die, else she'll betray more men.
Put out the light, and then put out the light.
If I quench thee, thou flaming minister,
I can again thy former light restore.
Should I repent me; but once put out thy light,   10
Thou cunning'st pattern of excelling nature,
I know not where is that Promethean heat
That can thy light relume. When I have pluck'd the rose,
I cannot give it vital growth again.
It needs must wither. I'll smell thee on the tree.
                                        [Kissing her.]

O balmy breath, that dost almost persuade
Justice to break her sword! One more, one more.
Be thus when thou art dead, and I will kill thee,
And love thee after. One more, and that's the last.
So sweet was ne'er so fatal. I must weep,   20
But they are cruel tears. This sorrow's heavenly;
It strikes where it doth love. She wakes.
DESDEMONA: Who's there? Othello?
OTHELLO: Ay, Desdemona.
DESDEMONA: Will you come to bed, my lord?
OTHELLO: Have you pray'd tonight, Desdemon?
DESDEMONA: Ay, my lord.
OTHELLO: If you bethink yourself of any crime
Unreconcil'd as yet to heaven and grace,
Solicit for it straight.
DESDEMONA: Alack, my lord, what may you mean by that?
OTHELLO: Well, do it, and be brief; I will walk by.   30
I would not kill thy unprepared spirit.
No, heaven forfend! I would not kill thy soul.
DESDEMONA: Talk you of killing?
OTHELLO: Ay, I do.
DESDEMONA: Then heaven
Have mercy on me!
OTHELLO: Amen, with all my heart!
DESDEMONA: If you say so, I hope you will not kill me.
OTHELLO: Hum!
DESDEMONA: And yet I fear you; for you're fatal then
When your eyes roll so. Why I should fear I know not,
Since guiltiness I know not; but yet I feel I fear.
OTHELLO: Think on thy sins.
DESDEMONA: They are loves I bear to you.   40
OTHELLO: Ay, and for that thou diest.
DESDEMONA: That death's unnatural that kills for loving.
Alas, why gnaw you so your nether lip?
Some bloody passion shakes your very frame.
These are portents; but yet I hope, I hope,
They do not point on me.
OTHELLO: Peace, and be still!
DESDEMONA: I will so. What's the matter?
OTHELLO: That handkerchief which I so lov'd and gave
    thee
Thou gav'st to Cassio.
DESDEMONA: No, by my life and soul!
Send for the man, and ask him.
OTHELLO: Sweet soul, take heed,   50
Take heed of perjury. Thou art on thy deathbed.
DESDEMONA: Ay, but not yet to die.
OTHELLO: Yes, presently.
Therefore confess thee freely of thy sin;
For to deny each article with oath
Cannot remove nor choke the strong conception
That I do groan withal. Thou art to die.
DESDEMONA: Then Lord have mercy on me!
OTHELLO: I say, amen.

---

92 fordoes undoes, ruins

55 conception belief (of your guilt)

V.ii. Location: A bedchamber in the citadel.
sd. in her bed (The bed is presumably "thrust out" on stage as the scene begins.) **1 cause** i.e., cause of justice, the offense itself, which Othello must correct as an agent of justice **12 Promethean heat** divine fire. (Alluding to the theft of fire from heaven by Prometheus.)
13 relume rekindle

DESDEMONA: And have you mercy too! I never did
Offend you in my life; never lov'd Cassio
But with such general warranty of heaven 60
As I might love. I never gave him token.
OTHELLO: By heaven, I saw my handkerchief in 's hand.
O perjur'd woman! Thou dost stone my heart,
And mak'st me call what I intend to do
A murder, which I thought a sacrifice.
I saw the handkerchief.
DESDEMONA: He found it then;
I never gave it him. Send for him hither;
Let him confess a truth.
OTHELLO: He hath confess'd.
DESDEMONA: What, my lord?
OTHELLO: That he hath us'd thee.
DESDEMONA: How? Unlawfully? 70
OTHELLO: Ay.
DESDEMONA: He will not say so.
OTHELLO: No, his mouth is stopp'd;
Honest Iago hath ta'en order for 't.
DESDEMONA: O, my fear interprets. What, is he dead?
OTHELLO: Had all his hairs been lives, my great revenge
Had stomach for them all.
DESDEMONA: Alas, he is betray'd and I undone!

[Weeps.]

OTHELLO: Out, strumpet! Weep'st thou for him to my face?
DESDEMONA: O, banish me, my lord, but kill me not!
OTHELLO: Down, strumpet!
DESDEMONA: Kill me tomorrow; let me live tonight! 80
OTHELLO: Nay, if you strive—
DESDEMONA: But half an hour!
OTHELLO: Being done, there is no pause.
DESDEMONA: But while I say one prayer!
OTHELLO: It is too late.

Smothers her.

EMILIA *[At the door]*: My lord, my lord? What, ho! My lord,
my lord!
OTHELLO: What noise is this? Not dead? Not yet quite
dead?
I that am cruel am yet merciful;
I would not have thee linger in thy pain.

[He dispatches her.]

So, so.
EMILIA *[Within]*: What, ho! My lord, my lord!
OTHELLO: Who's there?
EMILIA *[Within]*: O, good my lord, I would speak a word with
you!
OTHELLO: Yes, 'tis Emilia.—By and by.—She's dead. 90
'Tis like she comes to speak of Cassio's death.—
The noise was here. Ha! No more moving?
Still as the grave. Shall she come in? Were't good? —
I think she stirs again. No. What's best to do?
If she come in, she'll sure speak to my wife.
My wife! My wife! What wife? I have no wife.

O, insupportable! O heavy hour!
Methinks it should be now a huge eclipse
Of sun and moon, and that th' affrighted globe
Should yawn at alteration.
EMILIA *[Within]*:   I do beseech you 100
That I may speak with you, O, good my lord!
OTHELLO: I had forgot thee. O, come in, Emilia.—
Soft; by and by. Let me the curtains draw.—

[Closes bed-curtains and opens door.]

Where art thou?
Enter Emilia.
                    What's the matter with thee now?
EMILIA: O, my good lord, yonder's foul murders done!
OTHELLO: What, now?
EMILIA: But now, my lord.
OTHELLO: It is the very error of the moon;
She comes more nearer earth than she was wont,
And makes men mad.
EMILIA: Cassio, my lord, hath kill'd a young Venetian 110
Call'd Roderigo.
OTHELLO: Roderigo kill'd?
And Cassio kill'd?
EMILIA: No, Cassio is not kill'd.
OTHELLO: Not Cassio kill'd? Then murder's out of tune,
And sweet revenge grows harsh.
DESDEMONA: O, falsely, falsely murder'd!
EMILIA: O lord, what cry is that?
OTHELLO: That? What?
EMILIA: Out, and alas, that was my lady's voice.

[She opens the bed-curtains.]

Help, help, ho, help! O lady, speak again!
Sweet Desdemona! O sweet mistress, speak!
DESDEMONA: A guiltless death I die. 120
EMILIA: O, who hath done this deed?
DESDEMONA: Nobody; I myself. Farewell.
Commend me to my kind lord. O, farewell!

[Dies.]

OTHELLO: Why, how should she be murd'red?
EMILIA: Alas, who knows?
OTHELLO: You heard her say herself, it was not I.
EMILIA: She said so. I must needs report the truth.
OTHELLO: She's like a liar gone to burning hell!
'Twas I that kill'd her.
EMILIA: O, the more angel she,
And you the blacker devil!
OTHELLO: She turn'd to folly, and she was a whore. 130
EMILIA: Thou dost belie her, and thou art a devil.
OTHELLO: She was false as water.
EMILIA: Thou art rash as fire, to say
That she was false. O, she was heavenly true!
OTHELLO: Cassio did top her; ask thy husband else.
O, I were damn'd beneath all depth in hell
But that I did proceed upon just grounds
To this extremity. Thy husband knew it all.

---

63 **stone** turn to stone, harden   72 **ta'en order** taken measures   82 **Being done** i.e., since justice has begun its relentless course

100 **yawn** gape in amazement, i.e., move in an earthquake. (According to Pliny, earthquakes often happen during eclipses.)   107 **error** aberration, irregularity

EMILIA: My husband?
OTHELLO: Thy husband.
EMILIA: That she was false to wedlock? 140
OTHELLO: Ay, with Cassio. Nay, had she been true,
If heaven would make me such another world
Of one entire and perfect chrysolite,
I'd not have sold her for it.
EMILIA: My husband?
OTHELLO: Ay, 'twas he that told me on her first.
An honest man he is, and hates the slime
That sticks on filthy deeds.
EMILIA: My husband?
OTHELLO: What needs this iterance, woman? I say thy
husband.
EMILIA: O mistress, villainy hath made mocks with love!
My husband say she was false?
OTHELLO: He, woman; 150
I say thy husband. Dost understand the word?
My friend, thy husband, honest, honest Iago.
EMILIA: If he say so, may his pernicious soul
Rot half a grain a day! He lies to th' heart.
She was too fond of her most filthy bargain.
OTHELLO: Ha?

[He draws.]

EMILIA: Do thy worst!
This deed of thine is no more worthy heaven
Than thou wast worthy her.
OTHELLO: Peace, you were best.
EMILIA: Thou hast not half that pow'r to do me harm 160
As I have to be hurt. O gull! O dolt!
As ignorant as dirt! Thou hast done a deed—
I care not for thy sword; I'll make thee known,
Though I lost twenty lives.—Help! Help, ho, help!
The Moor hath kill'd my mistress! Murder, murder!
Enter Montano, Gratiano, and Iago [with others].
MONTANO: What is the matter? How now, general?
EMILIA: O, are you come, Iago? You have done well,
That men must lay their murders on your neck.
GRATIANO: What is the matter?
EMILIA: Disprove this villain, if thou be'st a man. 170
He says thou told'st him that his wife was false.
I know thou didst not; thou 'rt not such a villain.
Speak, for my heart is full.
IAGO: I told him what I thought, and told no more
Than what he found himself was apt and true.
EMILIA: But did you ever tell him she was false?
IAGO: I did.
EMILIA: You told a lie, an odious, damned lie!
Upon my soul, a lie, a wicked lie.
She false with Cassio? Did you say with Cassio? 180
IAGO: With Cassio, mistress. Go to, charm your tongue.
EMILIA: I will not charm my tongue; I am bound to speak.
My mistress here lies murdered in her bed—
ALL: O heavens forfend!
EMILIA: And your reports have set the murder on.

OTHELLO: Nay, stare not, masters. It is true indeed.
GRATIANO: 'Tis a strange truth.
MONTANO: O monstrous act!
EMILIA: Villainy, villainy, villainy!
I think upon 't—I think I smell 't! O villainy!
I thought so then—I'll kill myself for grief— 190
O villainy, villainy!
IAGO: What, are you mad? I charge you, get you home.
EMILIA: Good gentlemen, let me have leave to speak.
'Tis proper I obey him, but not now.
Perchance, Iago, I will ne'er go home.
OTHELLO: O! O! O!

[He falls on the bed.]

EMILIA: Nay, lay thee down and roar;
For thou hast kill'd the sweetest innocent
That e'er did lift up eye.
OTHELLO [Rising]: O, she was foul!
I scarce did know you, uncle. There lies your niece,
Whose breath, indeed, these hands have newly stopp'd. 200
I know this act shows horrible and grim.
GRATIANO: Poor Desdemona! I am glad thy father's dead.
Thy match was mortal to him, and pure grief
Shore his old thread in twain. Did he live now,
This sight would make him do a desperate turn,
Yea, curse his better angel from his side,
And fall to reprobance.
OTHELLO: 'Tis pitiful; but yet Iago knows
That she with Cassio hath the act of shame
A thousand times committed. Cassio confess'd it; 210
And she did gratify his amorous works
With that recognizance and pledge of love
Which I first gave her. I saw it in his hand;
It was a handkerchief, an antique token
My father gave my mother.
EMILIA: O God! O heavenly God!
IAGO: 'Zounds, hold your peace.
EMILIA: 'Twill out, 'twill out! I peace?
No, I will speak as liberal as the north.
Let heaven and men and devils, let them all,
All, all, cry shame against me, yet I'll speak.
IAGO: Be wise, and get you home.
EMILIA: I will not.

[Iago offers to stab Emilia.]

GRATIANO: Fie! 220
Your sword upon a woman?
EMILIA: O thou dull Moor! That handkerchief thou
speak'st of
I found by fortune and did give my husband;
For often, with a solemn earnestness,
More than indeed belong'd to such a trifle,
He begg'd of me to steal it.
IAGO: Villainous whore!
EMILIA: She give it Cassio? No, alas! I found it,
And I did give't my husband.
IAGO: Filth, thou liest!

---

143 chrysolite precious topaz   148 iterance iteration, repetition
149 made mocks with derided, made sport of   161 to be hurt i.e., to endure
hurt   181 charm keep silent (as though by a magic spell)

190 then (i.e., probably at IV.ii.130–144.)   201 shows looks
204 Shore sheared, cut   207 reprobance damnation   212 recognizance token
217 liberal as the north freely as the north wind (blows)

EMILIA: By heaven, I do not, I do not, gentlemen.
O murd'rous coxcomb, what should such a fool   230
Do with so good a wife?
    OTHELLO: Are there no stones in heaven
But what serves for the thunder?—Precious villain!
    [He runs at Iago; Montano disarms Othello. Iago, from
              behind, stabs Emilia, and exit.]
    GRATIANO: The woman falls! Sure he hath kill'd his wife.
    EMILIA: Ay, ay. O, lay me by my mistress' side.
    GRATIANO: He's gone, but his wife's kill'd.
    MONTANO: 'Tis a notorious villain. Take you this weapon,
Which I have here recover'd from the Moor.
Come, guard the door without; let him not pass,
But kill him rather. I'll after that same villain,
For 'tis a damned slave.   240
              Exit [with all but Othello and Emilia,
              who has been laid by Desdemona's side].
    OTHELLO: I am not valiant neither,
But every puny whipster gets my sword.
But why should honor outlive honesty?
Let it go all.
    EMILIA: What did thy song bode, lady?
Hark, canst thou hear me? I will play the swan,
And die in music.
[Sings.] "Willow, willow, willow."
Moor, she was chaste. She lov'd thee, cruel Moor;
So come my soul to bliss, as I speak true.
So speaking as I think, alas, I die.   250
                    [Dies.]
    OTHELLO: I have another weapon in this chamber;
It is a sword of Spain, the ice-brook's temper—
O, here it is. *[Finds a sword.]* Uncle, I must come forth.
    GRATIANO *[Within]*: If thou attempt it, it will cost thee
    dear.
Thou hast no weapon, and perforce must suffer.
    OTHELLO: Look in upon me then and speak with me,
Or, naked as I am, I will assault thee.
[Enter Gratiano.]
    GRATIANO: What is the matter?
    OTHELLO: Behold, I have a weapon;
A better never did itself sustain
Upon a soldier's thigh. I have seen the day   260
That, with this little arm and this good sword,
I have made my way through more impediments
Than twenty times our stop. But, O vain boast!
Who can control his fate? 'Tis not so now.
Be not afraid, though you do see me weapon'd;
Here is my journey's end, here is my butt
And very sea-mark of my utmost sail.
              [Gratiano steps back.]
Do you go back dismay'd? 'Tis a lost fear;
Man but a rush against Othello's breast,
And he retires. Where should Othello go?   270
              [He turns to Desdemona.]
Now, how dost thou look now? O ill-starr'd wench!

Pale as thy smock! When we shall meet at compt,
This look of thine will hurl my soul from heaven,
And fiends will snatch at it. Cold, cold, my girl?
Even like thy chastity.
O cursed, cursed slave! Whip me, ye devils,
From the possession of this heavenly sight!
Blow me about in winds! Roast me in sulphur!
Wash me in steep-down gulfs of liquid fire!
O Desdemon! Dead, Desdemon! Dead! Oh! Oh!   280
Enter Lodovico, Cassio [carried in a litter], Montano, and
Iago [prisoner], with Officers.
    LODOVICO: Where is this rash and most unfortunate man?
    OTHELLO: That's he that was Othello. Here I am.
    LODOVICO: Where is that viper? Bring the villain forth.
              [Iago is led forward.]
    OTHELLO: I look down towards his feet; but that's a fable.
If that thou be'st a devil, I cannot kill thee.
              [Wounds Iago.]
    LODOVICO: Wrench his sword from him.
              [Othello is disarmed.]
    IAGO: I bleed, sir, but not kill'd.
    OTHELLO: I am not sorry neither. I'd have thee live;
For, in my sense, 'tis happiness to die.
    LODOVICO: O thou Othello, that was once so good,
Fall'n in the practice of a damned slave,   290
What shall be said to thee?
    OTHELLO: Why, anything.
An honorable murderer, if you will;
For nought I did in hate, but all in honor.
    LODOVICO: This wretch hath part confess'd his villainy.
Did you and he consent in Cassio's death?
    OTHELLO: Ay.
    CASSIO: Dear general, I never gave you cause.
    OTHELLO: I do believe it, and I ask your pardon.
Will you, I pray, demand that demi-devil
Why he hath thus ensnar'd my soul and body?   300
    IAGO: Demand me nothing. What you know, you know.
From this time forth I never will speak word.
    LODOVICO: What, not to pray?
    GRATIANO: Torments will ope your lips.
    OTHELLO: Well, thou dost best.
    LODOVICO: Sir, you shall understand what hath befall'n,
Which, as I think, you know not. Here is a letter
Found in the pocket of the slain Roderigo;
And here another. *[Produces letters.]* The one of them
    imports
The death of Cassio to be undertook
By Roderigo.
    OTHELLO: O villain!
    CASSIO: Most heathenish and most gross!   310
    LODOVICO: Now here's another discontented paper,
Found in his pocket too. *[Shows another paper.]* And this,
    it seems,
Roderigo meant t' have sent this damned villain;
But that belike Iago in the nick

---

230 coxcomb fool. (Addressed to Othello.)   **231 stones** bolts, such as those used for thunderbolts   **242 whipster** contemptible fellow **243 honor** i.e., the bravery for which one enjoys a soldier's reputation **honesty** true integrity   **252 the ice-brook's temper** tempered in ice-cold water **257 naked** unarmed   **263 stop** power (to stop)   **266 butt** goal, limit. (An archery term.)   **267 sea-mark** beacon (marking his destination or limit) **268 lost** wasted, unneeded   **269 Man . . . rush** wield no more than a reed

272 compt account, judgment day   **284 towards his feet** i.e., to see if they are cloven like a devil's   **290 practice** plotting

Came in and satisfied him.

OTHELLO: O thou pernicious caitiff!—
How came you, Cassio, by that handkerchief
That was my wife's?

CASSIO: I found it in my chamber;
And he himself confess'd but even now
That there he dropp'd it for a special purpose
Which wrought to his desire.

OTHELLO: O fool, fool, fool!   320

CASSIO: There is besides, in Roderigo's letter,
How he upbraids Iago, that he made him
Brave me upon the watch, whereon it came
That I was cast; and even but now he spake,
After long seeming dead, Iago hurt him,
Iago set him on.

LODOVICO: You must forsake this room and go with us.
Your power and your command is taken off,
And Cassio rules in Cyprus. For this slave,
If there be any cunning cruelty   330
That can torment him much and hold him long,
It shall be his. You shall close prisoner rest,
Till that the nature of your fault be known
To the Venetian state. Come, bring away.

OTHELLO: Soft you; a word or two before you go.
I have done the state some service, and they know 't.
No more of that. I pray you, in your letters,
When you shall these unlucky deeds relate,
Speak of me as I am; nothing extenuate,
Nor set down aught in malice. Then must you speak   340
Of one that lov'd not wisely but too well;
Of one not easily jealous, but, being wrought,
Perplex'd in the extreme; of one whose hand,
Like the base Indian, threw a pearl away
Richer than all his tribe; of one whose subdu'd eyes,
Albeit unused to the melting mood,
Drops tears as fast as the Arabian trees
Their medicinable gum. Set you down this;
And say besides, that in Aleppo once,
Where a malignant and a turban'd Turk   350
Beat a Venetian and traduc'd the state,
I took by th' throat the circumcised dog,
And smote him, thus.

                      [Stabs himself.]

LODOVICO: O bloody period!

GRATIANO: All that is spoke is marr'd.

OTHELLO: I kiss'd thee ere I kill'd thee. No way but this,
Killing myself, to die upon a kiss.

                [Falls on the bed, and dies.]

CASSIO: This did I fear, but thought he had no weapon;
For he was great of heart.

LODOVICO *[To Iago]*:   O Spartan dog,
More fell than anguish, hunger, or the sea!
Look on the tragic loading of this bed;   360
This is thy work. The object poisons sight;

Let it be hid. Gratiano, keep the house,

                [The bed-curtains are drawn.]
And seize upon the fortunes of the Moor,
For they succeed on you. To you, Lord Governor,
Remains the censure of this hellish villain,
The time, the place, the torture. O, enforce it!
Myself will straight aboard, and to the state
This heavy act with heavy heart relate.

                        Exeunt.

—————◆—————

SUMMARY

The sixteenth century was a time of rapid change marked by growing secularism, advancing technology, and European geographic expansion. It was also an age of profound religious and social upheaval. Northern European humanists, led by Erasmus of Rotterdam, made critical studies of early Christian literature and urged a return to the teachings of Jesus and the early church fathers. Demands for Church reform went hand in hand with the revival of Early Christian writings to culminate in the Protestant Reformation.

Aided by Gutenberg's printing press, Martin Luther contested the authority of the Church of Rome. He held that Scripture was the sole basis for religious interpretation and emphasized the idea of salvation through faith in God's grace rather than through good works. As Lutheranism and other Protestant sects proliferated throughout Europe, the unity of medieval Christendom was shattered.

The music and art of the Northern Renaissance reflect the mood of religious reform. In music, the Lutheran chorale became the vehicle of Protestant piety. In art, the increasing demand for illustrated devotional literature and private devotional art stimulated the production of woodcuts and metal engravings. The works of Dürer and Grünewald exhibit the Northern Renaissance passion for realistic detail and graphic expression, while the fantastic imagery of Hieronymus Bosch suggests a pessimistic and typically Northern concern with sin and death. Bosch's preoccupation with the palpable forces of evil found its counterpart in the witch-hunts of the sixteenth century. In painting, too, such secular subjects as portraiture, landscapes, and scenes of everyday life mirrored the tastes of a growing middle-class audience for an unidealized record of the material world.

---

323 Brave defy   **324 cast** dismissed   **344 Indian** (This reading pictures an ignorant savage who cannot recognize the value of a precious jewel. [An alternative reading, *Indean or Judean*, i.e., infidel or disbeliever, may refer to Herod, who slew Miriamne in a fit of jealousy, or to Judas Iscariot, the betrayer of Christ.)   **345 subdu'd** i.e., by grief   **354 period** termination, conclusion   **358 Spartan dog** (Spartan dogs were noted for their savagery and silence.)   **359 fell** cruel

362 Let it be hid i.e., draw the bed-curtains (No stage direction specifies that the dead are to be carried off stage at the end of the play.)

Northern Renaissance writers took a generally skeptical and pessimistic view of human nature. Erasmus, More, Cervantes, and Rabelais lampooned individual and societal failings and described the ruling influence of folly in all aspects of human conduct. In France, Montaigne devised the essay as an intimate form of rational reflection. The most powerful form of literary expression to evolve in the late sixteenth century, however, was secular drama. In the hands of William Shakespeare, drama became the ultimate expression of the quest to understand the workings of the individual imagination. Shakespeare's plays (as opposed, for instance, to Montaigne's essays) reveal the human condition through overt action, rather than through private reflection. In European drama, however, as in Japanese Nō drama, the stage play worked as a metaphor describing human experience, even as it provided communal confirmation of the literary and historical past.

By the end of the sixteenth century, national loyalties, religious fanaticism, and commercial rivalries had splintered the European community, rendering ever more complex the society of the West. And yet, on the threshold of modernity, the challenges to the human condition—economic survival, communality, self-knowledge, and the inevitability of death—were no less pressing than they had been two thousand years earlier. If the technology of the sixteenth century was more sophisticated than that of ancient times—giving human beings greater control over nature than ever before—it also provided more devastating weapons of war and destruction. In the centuries to come, the humanistic tradition would be shaped and reshaped by changing historical circumstances and the creative imagination of indomitable humankind.

GLOSSARY

blank verse unrhymed lines of iambic pentameter, that is, lines consisting of ten syllables each with accents on every second syllable

chorale a congregational hymn, first sung in the Lutheran churches of Germany in the early sixteenth century

couplet two successive lines of verse with similar end-rhymes

engraving the process by which lines are incised on a metal plate, then inked and printed; see Figure 18.5

essay a short piece of expository prose that examines a single subject or idea

genre painting painting that depicts scenes from everyday life; not to be confused with "genre," a term used to designate a particular branch or category in literature or art, such as the essay (in literature) and portraiture (in painting)

iconoclast one who opposes the use of images in religious worship

quatrain a four-line stanza

triptych a picture or altarpiece with a central panel and two flanking panels; see also "diptych" in Glossary, chapter 9

woodcut a relief printing process by which all parts of a design are cut away except those that will be inked and printed; see Figure 18.4

SUGGESTIONS FOR READING

Bainton, Roland H. *Here I Stand: A Life of Martin Luther*. New York: Abingdon-Cokesbury, 1950.

Benesch, Otto. *The Art of the Renaissance in Northern Europe*, rev. ed. New York: Phaidon, 1965.

Eisenstein, Elizabeth L. *The Printing Press as an Instrument of Change*. Cambridge, U.K. Cambridge University Press, 1979.

Farrell, Kirby. *Play, Death, and Heroism in Shakespeare*. Chapel Hill. N.C.: University of North Carolina Press, 1989.

Holl, Karl. *The Cultural Significance of the Reformation*, translated by K. and B. Herz and J. H. Lichtblau. Cleveland, Ohio: Meridian, 1962.

Hillerbrand, Hans J. *Men and Ideas in the Sixteenth Century*. Chicago: Rand McNally, 1969.

Kinsman, R. S. *The Darker Vision of the Renaissance: Beyond the Fields of Reason*. Berkeley, Calif.: University of California Press, 1975.

Schoeck, Richard. *Erasmus of Europe: Prince of the Humanists 1501–1536*. New York: Columbia University Press, 1995.

Snyder, James. *Northern Renaissance Art*. Englewood Cliffs, N.J.: Prentice-Hall, 1985.

Spitz, E. W. *The Protestant Reformation*. New York: Harper and Row, 1985.

Tillyard, E. M. W. *The Elizabethan World Picture*. New York: Random House, 1964.

19
Africa, the Americas, and Cross-Cultural Encounter

Cross-Cultural Encounter

The period between 1400 and 1600 was the greatest age of trans-Eurasian travel since the days of the Roman Empire. However, even earlier, and especially after 1000 C.E., long-range trade, religious pilgrimage, missionary activity, and just plain curiosity had stimulated cross-cultural contact between East and West. Arab merchants dominated North African trade routes. Converts to Islam—especially Turks and Mongols—carried the Muslim faith across Asia into India and Anatolia. Mongol tribes traversed the vast overland Asian Silk Route, which stretched from Constantinople to the Pacific Ocean. Enterprising families, like that of the Venetian voyager Marco Polo (ca. 1253–1324), established cultural and commercial links with the court of

Map 19.1 World Exploration, 1271–1295; 1486–1611.

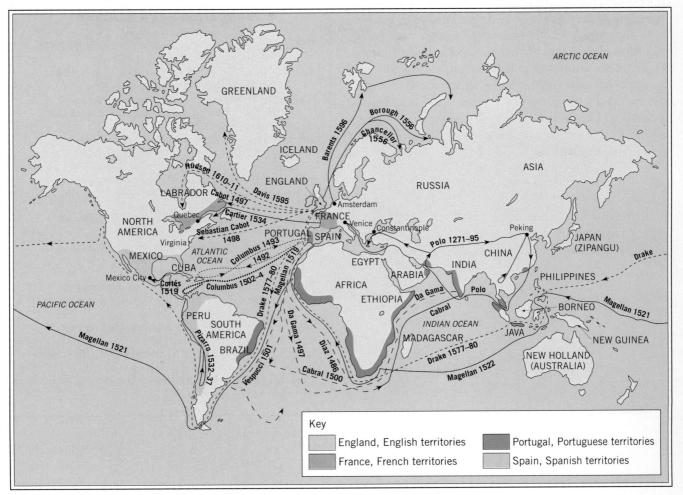

Key
England, English territories
France, French territories
Portugal, Portuguese territories
Spain, Spanish territories

the Mongol emperor of China, Kubilai Khan. Boasting that "brotherhood among peoples" had reached a new height during his rule (1260–1294), Kubilai encouraged long-distance travel and cross-cultural dialogue. The same roads that brought thirteenth-century Franciscan and Dominican monks into China sped the exchange of goods and religious beliefs between Muslims and Hindus, Confucianists and Buddhists. Even after Mongol rule came to an end in China, policies of outreach prevailed: During the brief period from 1405 to 1433, Chinese ships—the largest wooden vessels ever constructed—sailed the Indian Ocean to the coasts of India and Africa as China moved to expand its political and commercial influence.

Although the great plague that swept through Asia and Europe interrupted long-established patterns of East-West exchange, the appearance of fourteenth-century handbooks, such as that written by the Florentine merchant Francesco Pegolotti, suggests that global travel did not completely disappear (Pegolotti journeyed as far as China). Nor did regional travel cease: Chaucer's pilgrims traveled to local Christian shrines, while Buddhists visited their sanctuaries throughout East Asia, and Muslims often made even longer journeys to participate in the ritual of the *hajj*, that is, the pilgrimage to Mecca.

By the mid-fifteenth century, new factors fueled the enterprise of cross-cultural encounter. In 1453 the formidable armies of the Ottoman Empire captured Constantinople, bringing a thousand years of Byzantine civilization to an end. At the height of Ottoman power, as the Turkish presence in Southwest Asia threatened the safety of European overland caravans to the East, Western rulers (like the Duke of Venice in Shakespeare's *Othello*) explored offensive strategies: warfare against the Turks and the search for all-water routes to the East. Natural curiosity and greed for gold, slaves, and spices—the major commodities of Africa and Asia—also encouraged the emerging European nations to compete with Arab and Turkish traders for control of foreign markets and, thus, to seek faster and more efficient routes to East Asia. The technology of navigation

was crucial to the success of these ventures. Europeans improved such older Arab navigational devices as the compass and the astrolabe (an instrument that measures the angle between the horizon and heavenly bodies and thus fixes latitude; see chapter 10). With the early fifteenth-century Latin translation of Ptolemy's *Geography*, mapmakers began to order geographic space with the coordinates of latitude and longitude. The Portuguese, encouraged by Prince Henry the Navigator (1394–1460), came to produce maps and charts that exceeded the accuracy of those drafted by classical and Muslim cartographers. Portugal and Spain adopted the Arab lateen sail and built three-masted caravels with multiple sails—ships that were faster, safer, and more practical for rough ocean travel than the oar-driven galleys that sailed the Mediterranean Sea. The new caravels were outfitted with brass cannons and sufficient firepower to fend off severe enemy attack. By 1520, Vasco da Gama (1460–1524) had navigated around Southern Africa to establish Portuguese trading posts in India. Christopher Columbus (1451–1506), an Italian in the employ of Spain, sailed west in search of an all-water route to China. His discovery of the Americas—the existence of which no Europeans had ever suspected—was to change the course of world history. While the Spanish sought an all-water route to China by traveling west, that is, across the Atlantic Ocean, the Portuguese traveled eastward around Africa and across the Indian Ocean (Map 19.1). These enterprises initiated an era of exploration and cross-cultural encounter the consequences of which would transform the destiny of Africa.

The African Cultural Heritage

Africa, long known to Europeans as the "Dark Continent," was unaffected by the civilizations of both Asia and the West for thousands of years. Even after the Muslim conquest of North Africa in the seventh century and the impact of Arab trade, many parts of Africa remained independent of foreign influence and Africans continued to preserve local traditions and culture.

Diversity has characterized all aspects of African history, for Africa is a continent of widely varying geographic regions and more than eight hundred different native languages. The political organization of African territories over the centuries has ranged from small village communities to large states and empires.

Despite their geographic, linguistic, and political differences, however, Africans share some distinct cultural characteristics, including and especially a kinship

1405	China launches the first of seven overseas expeditions with over three hundred of the largest wooden ships ever built
1418	Prince Henry of Portugal opens a school of navigation
1420	the Portuguese develop the three-masted caravel for ocean travel
1448	Andreas Walsperger (Flemish) uses the coordinates of longitude, latitude, and climatic divisions in his *mappa mundi* (world map)
1522	the circumnavigation of the globe (begun by Magellan) is completed

system that emphasizes the importance and well-being of the group as essential to that of the individual. A Yoruba proverb proclaims, "I am because we are; What I am is what we are." Historically, the African kinship system was based on the extended family, a group of people who were both related to each other and dependent on each other for survival. The tribe consisted of a federation of extended families or clans ruled by chiefs or elders—either hereditary or elected—who held semidivine status. All those who belonged to the same family, clan, or tribe—the living, the dead, and the yet unborn—made up a single cohesive community irrevocably linked in time and space. While this form of social organization was not unique to Africa—indeed, it has characterized most agricultural societies in world history—it played an especially important role in shaping the character of African society and culture.

While tribal structure was traditionally the primary feature of African culture, **animism**—the belief that spirits inhabit all things in nature—was equally characteristic. Africans perceived the natural world as animated by supernatural spirits (including those of the dead). Though most Africans honored a Supreme Creator, they also recognized a great many lesser deities and spirits. For Africans, the spirits of ancestors, as well as those of natural objects, carried great potency. Since the spirits of the dead and the spirits of natural forces (rain, wind, forests, and so on) were thought to influence the living and to act as guides and protectors, honoring them was essential to tribal security. Hence, ritual played a major part in assuring the well-being of the community, and the keepers of ritual—shamans, diviners, and priests—held prominent positions in African society.

Map 19.2 Africa, 1000–1500

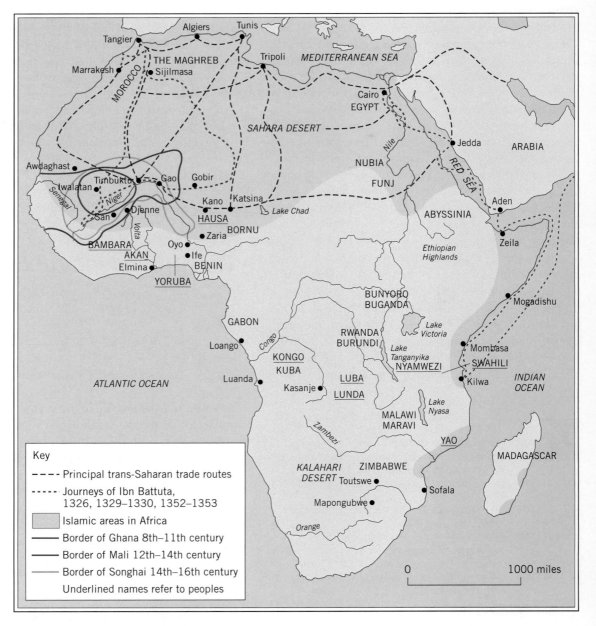

Key

- - - - Principal trans-Saharan trade routes

········· Journeys of Ibn Battuta, 1326, 1329–1330, 1352–1353

▨ Islamic areas in Africa

——— Border of Ghana 8th–11th century

——— Border of Mali 12th–14th century

——— Border of Songhai 14th–16th century

Underlined names refer to peoples

West African Kingdoms

From earliest times, most of Africa consisted of villages united by kinship ties and ruled by chieftains. However, by the ninth century (encouraged by the demands of Muslim merchants and a lucrative trans-Saharan trade) the first of a number of African states emerged in the *Sudan* (the word means "Land of the Blacks"): the region that stretches across Africa south of the Sahara Desert (Map 19.2). The very name of the first Sudanic state, Ghana, which means "war chief," suggests the manner in which centralization came about: A single powerful chieftain took control of the surrounding villages. Ghana's rulers, who were presumed to have divine ancestors, regulated the exportation of gold to the north and the importation of salt from the desert fringes. These two products—gold and salt—along with iron, slaves, and ivory, were the principal African commodities. After Ghana fell to the Muslims in the eleventh century, the native kings, along with much of the local culture, came under Arabic influence. The history of Ghana and other ancient African kingdoms is recorded primarily in Arabic sources describing the courts of kings, but little is known of African life in areas removed from the centers of power. Scholars estimate that in the hands of the Muslims, the trans-Saharan market in slaves—war captives, for the most part—increased from roughly three hundred thousand in the ninth century to over a million in the twelfth century.

During the thirteenth century, West Africans speaking the Mande language brought much of the Sudan under their dominion to form the Mali Empire. This dramatic development is associated with the powerful warrior-king Sundiata, who ruled Mali from around 1230 to 1255. The wealth and influence of the Mali Empire, which reached its zenith in the early fourteenth century, lay in its control of northern trade routes. On one of these routes lay the prosperous city of Timbuktu (see Map 19.2), the greatest of early African trading centers and the site of an Islamic university. In Mali, as in many of the African states, the rulers were converts to Islam; they employed Muslim scribes and jurists and used Arabic as the language of administration. The hallmarks of Islamic culture—its great mosques (Figure 19.1) and libraries and the Arabic language itself—did not penetrate deeply into the vast inte-

Figure 19.1 Prostrate Muslims in front of a mosque in the town of San, Mali, 1971. Photographic Archives, National Museum of African Art, Smithsonian Institution, Washington, D.C. (neg. no. VII–11, 37). Photo: Eliot Elisofon. The worshipers pray facing Mecca, birthplace of Muhammad and the holiest city of Islam.

Figure 19.2 The *oba* (ruler) of Ife wearing a bead crown and plume, from Benin, thirteenth to fourteenth centuries. Bronze. Reproduced by courtesy of the Trustees of the British Museum, London.

rior of Africa, however, where native African traditions dominated everyday life.

Prior to the fourteenth century, neither Arabs nor Europeans traveled to the parts of Africa south of the great savanna, a thickly vegetated area of tropical rain forest. Here, at the mouth of the Niger, in the area of present-day Nigeria, emerged the culture known as Benin, which absorbed the traditions of the Nok and Ife cultures that had preceded it. By the twelfth century, Benin dominated most of the West African territories north of the Niger delta. The Benin *oba* (kings) established an impressive royal tradition, building large, walled cities and engaging in trade with other African states. Like most African rulers, the *oba* of Benin regarded themselves as descendants of the gods. Craftspeople specially trained in the technique of lost-wax bronze casting—a process probably begun in Mesopotamia (see chapter 1)—immortalized the *oba* and their queens in magnificent portraits that capture their dignity and authority (Figures **19.2, 19.3**). Benin culture reached its peak during the sixteenth century.

African Literature

Black Africa transmitted native folk traditions orally rather than in writing. As a result, the literary contributions of Africans remained unrecorded for hundreds of years—in some cases until the nineteenth century and thereafter. During the tenth century, Arab scholars in Africa began to transcribe popular native tales and stories into Arabic. More recently, African literature has assumed the written forms of the various African languages. Even to this day, however, a highly prized oral tradition dominates African literature.

Ancient Africa's oral tradition was the province of *griots*, a special class of professional poet-historians who preserved the legends of the past by chanting or singing them from memory. Like the *jongleurs* of the early Middle Ages, the *griots* of Africa transmitted the history of the people in stories that had been handed down from generation to generation. The most notable of these narratives is *Sundiata*, an epic describing the formative phase of Mali history. Recounted by a *griot*, who identifies himself in the opening passages, the epic immortalizes the adventures of Sundiata, the champion and founder of the Mali Empire. In the tradition of such Western heroes as Gilgamesh, Achilles, Alexander, and Roland, the "lion-child" Sundiata performs extraordinary deeds that bring honor and glory to himself and his people. The following excerpt includes the *griot*'s introduction to the poem, the story of the battle of Tabon, and a brief description of the lively festival that celebrates Sundiata's triumphs. In the final passages of the poem, Mali is pictured as a place of peace and prosperity; it is eternal in the memory of those who know its history.

READING 3.19

From *Sundiata: An Epic of Old Mali*

I am a griot. It is I, Djeli Mamoudou Kouyaté, son of   1
Bintou Kouyaté and Djeli Kedian Kouyaté, master in the
art of eloquence. Since time immemorial the Kouyatés
have been in the service of the Keita[1] princes of Mali; we
are vessels of speech, we are the repositories which
harbor secrets many centuries old. The art of eloquence
has no secrets for us; without us the names of kings
would vanish into oblivion, we are the memory of
mankind; by the spoken word we bring to life the deeds
and exploits of kings for younger generations.   10

I derive my knowledge from my father Djeli Kedian,
who also got it from his father; history holds no mystery
for us; we teach to the vulgar just as much as we want to
teach them, for it is we who keep the keys to the twelve
doors of Mali.[2]

I know the list of all the sovereigns who succeeded to
the throne of Mali. I know how the black people divided
into tribes, for my father bequeathed to me all his
learning; I know why such and such is called Kamara,
another Keita, and yet another Sibibé or Traoré; every   20
name has a meaning, a secret import.

I teach kings the history of their ancestors so that the
lives of the ancients might serve them as an example, for
the world is old, but the future springs from the past.

My word is pure and free of all untruth; it is the word
of my father; it is the word of my father's father. I will
give you my father's words just as I received them; royal
griots do not know what lying is. When a quarrel breaks
out between tribes it is we who settle the difference, for
we are the depositaries of oaths which the ancestors   30
swore.

Listen to my word, you who want to know; by my
mouth you will learn the history of Mali.

By my mouth you will get to know the story of the
ancestor of great Mali, the story of him who, by his
exploits, surpassed even Alexander the Great; he who,
from the East, shed his rays upon all the countries of the
West.

Listen to the story of the son of the Buffalo, the son of
the Lion.[3] I am going to tell you of Maghan Sundiata, of   40
Mari-Djata, of Sogolon Djata, of Naré Maghan Djata; the
man of many names against whom sorcery could avail
nothing.

. . . .

Kings have prescribed destinies just like men, and
seers who probe the future know it. They have knowledge
of the future, whereas we griots are depositaries of the
knowledge of the past. But whoever knows the history of
a country can read its future.

Other peoples use writing to record the past, but this
invention has killed the faculty of memory among them.   50

Figure 19.3 Edo head of a queen mother, from Benin. Cast copper alloy and iron, height 4 ft. 3 in. The Metropolitan Museum of Art, New York (1991.17.146).

They do not feel the past any more, for writing lacks the
warmth of the human voice. With them everybody thinks
he knows, whereas learning should be a secret. The
prophets did not write and their words have been all the
more vivid as a result. What paltry learning is that which
is congealed in dumb books!

I, Djeli Mamoudou Kouyaté, am the result of a long
tradition. For generations we have passed on the history
of kings from father to son. The narrative was passed on
to me without alteration and I deliver it without   60
alteration, for I received it free from all untruth.

. . . .

---

[1]The ruling Muslim family, the Mali emperors identified themselves as
descendants of the prophet Muhammad.
[2]The twelve provinces of which Mali was originally composed.
[3]According to tradition, the buffalo was the totem of Sundiata's mother,
Sogolon, while the lion was the totem of his father.

Every man to his own land! If it is foretold that your destiny should be fulfilled in such and such a land, men can do nothing against it. Mansa Tounkara could not keep Sundiata back because the destiny of Sogolon's son was bound up with that of Mali. Neither the jealousy of a cruel stepmother, nor her wickedness, could alter for a moment the course of great destiny.

The snake, man's enemy, is not long-lived, yet the serpent that lives hidden will surely die old. Djata[4] was strong enough now to face his enemies. At the age of eighteen, he had the stateliness of the lion and the strength of the buffalo. His voice carried authority, his eyes were live coals, his arm was iron, he was the husband of power.

Moussa Tounkara, king of Mema, gave Sundiata half of his army. The most valiant came forward of their own free will to follow Sundiata in the great adventure. The cavalry of Mema, which he had fashioned himself, formed his iron squadron. Sundiata, dressed in the Muslim fashion of Mema, left the town at the head of his small but redoubtable army. The whole population sent their best wishes with him. He was surrounded by five messengers from Mali and Manding Bory rode proudly at the side of his brother. The horsemen of Mema formed behind Djata a bristling iron squadron. The troop took the direction of Wagadou, for Djata did not have enough troops to confront Soumaoro directly, and so the king of Mema advised him to go to Wagadou and take half of the men of the king, Soumaba Cissé. A swift messenger had been sent there and so the king of Wagadou came out in person to meet Sundiata and his troops. He gave Sundiata half of his cavalry and blessed the weapons. Then Manding Bory said to his brother, "Djata, do you think yourself able to face Soumaoro now?"

"No matter how small a forest may be, you can always find there sufficient fibers to tie up a man. Numbers mean nothing; it is worth that counts. With my cavalry I shall clear myself a path to Mali."

Djata gave out his orders. They would head south, skirting Soumaoro's kingdom. The first objective to be reached was Tabon, the iron-gated town in the midst of the mountains, for Sundiata had promised Fran Kamara that he would pass by Tabon before returning to Mali. He hoped to find that his childhood companion had become king. It was a forced march and during the halts the divines, Singbin Mara Cissé and Mandjan Bérété, related to Sundiata the history of Alexander the Great[5] and several other heroes, but of all of them Sundiata preferred Alexander, the king of gold and silver, who crossed the world from west to east. He wanted to outdo his prototype both in the extent of his territory and the wealth of his treasury. . . .

In the evening, after a long day's march, Sundiata arrived at the head of the great valley which led to Tabon. The valley was quite black with men, for Sosso Balla had deployed his men everywhere in the valley, and some were positioned on the heights which dominated the way through. When Djata saw the layout of Sosso Balla's men he turned to his generals laughing.

"Why are you laughing, brother, you can see that the road is blocked."

"Yes, but no mere infantrymen can halt my course towards Mali," replied Sundiata.

The troops stopped. All the war chiefs were of the opinion that they should wait until the next day to give battle because, they said, the men were tired.

"The battle will not last long," said Sundiata, "and the men will have time to rest. We must not allow Soumaoro the time to attack Tabon."

Sundiata was immovable, so the orders were given and the war drums began to beat. On his proud horse Sundiata turned to right and left in front of his troops. He entrusted the rearguard, composed of a part of the Wagadou cavalry, to his younger brother, Manding Bory. Having drawn his sword, Sundiata led the charge, shouting his war cry.

The Sossos were surprised by this sudden attack for they all thought that the battle would be joined the next day. The lightning that flashes across the sky is slower, the thunderbolts less frightening and floodwaters less surprising than Sundiata swooping down on Sosso Balla and his smiths.[6] In a trice, Sundiata was in the middle of the Sossos like a lion in the sheepfold. The Sossos, trampled under the hooves of his fiery charger, cried out. When he turned to the right the smiths of Soumaoro fell in their tens, and when he turned to the left his sword made heads fall as when someone shakes a tree of ripe fruit. The horsemen of Mema wrought a frightful slaughter and their long lances pierced flesh like a knife sunk into a paw-paw.[7] Charging ever forwards, Sundiata looked for Sosso Balla; he caught sight of him and like a lion bounded towards the son of Soumaoro, his sword held aloft. His arm came sweeping down but at that moment a Sosso warrior came between Djata and Sosso Balla and was sliced like a calabash.[8] Sosso Balla did not wait and disappeared from amidst his smiths. Seeing their chief in flight, the Sossos gave way and fell into a terrible rout. Before the sun disappeared behind the mountains there were only Djata and his men left in the valley.

. . . .

The festival began. The musicians of all the countries were there. Each people in turn came forward to the dais under Sundiata's impassive gaze. Then the war dances began. The sofas[9] of all the countries had lined themselves up in six ranks amid a great clatter of bows and spears knocking together. The war chiefs were on horseback. The warriors faced the enormous dais and at a signal from Balla Fasséké, the musicians, massed on the right of the dais, struck up. The heavy war drums thundered, the bolons[10] gave off muted notes while the griot's voice gave the throng the pitch for the "Hymn to

---

[4]Sundiata.
[5]In Mali tradition, it is said that Alexander was the second great conqueror and Sundiata the seventh and last.
[6]Metalsmiths, within the clan, a powerful caste of men who were noted as makers of weapons and sorcerers or soothsayers.
[7]Papaya.
[8]The common bottle gourd.
[9]Sudanese infantrymen or soldiers.
[10]Large harps with three or four strings.

the Bow."[11] The spearmen, advancing like hyenas in the night held their spears above their heads; the archers of Wagadou and Tabon,[12] walking with a noiseless tread, seemed to be lying in ambush behind bushes. They rose suddenly to their feet and let fly their arrows at imaginary enemies. In front of the great dais the Kéké-Tigui, or war chiefs, made their horses perform dance steps under the eyes of the Mansa.[13] The horses whinnied and reared, then, overmastered by the spurs, 180 knelt, got up and cut little capers, or else scraped the ground with their hooves.

The rapturous people shouted the "Hymn to the Bow" and clapped their hands. The sweating bodies of the warriors glistened in the sun while the exhausting rhythm of the tam-tams[14] wrenched from them shrill cries. But presently they made way for the cavalry, beloved by Djata. The horsemen of Mema threw their swords in the air and caught them in flight, uttering mighty shouts. A smile of contentment took shape on Sundiata's lips, for he was 190 happy to see his cavalry manoeuvre with so much skill. . . .

. . . .

After a year Sundiata held a new assembly at Niani, but this one was the assembly of dignitaries and kings of the empire. The kings and notables of all the tribes came to Niani. The kings spoke of their administration and the dignitaries talked of their kings. Fakoli, the nephew of Soumaoro, having proved himself too independent, had to flee to evade the Mansa's anger. His lands were confiscated and the taxes of Sosso were paid directly into the granaries of Niani. In this way, every year, 200 Sundiata gathered about him all the kings and notables; so justice prevailed everywhere, for the kings were afraid of being denounced at Niani.

Djata's justice spared nobody. He followed the very word of God. He protected the weak against the strong and people would make journeys lasting several days to come and demand justice of him. Under his sun the upright man was rewarded and the wicked one punished.

In their new-found peace the villages knew prosperity again, for with Sundiata happiness had come into 210 everyone's home. Vast fields of millet, rice, cotton, indigo and fonio[15] surrounded the villages. Whoever worked always had something to live on. Each year long caravans carried the taxes in kind[16] to Niani. You could go from village to village without fearing brigands. A thief would have his right hand chopped off and if he stole again he would be put to the sword.

New villages and new towns sprang up in Mali and elsewhere. "Dyulas," or traders, became numerous and during the reign of Sundiata the world knew happiness. 220

There are some kings who are powerful through their military strength. Everybody trembles before them, but when they die nothing but ill is spoken of them. Others do neither good nor ill and when they die they are forgotten. Others are feared because they have power,

but they know how to use it and they are loved because they love justice. Sundiata belonged to this group. He was feared, but loved as well. He was the father of Mali and gave the world peace. After him the world has not seen a greater conqueror, for he was the seventh and last 230 conqueror. He had made the capital of an empire out of his father's village, and Niani became the navel of the earth. In the most distant lands Niani was talked of and foreigners said, "Travellers from Mali can tell lies with impunity," for Mali was a remote country for many peoples.

The griots, fine talkers that they were, used to boast of Niani and Mali saying: "If you want salt, go to Niani, for Niani is the camping place of the Sahel[17] caravans. If you want gold, go to Niani, for Bouré, Bambougou and 240 Wagadou work for Niani. If you want fine cloth, go to Niani, for the Mecca road passes by Niani. If you want fish, go to Niani, for it is there that the fishermen of Maouti and Djenné come to sell their catches. If you want meat, go to Niani, the country of the great hunters, and the land of the ox and the sheep. If you want to see an army, go to Niani, for it is there that the united forces of Mali are to be found. If you want to see a great king, go to Niani, for it is there that the son of Sogolon lives, the man with two names." 250

This is what the masters of the spoken word used to sing. . . .

How many piled-up ruins, how much buried splendour! But all the deeds I have spoken of took place long ago and they all had Mali as their background. Kings have succeeded kings, but Mali has always remained the same.

Mali keeps its secrets jealously. There are things which the uninitiated will never know, for the griots, their depositaries, will never betray them. Maghan Sundiata, 260 the last conqueror on earth, lies not far from Niani-Niani at Balandougou, the weir town.

After him many kings and many Mansas reigned over Mali and other towns sprang up and disappeared. Hajji Mansa Moussa, of illustrious memory, beloved of God, built houses at Mecca for pilgrims coming from Mali, but the towns which he founded have all disappeared, Karanina, Bouroun-Kouna—nothing more remains of these towns. Other kings carried Mali far beyond Djata's frontiers, for example Mansa Samanka and Fadima 270 Moussa, but none of them came near Djata.

Maghan Sundiata was unique. In his own time no one equalled him and after him no one had the ambition to surpass him. He left his mark on Mali for all time and his taboos still guide men in their conduct.

Mali is eternal. To convince yourself of what I have said go to Mali.

. . .

Men of today, how small you are beside your ancestors, and small in mind too, for you have trouble in grasping the meaning of my words. Sundiata rests near Niani- 280

---

[11]A traditional song among the people of Mali.
[12]Kingdoms near Mali.
[13]Emperor.
[14]Large, circular gongs.
[15]A crabgrass with seeds that are used as a cereal.
[16]In produce or goods instead of money.

[17]A region of the Sudan bordering on the Sahara.

Figure 19.4 Bambara ritual *chi wara* dance, Mali. Photographic Archives, National Museum of African Art, Smithsonian Institution, Washington, D.C. (neg. no. VIII–58, 4A). Photo: Eliot Elisofon.

Niani, but his spirit lives on and today the Keitas still come and bow before the stone under which lies the father of Mali.

To acquire my knowledge I have journeyed all round Mali. At Kita I saw the mountain where the lake of holy water sleeps; at Segou, I learnt the history of the kings of Do and Kri; at Fadama, in Hamana, I heard the Kondé griots relate how the Keitas, Kondés and Kamaras conquered Wouroula. At Keyla, the village of the great masters, I learnt the origins of Mali and the art of speaking. Everywhere I was able to see and understand what my masters were teaching me, but between their hands I took an oath to teach only what is to be taught and to conceal what is to be kept concealed.   290

◆

As lines 161–191 of this excerpt suggest, in African ritual celebration, the arts of music, dance, poetry, and decorative display formed a synthesis that mirrored shared spiritual and communal values (Figure 19.4). Similarly, within the African community, the telling of stories was a group enterprise and an expression of social unity. Seated around the communal fire, the members of the tribe recited tales serially and from memory. Traditionally, such tales were told only after sundown, because, as favored entertainments, they might otherwise distract the group from daily labor.

Among the many genres of African literature was the mythical tale that accounted for the origins of the universe, of the natural forces, and of the community. African creation myths—like those of the Hebrews, Egyptians, and Mesopotamians—explained the beginnings of the world, the creation of human beings, and the workings of nature, while still other myths dealt with the origin of death. The following brief examples, which come from three different parts of Africa, represent only a sampling of the many African tales that explain how death came into the world.

READING 3.20

Three African Myths on the Origin of Death

1

In the beginning, Nzambi slid down to earth on a rainbow, and there created the animals and the trees. After this he also created a man and a woman, and he told them to marry and have children. Nzambi imposed only one prohibition upon men, that they should not sleep when the moon was up. If they disobeyed this command, they would be punished with death. When the first man had become old and had poor eyesight, it once happened that the moon was veiled behind the clouds, so that he could not see it shine. He went to sleep and died in his sleep. Since then all men have died, because they are unable to keep awake when the moon is up.

(Lunda)

2

One day God asked the first human couple who then lived in heaven what kind of death they wanted, that of the moon or that of the banana. Because the couple wondered in dismay about the implications of the two modes of death, God explained to them: the banana puts forth shoots which take its place, and the moon itself comes back to life. The couple considered for a long time before they made their choice. If they elected to be childless they would avoid death, but they would also be very lonely, would themselves be forced to carry out all the work, and would not have anybody to work and strive for. Therefore they prayed to God for children, well aware of the consequences of their choice. And their prayer was granted. Since that time man's sojourn is short on this earth.

(Madagascar)

3

Formerly men had no fire but ate all their food raw. At that time they did not need to die for when they became old God made them young again. One day they decided to beg God for fire. They sent a messenger to God to convey their request. God replied to the messenger that he would give him fire if he was prepared to die. The man took the fire from God, but ever since then all men must die.

(Darasa, Gada)

◆

These myths offer valuable insights into ancient African culture. The directness with which the characters in these tales address the gods suggests the basic intimacy between Africans and the spirit world. Moreover, the tales stress human fallibility (as in the disastrous blunder of the nearly blind "first man"), rather than (as in most Christian literature) human sinfulness. They describe a gentle and casual, rather than a forbidding and patriarchal, relationship between divine and human realms. Finally, as the second myth suggests, Africans placed great value on their children; as was the case in most agricultural societies, children were prized as helpers and as perpetuators of tradition. One African proverb reads, "There is no wealth where there are no children"; another asserts, "Children are the wisdom of the nation."

Africans invented a huge and colorful literature of tales, proverbs, and riddles. The animal tale explains why certain creatures look and act as they do. In the trickster tale, a small animal, such as a hare or spider, outwits a larger one, such as a hyena or elephant. Explanatory tales treat such themes as "Why some people are good-looking" and "Why one never tells a woman the truth." African tales, proverbs, and riddles—often playfully swapped—functioned as sources of instruction and entertainment. Like most forms of African expression, they were characterized by animism: Consider, for instance, the riddle "who goes down the street and passes the king's house without greeting the king?" The answer is "rainwater." Many proverbs call attention to the immutability of nature's laws. One states, "When it rains, the roof always drips in the same way." Africans used their riddles and proverbs to help teach moral values and even to litigate tribal disputes.

African Poetry

In ancient Africa, religious rituals and rites of passage featured various kinds of chant. Performed by shamans and priests, but also by nonprofessionals, the chanting of poems, often integrated with mime and dance, created a unified texture not unlike that of modern rap and Afro-pop music. Poets addressed the fragility of human life, celebrated the transition from one stage of growth to another, honored the links between the living and the dead, praised heroes and rulers, and recounted the experiences of everyday life. African poetry does not share the satiric flavor of Roman verse, the erotic mood of Indian poetry, the intimate tone of the Petrarchan or Shakespearean sonnet, or the reclusive spirit of Chinese verse; it is, rather, a frank and intensely personal form of vocal music.

African poetry is characterized by strong percussive qualities, by **anaphora** (the repetition of a word or words at the beginning of two or more lines), and by tonal patterns that—much like Chinese poetry—are based on voice inflections. Repetition of key phrases and call-and-response "conversations" between narrator and listeners add texture to oral performance. The rhythmic energy and raw vitality of African poetry set it apart from most other kinds of world poetry, including Chinese, which seems controlled and intellectualized by comparison. The poem of praise for the *oba* of Benin, reproduced in Reading 3.21, throbs with rhythms that invite accompanying drumbeats or hand-clapping of the kind familiar to us in gospel singing and contemporary rock music. African poetry is also notable for its inventive similes and metaphors. In the Yoruba poem "The God of War," warfare is likened to a needle "that pricks at both ends," a vivid image of the perils of combat—compare the plainspoken ode "On Civil War" by the Roman poet Horace (see chapter 7). And in the "Song for the Sun," the Hottentot poet invents the memorable image of God collecting the stars and piling them into a basket "like a woman who collects lizards and piles them in her pot."

READING 3.21

Selections from African Poetry

Song for the Sun that Disappeared behind the Rainclouds

The fire darkens, the wood turns black.   1
The flame extinguishes, misfortune upon us.
God sets out in search of the sun.
The rainbow sparkles in his hand,
the bow of the divine hunter.   5
He has heard the lamentations of his children.
He walks along the milky way, he collects the stars.
With quick arms he piles them into a basket
piles them up with quick arms
like a woman who collects lizards   10
and piles them into her pot, piles them up
until the basket overflows with light.

(Hottentot)

Longing for Death

I have been singing, singing I have cried bitterly   1
I'm on my way.
How large this world!
Let the ferryman bring his boat
on the day of my death.   5
I'll wave with my left hand,
I'm on my way.
I'm on my way,
the boat of death is rocking near,
I'm on my way,   10
I who have sung you many songs.

(Ewe)

The Oba of Benin

He who knows not the Oba   1
let me show him.
He has mounted the throne,
he has piled a throne upon a throne.
Plentiful as grains of sand on the earth   5
are those in front of him.
Plentiful as grains of sand on the earth
are those behind him.
There are two thousand people
to fan him.   10
He who owns you
is among you here.
He who owns you
has piled a throne upon a throne.
He has lived to do it this year;   15
even so he will live to do it again.

(Bini)

The God of War

He kills on the right and destroys on the left.   1
He kills on the left and destroys on the right.
He kills suddenly in the house and suddenly in the field.
He kills the child with the iron with which it plays.
He kills in silence.   5
He kills the thief and the owner of the stolen goods.
He kills the owner of the slave—and the slave runs away.
He kills the owner of the house—and paints the hearth
    with his blood.
He is the needle that pricks at both ends.
He has water but he washes with blood.   10

(Yoruba)

The Poor Man

The poor man knows not how to eat with the rich man.   1
When they eat fish, he eats the head.

Invite a poor man and he rushes in
licking his lips and upsetting the plates.

The poor man has no manners, he comes along   5
with the blood of lice under his nails.

The face of the poor man is lined
from the hunger and thirst in his belly.

Poverty is no state for any mortal man.
It makes him a beast to be fed on grass.   10

Poverty is unjust. If it befalls a man,
though he is nobly born, he has no power with God.

(Swahili)

A Baby is a European

A baby is a European   1
he does not eat our food:
he drinks from his own water pot.

A baby is a European
he does not speak our tongue: 5
he is cross when the mother understands him not.

A baby is a European
he cares very little for others;
he forces his will upon his parents.

A baby is a European   10
he is always very sensitive:
the slightest scratch on his skin results in an ulcer.

(Ewe)

The Moon

The moon lights the earth   1
it lights the earth but still
the night must remain the night.
The night cannot be like the day.
The moon cannot dry our washing.   5
Just like a woman cannot be a man
just like black can never be white.

(Soussou)

————————————◆————————————

African Music and Dance

African music shares the vigorous rhythms of poetry and dance. In texture, it consists of a single line of melody without harmony. As with most African dialects, where pitch is important in conveying meaning, variations of musical effect derive from tonal inflection and timbre. The essentially communal spirit of African culture is reflected in the use of responsorial chants involving call-and-answer patterns similar to those of African poetry. The most compelling characteristic of African music, however, is its polyrhythmic structure. A single piece of music may simultaneously engage five to ten different rhythms, many of which are repeated over and over.[§] African dance, also communally performed, shares the distinctively dense polyrhythmic qualities of African music. The practice of playing "against" or "off" the main beat provided by the instruments is typical of much West African music and is preserved in the "off-beat" patterns of early modern jazz (see chapter 36).

A wide variety of percussion instruments, including various types of drums and rattles, are used in the performance of African poetry and dance. Also popular are the *balafo* (a type of xylophone), the *bolon* or *kora* (a large harp), and the *sansa* (an instrument consisting of a number of metal tongues attached to a small wooden soundboard). The latter two of these instruments, used to accompany storytelling, were believed to contain such potent supernatural power that they were considered dangerous and were outlawed among some African tribes, except for use by *griots*. Africa was the place of origin for the banjo, which (since bells, drums, and other instruments were forbidden) may have been the only musical instrument permitted on the slave ships that traveled across the Atlantic in the sixteenth century. African culture is notably musical, and the dynamic convergence of chant, dance, music, and bodily ornamentation generates a singularly dramatic experience that has a binding effect on the participants.

African Sculpture

Perhaps no other art prior to the twentieth century confronts the viewer as boldly as African art or speaks as directly to the subconscious. The twentieth-century Spanish master Pablo Picasso, who tried to capture in his own work the power of African art, referred to African sculptures as "magical things" (see chapter 32). Picasso perceived that African sculpture was of a magico-religious character, and that, like so much ancient and medieval art, it was inseparable from sacred ritual. Yet African sculpture has a fierce, forbidding

Figure 19.5 Bakota reliquary figure, from Gabon. Wood covered with strips of copper and brass. © Lee Boltin Picture Library, Crotin-on-Hudson, New York.

intensity that is not found in any art produced in the European West or, for that matter, in any other culture. This phenomenon is explained by the fact that most African art was designed to ward off evil or attract good—that is, to influence the spirit world or to channel supernatural energy. The Gabon-Bakota statue (Figure 19.5), which once stood above a container holding the bones of an ancestor, worked to guard and protect the dead from evil. It was not a symbol of occult power or (like the medieval reliquary) a representation of the deceased, but, rather, a **fetish**—that is, an object believed to have magical power. Perhaps for that reason, it resembles nothing in the ordinary world. Its aesthetic force derives from the unique synthesis of expressive abstraction, exaggeration, and distortion.

Most African sculpture is made of wood or, as in the case of Figure 19.5, wood covered with strips of metal. Using axes, knives, and chisels, professional sculptors carved their images from green or semidry timber. Rarely monumental in size, these objects still bear the rugged imprint of the artists' tools. And, like the trunks of the trees from which they were hewn, they are often rigid, tubular, and symmetrical (Figure 19.6). African artists respected and patronized the life force that resided within the medium. Wooden caryatid stools like that shown in Figure 19.6 translated the power of the female as source of life to the seated ruler. Feathers, shells, teeth, beads, raffia, hair, and other materials might be added to a fetish to increase textural contrast and enhance its vital powers (see Figure 19.4). And the surfaces of the fetish might be embellished with symbolic colors: red to represent danger, blood, and power; black to symbolize chaos and evil; and white to mean death.

African sculpture served in conjunction with ceremonies that channeled the spirits of ancestors, honored a **totem** (the heraldic emblem of the tribe, family, or clan), marked rites of passage, or operated to bring forth some special desired state. The Congo nail fetish (Figure 19.7)—a nineteenth-century example of the long tradition of African wood sculpture—was a power-object used by a healer-priest in a ritual that protected against evil spirits or attempted to cure (or inflict) disease.

Figure 19.6 Front and back of Kuba stool with caryatid, from Zaire. Wood and glass beads, height 23¼ in. © Lee Boltin Picture Library, Crotin-on-Hudson, New York.

 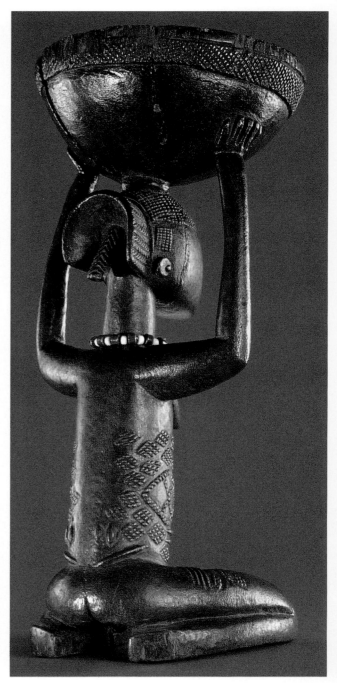

The act of driving a nail or sharp wedge into the figure was believed to invoke or liberate powers that, like the medicines the shaman inserted into the cavity ("stomach") of the figure, resided deep within. Both the nail fetish and the reliquary figure (see Figure 19.5), then, served to mediate between the sacred and profane worlds, to ward off evil and restore good.

African masks and headdresses, usually worn with elaborate cloth and fiber costumes, were essential to rituals of exorcism, initiation, purification, and burial. The mask not only disguised the wearer's identity; it also invited the spirit to enter the mask and make the wearer the agent of its supernatural power. A fetish, or power-object, the mask worked to transform the wearer. Religious rites and festivals of various cultures throughout the world—from ancient Greek Dionysian ceremonies to the Catholic Mardi Gras carnival—have featured the act of masking, usually as part of a larger performance of music and dance. Among the black Mardi Gras "Indians" of New Orleans, such traditions prevail to this day.

The people of Mali have long regarded the antelope as the mythical creature which taught humankind how to cultivate the land; hence, Mali rituals feature masks with huge crests for tribal dances whose movements imitate those of the antelope (see Figure 19.4). The antelope headpiece produced by the Bambara ancestors of the Mali people epitomizes the African taste for expressive simplification and geometric design (Figure 19.8). The triangular head of the beast is echoed in the chevron patterns of the neck and the zigzags of the mane. In the Songe mask (Figure 19.9), whose neck holes indicate that it was attached to some type of costume, expressive linear patterns recreate the effects of **scarification**: the process of incising the flesh (see also Figure 19.6). Scarification served as a form of identification or rank among some African tribes, but, somewhat like tattooing, it also had symbolic and aesthetic significance. In the Songe mask, the artist has distorted and exaggerated the features so as to compress emotion and energy and render the face dynamic and forbidding.

Not all African sculpture is as abstract as that from Gabon and Mali. Between the twelfth and seventeenth centuries, the royal craftsmen of Benin used the lost-wax method of bronze casting to produce realistic portraits (see Figures 19.2, 19.3). Often placed on altars that honored the spirit of a deceased *oba*, the Benin bronzes had both commemorative and ritual functions. Though many bronze, terra-cotta, gold, and ivory sculptures have outlasted the oldest African cultures, few examples in wood survive from before the nineteenth century. Eleventh-century Arab chronicles confirm, however, that the rich tradition of wood sculpture evidenced in the artworks illustrated here reaches far back into earlier African history.

Figure 19.7 Congo nail fetish, 1875–1900. Wood with screws, nails, blades, cowrie shell, and other material, height 3 ft. 10 in. Photograph © 1997 The Detroit Institute of Arts. Founders Society Purchase, Eleanor Clay Ford Fund for African Art. 76.79.

Figure 19.8 Bambara antelope headpiece, from Mali. Wood, height 35¾ in., width 15¾ in. The Metropolitan Museum of Art, New York. The Michael C. Rockefeller Memorial Collection of Primitive Art. Gift of Nelson A. Rockefeller, 1964 (1978.412.435.436).

African Architecture

As with the sculpture of ancient Africa, little survives of African architecture from past centuries, and that which does suggests a wide diversity of structural forms. A survey of traditional African house forms lists almost three dozen different types of structure. Construction materials consist of mud, stones, and brushwood, or adobe brick—a sun-dried mixture of clay and straw. At the tribal level of social organization, Africans seem to have had little need for permanent religious or administrative buildings. But at the ancient trade center of Zimbabwe, in South Central Africa, where a powerful kingdom developed before the year 1000, the remains of huge stone walls and towers indicate the presence of a royal residence or palace complex.

If rural Africans confirmed their sense of community in ways other than the construction of monumental architecture, urban Africans in Muslim-dominated cities built some of the most visually striking structures in the history of world architecture. The adobe mosques of Mali, for instance, with their bulging, organic contours, bulbous towers, and egglike finials (native symbols of fertility) resemble fantastic sand castles (see Figure 19.1). They have proved to be almost as impermanent: Some have been rebuilt (and replastered) continuously since the twelfth century, hence their walls and towers bristle with sticks or wooden beams that provide a permanent scaffolding for restoration. African mosques are testimonials to the fusion of Muslim and local ancestral traditions. Domical mounds that resemble the primordial mountain and womblike shapes of most ancient temples and shrines (see chapters 1 and 9), these vernacular structures call to mind the eternal link between Mother Earth and the human community. Even the wooden pickets that serve as scaffolding have a sacred significance: Used at Bambara initiation ceremonies and often buried with the dead, such tree branches are symbols of rebirth and regeneration.

Cross-Cultural Encounter

Ibn Battuta in West Africa

Islam was present in West Africa from at least the eighth century, and the religion increased in influence as Muslims came to dominate trans-Saharan trade. Although occasional efforts to spread Islam by force were generally unsuccessful, the Islamization of the Sudan ultimately succeeded as the result of the peaceful and prosperous activities of Muslim merchants, administrators, and scholars. Mali's most famous ruler, Mansa ("King") Musa (1312–1337), came to symbolize the largesse of the African Muslim elite when, during his *hajj* of 1324, he and his retinue scattered large amounts of gold from Mali to Mecca. West African rulers like Musa patronized the arts, commissioned the construction of mosques, and encouraged conversion to Islam.

Nowhere in the literature of the age are the realities of cross-cultural encounter so well expressed as in the journal of the fourteenth-century Muslim traveler-scholar, Ibn Battuta (1304–1369). Born into an upper-class Muslim family in the North African city of Tangier,

Figure 19.9 Songe mask, from Zaire. Wood and paint, height 17 in. The Metropolitan Museum of Art, New York. The Michael C. Rockefeller Memorial Collection of Primitive Art. Bequest of Nelson A. Rockefeller, 1979 (1979.206.83).

Battuta was educated in law and Arabic literature before he made the first of his seven pilgrimages in 1325. Over the course of his lifetime, this inveterate tourist journeyed on foot or by camel caravan some 75,000 miles, visiting parts of China, Indonesia, Persia, India, Burma, Spain, Arabia, Russia, Asia Minor, Egypt, and East and West Africa. Although his initial motives for travel were religious, he shared with other itinerant Muslim scholars an interest in Islamic law and a curiosity concerning the customs of Muslim communities throughout the world. In 1354, Battuta narrated the history of his travels, including his two-year trip from Morocco to Mali—his last recorded journey—to a professional scribe who recorded it in a *ribla* ("book of travels"). That portion of the *ribla* which recounts Battuta's visit to Mali is the only existing eyewitness account of the kingdom at the height of its power. It documents Battuta's keen powers of observation and his efforts to evaluate social and cultural practices that differed sharply from his own.

READING 3.22
From Ibn Battuta's *Book of Travels*

. . . We reached the city of Īwālātan¹ at the beginning   1
of the month of Rabi'I² after a journey of two full months
from Sijilmāsa. It is the first district of the country of the
Blacks. . . .

When we arrived the merchants deposited their goods
in an open space and the Blacks took responsibility for
them. The merchants went to the Farbā who was sitting
on a rug under a shelter; his officials were in front of him
with spears and bows in their hands. The Massūfa³
notables were behind him. The merchants stood in front   10
of him and he spoke to them through an interpreter as a
sign of his contempt for them, although they were close
to him. At this I was sorry I had come to their country,
because of their bad manners and contempt for white
people. I made for the house of the Ibn Baddā', a kind
man of Salā to whom I had written asking him to let⁴ a
house to me, which he did. . . .

. . . I stayed in Īwālātan about fifty days. Its people
treated me with respect and gave me hospitality. Among
them were the qāḍī⁵ of the town Muḥammad b. 'Abdallāh   20
b. Yanūmar, and his brother the jurist and professor
Yaḥyā. The town of Īwālātan is extremely hot. There are a
few small palms and they sow melons in their shade.
Water comes from underground sources. Mutton is
plentiful. Their clothes are of fine quality and Egyptian
origin. Most of the inhabitants belong to the Massūfa.
The women are of outstanding beauty and are more
highly regarded than the men.

Conditions among these people are remarkable and
their life style is strange. The men have no jealousy. No   30
one takes his name from his father, but from his maternal
uncle. Sons do not inherit, only sister's sons!⁶ This is
something I have seen nowhere in the world except
among the infidel Indians of al-Mulāibar. Nevertheless
these people are Muslims. They are strict in observing the
prayers, studying the religious law, and memorizing the
Qur'ān. Their women have no shame before men and do
not veil themselves, yet they are punctilious about their
prayers. Anyone who wants to take a wife among them
does so, but they do not travel with their husbands, and   40
even if one of them wished to, her family would prevent
her. Women there have friends and companions among
men outside the prohibited degrees for marriage, and in
the same way men have women friends in the same
category. A man goes into his house, finds his wife with
her man friend, and does not disapprove.

One day I called upon the qāḍī at Īwālātan after he had
given permission for me to enter. I found him with a
young and exceptionally beautiful woman. When I saw her
I hesitated and was going to go back, but she laughed at   50
me and showed no embarrassment. The qāḍī said to me:
"Why are you turning back? She is my friend." I was
astonished at them, for he was a jurist and a Ḥājj.⁷ I

¹Near Timbuktu in Mali.   ²April 1352.
³A Berber people of the Western Sahara.   ⁴Rent.
⁵Muslim judges.   ⁶In the matrilineal sub-Saharan tribes, the
mother's brother is considered the most important male.
⁷One who has made the pilgrimage to Mecca.

learnt that he had asked the Sultan's permission to go on pilgrimage that year with his female companion. I do not know whether this was the one or not, but permission was not given.

One day I called on Abū Muḥammad Yandakān al-Massūfi, in whose company we had arrived, and found him sitting on a rug. In the middle of the room was a 60 canopied couch and upon it was a woman with a man sitting and talking together. I said to him: "Who is this woman?" He said: "She is my wife." I said: "What about the man who is with her?" He said: "He is her friend." I said: "Are you happy about this, you who have lived in our country and know the content of the religious law?" He said: "The companionship of women and men among us is a good thing and an agreeable practice, which causes no suspicion; they are not like the women of your country." I was astonished at his silliness. I left him and 70 did not visit him again. Afterwards he invited me a number of times but I did not accept. . . .

The Blacks are the most respectful of people to their king and abase themselves most before him. . . . If he summons one of them at his session in the cupola we have mentioned, the man summoned removes his robe and puts on a shabby one, takes off his turban, puts on a dirty skull-cap and goes in with his robe and his trousers lifted half way to his knees. He comes forward humbly and abjectly, and strikes the ground hard with his 80 elbows. He stands as if he were prostrating himself in prayer, and hears what the Sultan says like this. If one of them speaks to the Sultan and he answers him, he takes his robe off his back, and throws dust on his head and back like someone making his ablutions with water. I was astonished that they did not blind themselves.

When the Sultan makes a speech in his audience those present take off their turbans from their heads and listen in silence. Sometimes one of them stands before him, recounts what he has done for his service, and says: 90 "On such and such a day I did such and such, and I killed so and so on such and such a day." Those who know vouch for the truth of that and he does it in this way. One of them draws the string of his bow, then lets it go as he would do if he were shooting. If the Sultan says to him: "You are right" or thanks him, he takes off his robe and pours dust on himself. That is good manners among them. . . .

Among their good practices are their avoidance of injustice; there is no people more averse to it, and their 100 Sultan does not allow anyone to practise it in any measure; the universal security in their country, for neither the traveller nor the resident there has to fear thieves or bandits; they do not interfere with the property of white men who die in their country, even if it amounts to vast sums; they just leave it in the hands of a trustworthy white man until whoever is entitled to it takes possession of it; their punctiliousness in praying, their perseverance in joining the congregation, and in compelling their children to do so; if a man does not 110 come early to the mosque he will not find a place to pray because of the dense crowd; it is customary for each man to send his servant with his prayer-mat to spread it out in a place reserved for him until he goes to the mosque himself; their prayer-mats are made of the leaves of a tree like the date-palm, but which has no fruit. They dress in clean white clothes on Fridays; if one of them has only a threadbare shirt he washes it and cleans it and wears it for prayer on Friday. They pay great attention to memorizing the Holy Qur'ān. If their children 120 appear to be backward in learning it they put shackles on them and do not remove them till they learn it. I called on the qāḍī on the Feast Day. His children were in shackles. I said to him: "Are you not going to free them?" He said: "Not till they learn the Qur'ān by heart." One day I passed by a handsome youth, who was very well dressed, with a heavy shackle on his foot. I said to the person with me: "What has he done? Has he killed someone?" The youth understood what I said and laughed. I was told: "He has been shackled to make him 130 memorize the Qur'ān."

Among their bad practices are that the women servants, slave-girls and young daughters appear naked before people, exposing their genitals. I used to see many like this in Ramaḍān,[8] for it is customary for the farārīs[9] to break the fast in the Sultan's palace, where their food is brought to them by twenty or more slave-girls, who are naked. Women who come before the Sultan are naked and unveiled, and so are his daughters. On the night of the twenty-seventh of Ramaḍān I have 140 seen about a hundred naked slave-girls come out of his palace with food; with them were two daughters of the Sultan with full breasts and they too had no veil. They put dust and ashes on their heads as a matter of good manners. There is the clowning we have described when poets recite their works. Many of them eat carrion, dogs and donkeys. . . .[10]

————————◆————————

The Europeans in Africa

European commercial activity in Africa was the product of the quest for better trade routes to the East, and for the markets in gold, salt, and slaves that had long made Africa a source of wealth for Muslim merchants. During the sixteenth century, Portugal intruded upon the well-established Muslim-dominated trans-Saharan commercial slave trade. The Portuguese slave trade in West Africa, the Congo, and elsewhere developed in agreement with local leaders such as the Benin, who reaped profits from supplying to the Europeans the victims of African wars or raids into the interior of the country. By the year 1500, the Portuguese controlled the flow of both gold and slaves to Europe. Transatlantic slave trade commenced in 1551, when the Portuguese began to ship thousands of slaves from Africa to work in the sugar plantations of Brazil, a "New World" territory claimed by Portugal. European forms of slavery were more brutal and exploitative than any previously practiced in Africa: Slaves shipped overseas were branded,

---

[8]The Muslim month of fasting; the daily fast ends at sunset.
[9]Chiefs.   [10]The Quran forbids the eating of unclean meat.

Figure 19.10 Benin plaque showing a Portuguese warrior surrounded by *manillas* (horseshoe-shaped metal objects used as a medium of exchange), from Nigeria, sixteenth century. Bronze. Museum für Volkerkunde, Vienna.

shackled in chains like beasts, underfed, and—if they survived the ravages of dysentery and disease—conscripted into oppressive kinds of physical labor (see chapter 25).

In their relations with the African states, especially those in coastal areas, the Europeans were equally brutal. They often ignored local laws and customs, pressured Africans to adopt European language and dress, and fostered economic rivalry. While in a spirit of missionary zeal and altruism they introduced Christianity and Western forms of education, they also brought ruin to some tribal kingdoms, and, in parts of Africa, they almost completely destroyed native black cultural life. These activities were but a prelude to the more disastrous

forms of exploitation that prevailed during the seventeenth and eighteenth centuries, when the transatlantic slave trade, now dominated by the Dutch, the French, and the English, reached massive proportions. Between the years 1600 and 1700, the number of Africans taken captive may have reached over one million.

Considering the repeated intrusion of outsiders over the centuries, it is remarkable that local traditions in the arts of Africa have continued to flourish. Indeed, although the Portuguese and other Europeans to a great extent determined the course of African history (Figure **19.10**), neither Western European styles nor Western forms of artistic expression would eclipse the unique characteristics of native African art, literature, and music.

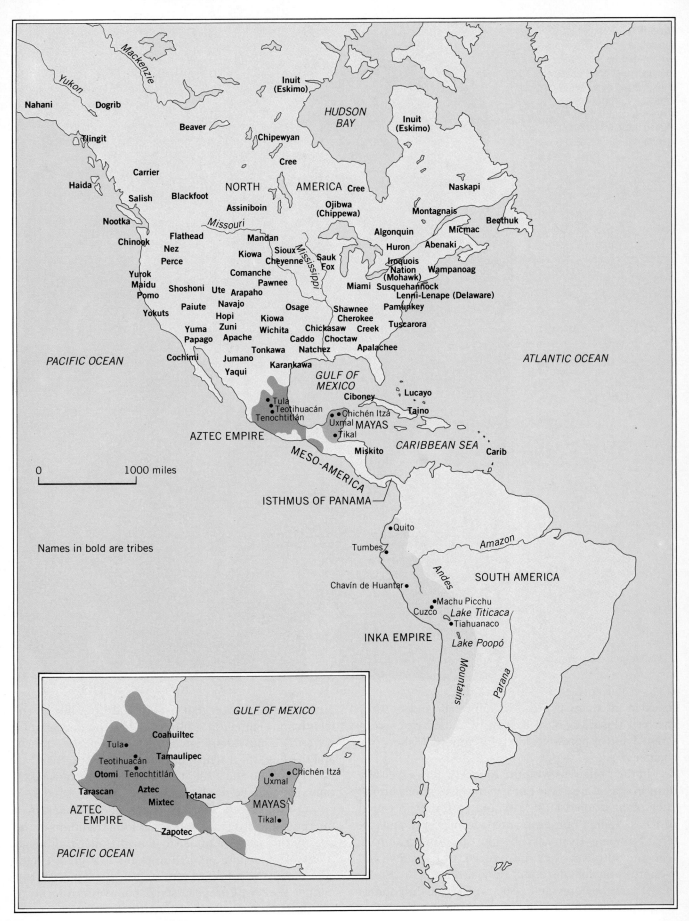

Map 19.3 The Americas Before 1500.

Names in bold are tribes

0 ——— 1000 miles

The Americas

Native American Cultures

Native cultures in the territories of North, Central, and South America began to develop at least twenty thousand years ago, following nomadic migrations of Asians across a land bridge that once linked Siberia and Alaska at the Bering Strait. Migrant populations then split into various groups that developed different ethnic and linguistic patterns. During the second millennium B.C.E., these migrant people established tribal communities throughout the Americas (Map 19.3). Like the ancient Africans, the Native Americans were culturally diverse; and although these cultures developed independently of each other over a period of many centuries, Africans and Native Americans held in common a strong sense of communion with nature and deeply felt tribal loyalties.

In the five centuries prior to the first European contacts with the Americas, some one thousand individual tribal societies flourished. And although many produced illustrious histories, only a few achieved the status of empire. In Middle (or Meso-) America (principally the Mexican highlands and Guatemala) and on the western coast of South America, villages grew into states that conquered or absorbed their rivals. Settlers of essentially tropical areas, these were agricultural peoples who traded only regionally and made frequent war on each other. Although after the ninth century copper came into use in Meso-America, iron was unknown until the arrival of the Spaniards in the fifteenth century. Most Native Americans fashioned their tools and weapons out of wood, stone, bone, and bits of volcanic glass. They had no draft animals and no wheeled vehicles. These facts make all the more remarkable the material achievements of the Maya, Inka, and Aztec civilizations, all three of which developed into empires of considerable authority in the pre-Columbian era.

The largest and most complex Native American states were theocratic: Rulers governed on behalf of the gods and rule was hereditary. An elite cadre of priests oversaw the spiritual life of the community—a population consisting of farmers and artisans at the lower end of the class structure and a ruling nobility at the upper end. In that the sun gave life to the crops, its sacred presence was honored over all other natural forces. Meso-Americans believed that the sun god was a fearsome deity with a special appetite for human blood. Since the blood of warriors was thought to nourish the sun and ensure its daily course in the sky (thus saving the world from destruction), human sacrifice was central to religious ritual. The idea that human blood

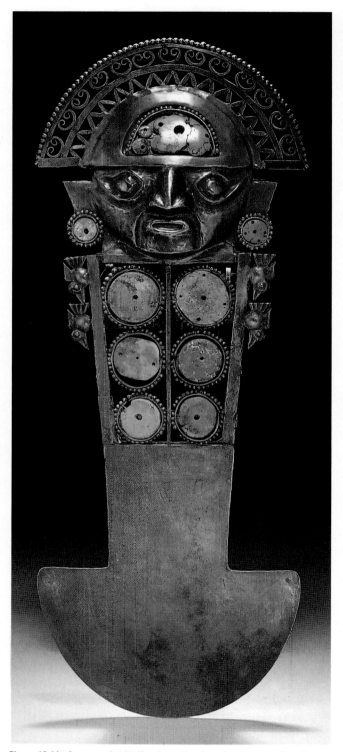

Figure 19.11 Ceremonial knife, from the Lambayeque valley, Peru, ninth to eleventh centuries. Hammered gold with turquoise inlay, 13 × 5⅛ in. The Metropolitan Museum of Art, New York. The Jan Mitchell Treasury for Precolumbian works of art in gold (1991.419.58).

provided food for the gods is a vivid example of the powerful sense of interdependence between earthly and spiritual realms. While blood served to feed the gods, gold—thought to contain the brightness and hence the power of the sun—served to glorify the authority of the ruler. And although sixteenth-century Europeans melted down or carried off much of the native gold, extant pieces from Mexico, Ecuador, and Peru suggest that goldworking was one of the technical specialties of Native American artists (Figure **19.11**).

The Arts of Native America

A holistic and animistic view of nature, similar to that held among Africans, characterizes Native American culture. Like the people of Africa, Native Americans perceive the world as infused with natural spirits, which they seek to influence by means of rituals and fetish objects. The Hopi people of Arizona still produce small wooden *kachinas* ("spirit beings") for the purpose of channeling supernatural powers (Figure **19.12**). These "dolls" are also given to children in order to familiarize them with the tribal gods. Masks, bowls, rattles, and charms picture gods and mythological heroes whose powers are sought in healing ceremonies and other sacred rites. Weaving, beadwork, pottery, and jewelry-making remain among the most technical and highly-prized of Native American crafts. The Haida folk of the Queen Charlotte Islands, located near British Columbia, have revived the ancient practice of raising wooden poles carved and painted with *totems*—that is, heraldic family symbols that served as powerful expressions of social status, spiritual authority, and ancestral pride. The Haida and Tlingit peoples of the Northwest Coast make portrait masks of spirits and ancestors whose powers help their shamans to cure the sick and predict events (Figure **19.13**). Tlingit dance masks and clan helmets—which, like African masks, draw on the natural elements of wood, human hair and teeth, animal fur, seashell, and feathers—capture the metamorphic vitality of Northwest Coast creatures such as the raven (see Reading 3.24).

In various parts of the American Southwest, Native Americans built elaborate towns, called "pueblos" by the Spaniards. Between the eighth and fifteenth centuries, the Anasazi (a Navajo word meaning "ancient ones") constructed multistory adobe structures with many rooms, storage areas, and underground ceremonial centers called *kivas*. Large enough to hold all of the male members of the community (women were not generally invited to attend sacred ceremonies), *kivas* served as cosmic symbols of the underworld from which the first humans emerged and as circular theaters for rites designed to maintain harmony with nature. The Cliff Palace at Mesa Verde, Colorado, positioned under

Figure 19.12 Hopi peoples, *Zuni Warrior Kachina*, from Arizona, ca. 1930. Wood, pigment, feathers, cotton, and yucca fiber, 18 × 11¼ in. Collection of New Orleans Museum of Art. Gift of Emerson Woelffer in memory of his wife Dina. 91.341.

an overhanging cliff and occupied between the eleventh and thirteenth centuries, is one of the largest cliff dwellings in America (Figure **19.14**). Its inhabitants—an estimated 250 people—engineered the tasks of quarrying sandstone, cutting logs (for beams and posts), and hauling water, sand, and clay (for the adobe core structure) entirely without the aid of wheeled vehicles, draft animals, or metal tools.

The pueblo tribes of the American Southwest, including the Anasazi and the Mimbres people who preceded them, produced some of the most elegant ceramic wares in the history of North American art. Lacking the potter's wheel, women handbuilt vessels for domestic and ceremonial uses. They embellished jars and bowls with designs that vary from a stark, geometric abstraction to stylized human, animal, and plant forms. One Mimbres bowl shows a rabbit-man carrying a basket on his back (Figure **19.15**): The shape of the creature, which subtly blends human and animal features, works harmoniously with the curves of the bowl and animates the negative space that surrounds the image. Mimbres pottery—usually pierced or ritually "killed" before being placed with its owner in the grave—testifies to the rich imagination and sophisticated artistry of pueblo culture.

Figure 19.13 Maskette representing a dying man, from a headdress worn in the healing ceremony, ca. 1850. Spruce, human hair, teeth of operculum, height approx. 6 in. American Museum of Natural History, New York. Photo: © McMichael Canadian Collection, Kleinburg, Ontario.

Native American religious rituals, like those of all ancient societies, blended poetry, music, and dance. The sun dance was a principal part of the annual ceremony that celebrated seasonal renewal. In the Navajo tribal community of the American Southwest, the shaman still conducts the healing ceremony known as the Night Chant.[§] Beginning at sunset and ending some nine days later at sunrise, the Night Chant calls for a series of meticulously executed sand paintings and the recitation of song cycles designed to remove evil and restore good. Characterized by monophonic melody and hypnotic repetition, the Night Chant is performed to the accompaniment of whistles and percussive instruments such as gourd rattles, drums, and rasps. Its compelling rhythms are evident in both the Music Listening Selection and in the "Prayer of the Night Chant" reproduced below. Rituals like the Night Chant are not mere curiosities but, rather, living practices that remain sacred to the Navajo people.

[§]See Music Listening Selections at end of chapter.

READING 3.23

"A Prayer of the Night Chant" (Navajo)

Tségihi.   1
House made of dawn.
House made of evening light.
House made of the dark cloud.
House made of male rain.   5
House made of dark mist.
House made of female rain.
House made of pollen.
House made of grasshoppers.
Dark cloud is at the door.   10
The trail out of it is dark cloud.
The zigzag lightning stands high upon it.
Male deity!
Your offering I make.
I have prepared a smoke for you.   15
Restore my feet for me.
Restore my legs for me.
Restore my body for me.
Restore my mind for me.
This very day take out your spell for me.   20
Your spell remove for me.
You have taken it away for me.
Far off it has gone.
Happily I recover.
Happily my interior becomes cool.   25
Happily I go forth.
My interior feeling cool, may I walk.
No longer sore, may I walk.
Impervious to pain, may I walk.
With lively feelings may I walk.   30
As it used to be long ago, may I walk.
Happily may I walk.
Happily, with abundant dark clouds, may I walk.
Happily, with abundant showers, may I walk.
Happily, with abundant plants, may I walk.   35
Happily, on a trail of pollen, may I walk.
Happily may I walk.
Being as it used to be long ago, may I walk.
May it be beautiful before me.
May it be beautiful behind me.   40
May it be beautiful below me.
May it be beautiful above me.
May it be beautiful all around me.
In beauty it is finished.

———————◆———————

Myths and folktales, transmitted orally for generations (and only recorded since the seventeenth century), feature themes that call to mind those of Africa. Creation myths, myths of destruction (or death), and myths that describe the way things are served to provide explanations of the workings of nature. Usually told by men who passed them down to boys, myths and tales

Figure 19.14 (opposite) Cliff Palace, Mesa Verde, Colorado, inhabited 1073–1272. Photo: Werner Forman Archive, London.

Figure 19.15 Classic Mimbres bowl showing rabbit-man with burden basket, from Cameron Creek village, New Mexico, 1000–1150. Black-on-white pottery, height 4⅜ in., diameter 10¾ in. Museum of Indian Arts and Culture/Laboratory of Anthropology, Santa Fe, New Mexico. Cat. 20420/11. Photo: Blair Clark.

often traveled vast distances, and, thus, may appear in many variant versions. As with African folklore, Native American myths feature heroes or heroines who work to transform nature; the heroes/tricksters may themselves be humans who are transformed into ravens, spiders, coyotes, wolves, or rabbits (see Figure 19.15). As with the African trickster tale, which usually points to a moral, the Native American trickster story means to teach or explain; nonetheless, heroes whose strategies involve deceit and cunning are often held in high regard.

READING 3.24

Two Native American Tales

How the Sun Came

There was no light anywhere, and the animal people   1
stumbled around in the darkness. Whenever one bumped
into another, he would say, "What we need in the world
is light." And the other would reply, "Yes, indeed, light is
what we badly need."
    At last, the animals called a meeting, and gathered
together as well as they could in the dark. The red-
headed woodpecker said, "I have heard that over on the
other side of the world there are people who have light."
    "Good, good!" said everyone.   10
    "Perhaps if we go over there, they will give us some
light," the woodpecker suggested.
    "If they have all the light there is," the fox said, "they
must be greedy people, who would not want to give any
of it up. Maybe we should just go there and take the
light from them."

"Who shall go?" cried everyone, and the animals all began talking at once, arguing about who was strongest and ran fastest, who was best able to go and get the light.

Finally, the 'possum said, "I can try. I have a fine big bushy tail, and I can hide the light inside my fur." 20

"Good! Good!" said all the others, and the 'possum set out.

As he traveled eastward, the light began to grow and grow, until it dazzled his eyes, and the 'possum screwed his eyes up to keep out the bright light. Even today, if you notice, you will see that the 'possum's eyes are almost shut, and that he comes out of his house only at night.

All the same, the 'possum kept going, clear to the other side of the world, and there he found the sun. He 30 snatched a little piece of it and hid it in the fur of his fine, bushy tail, but the sun was so hot it burned off all the fur, and by the time the 'possum got home his tail was as bare as it is today.

"Oh, dear!" everyone said. "Our brother has lost his fine, bushy tail, and still we have no light."

"I'll go," said the buzzard. "I have better sense than to put the sun on my tail. I'll put it on my head."

So the buzzard traveled eastward till he came to the place where the sun was. And because the buzzard flies 40 so high, the sun-keeping people did not see him, although now they were watching out for thieves. The buzzard dived straight down out of the sky, the way he does today, and caught a piece of the sun in his claws. He set the sun on his head and started for home, but the sun was so hot that it burned off all his head feathers, and that is why the buzzard's head is bald today.

Now the people were in despair. "What shall we do? What shall we do?" they cried. "Our brothers have tried hard; they have done their best, everything a man can 50 do. What else shall we do so we can have light?"

"They have done the best a man can do," said a little voice from the grass, "but perhaps this is something a woman can do better than a man."

"Who are you?" everyone asked. "Who is that speaking in a tiny voice and hidden in the grass?"

"I am your Grandmother Spider," she replied. "Perhaps I was put in the world to bring you light. Who knows? At least I can try, and if I am burned up it will still not be as if you had lost one of your great warriors." 60

Then Grandmother Spider felt around her in the darkness until she found some damp clay. She rolled it in her hands, and molded a little clay bowl. She started eastward, carrying her bowl, and spinning a thread behind her so she could find her way back.

When Grandmother Spider came to the place of the sun people, she was so little and so quiet no one noticed her. She reached out gently, gently, and took a tiny bit of the sun, and placed it in her clay bowl. Then she went back along the thread that she had spun, with the sun's 70 light growing and spreading before her, as she moved from east to west. And if you will notice, even today a spider's web is shaped like the sun's disk and its rays, and the spider will always spin her web in the morning, very early, before the sun is fully up.

"Thank you, Grandmother," the people said when she returned. "We will always honor you and we will always remember you."

And from then on pottery making became woman's work, and all pottery must be dried slowly in the shade 80 before it is put in the heat of the firing oven, just as Grandmother Spider's bowl dried in her hand, slowly, in the darkness, as she traveled toward the land of the sun.

(Cheyenne)

Raven and the Moon

One day Raven learnt that an old fisherman, living alone 1 with his daughter on an island far to the north, had a box containing a bright light called the moon. He felt that he must get hold of this wonderful thing, so he changed himself into a leaf growing on a bush near to the old fisherman's home. When the fisherman's daughter came to pick berries from the wild fruit patch, she pulled at the twig on which the leaf stood and it fell down and entered into her body. In time a child was born, a dark-complexioned boy with a long, hooked nose, almost like 10 a bird's bill. As soon as the child could crawl, he began to cry for the moon. He would knock at the box and keep calling, "Moon, moon, shining moon."

At first nobody paid any attention, but as the child became more vocal and knocked harder at the box, the old fisherman said to his daughter, "Well, perhaps we should give the boy the ball of light to play with." The girl opened the box and took out another box, and then another, from inside that. All the boxes were beautifully painted and carved, and inside the tenth there was a net 20 of nettle thread. She loosened this and opened the lid of the innermost box. Suddenly light filled the lodge, and they saw the moon inside the box; bright, round like a ball, shining white. The mother threw it towards her baby son and he caught and held it so firmly they thought he was content. But after a few days he began to fuss and cry again. His grandfather felt sorry for him and asked the mother to explain what the child was trying to say. So his mother listened very carefully and explained that he wanted to look out at the sky and see the stars in the 30 dark sky, but that the roof board over the smoke hole prevented him from doing so. So the old man said, "Open the smoke hole." No sooner had she opened the hole than the child changed himself back into the Raven. With the moon in his bill he flew off. After a moment he landed on a mountain top and then threw the moon into the sky where it remains, still circling in the heavens where Raven threw it.

(Northwest Coast)

———————◆———————

Maya Civilization

The most inventive of the ancient Native American peoples were the Maya, whose civilization reached the classic phase between 250 and 900 C.E. and survived with considerable political and economic vigor until roughly 1600. At sites in Southern Mexico, Honduras, Guatemala, and the Yucatán Peninsula, the Maya constructed fortified cities consisting of elaborate palace complexes that are hauntingly reminiscent of those

Figure 19.16 Reconstruction drawing of post-classic Maya fortress city of Chutixtiox, Quiche, Guatemala, ca. 1000, from Richard Adams, *Prehistoric Mesoamerica*. Boston: Little Brown, 1977.

Figure 19.17 Castillo, Chichén Itzá, Yucatán, Mexico. © Lee Boltin Picture Library, Crotin-on-Hudson, New York.

from ancient Mesopotamia (Figure **19.16**; see chapter 3). Like the Mesopotamian ziggurat (see chapter 2), the Maya temple was a terraced pyramid with a staircase ascending to a platform on which stood a shrine capped with a sculpted crest (Figure **19.17**).

A shrine and sanctuary that might also serve as a burial place for priests or rulers, the Maya temple was the physical link between earth and the heavens. On the limestone facades of temples and palaces, the Maya carved and painted scenes of religious ceremonies and war, as well as images of their gods: Tlaloc, the long-snouted rain deity, and Quetzalcoatl, the feathered serpent and legendary hero-god of Meso-America (Figure **19.18**). A key feature of almost all Meso-American sacred precincts was the ballpark. It was used for the performance of ceremonial games played by two teams of nine to eleven men each. The object of the game was to propel a five-pound rubber ball through the stone rings at either side of a high-walled court. Members of the losing team lost more than glory: They were sacrificed to the sun god, their hearts torn from their bodies on ritual altars adjacent to the court.

Maya pride in the power of individual leaders is conveyed by the confident stance, upturned head, and ritually scarified face of a ceramic warrior from the late classic period (Figure 19.19). The full-figured portrait, which combines realistic detail and powerful idealization, testifies to the Maya genius for uniting representational and symbolic modes of expression.

The Maya were the only known Stone Age culture to produce a written language. This ancient script, comprised of hieroglyphs, was decoded during the second half of the twentieth century. Indeed, only since 1995 have the glyphs been recognized as a system of phonetic signs that operate like spoken syllables*—a discovery made, in part, by studying the living language of modern-day descendants of the Maya who inhabit the Guatemalan highlands and the Yucatán. Despite the survival of some codices and many stone inscriptions, nearly all of the literary evidence of this people was destroyed during the sixteenth century by Spanish missionaries and colonial settlers. Perhaps the most important source of Meso-American mythology, however,

*See Michael D. Coe, *Breaking the Maya Code*. London: Thames and Hudson, 1995.

Figure 19.18 Facade of the late classic Maya temple called "the Nunnery," Uxmal, Yucatán, Mexico, 600–1000 C.E. Photo: Ancient Art and Architecture Collection, Middlesex, U.K.

Figure 19.19 Late classic Maya warrior, 700–900 C.E. Ceramic. Denver Art Museum, Acquisition #1969.308.

survives in the form of an oral narrative transcribed into Spanish by a sixteenth-century Maya nobleman. This narrative, known as the *Popol Vuh* (see chapter 1), recounts the creation of the world. According to the Maya, the gods fashioned human beings out of maize— the principal Native American crop—but chose deliberately to deprive them of perfect understanding. As if to challenge the gods, the Maya became accomplished mathematicians and astronomers. Carefully observing the earth's movements around the sun, they devised a calendar that was more accurate than any used in medieval Europe before the twelfth century. Having developed a mathematical system that recognized "zero," they computed planetary and celestial cycles

1500	Maya in the Yucatán utilize vegetable-based molds to treat wounds and infections
1568	Gerhard Kremen (Flemish) produces the first Mercator projection map
1596	Korean naval architects launch the first ironclad warship

with some accuracy, tracked the paths of Venus, Jupiter, and Saturn, and successfully predicted eclipses of the sun and moon. They recorded their findings in stone, on the limestone-covered bark pages of codices and on the facades of temples, some of which may have functioned as planetary observatories. At the principal pyramid at Chichén Itzá in the Yucatán (see Figure 19.17), the ninety-one steps on each of four sides, plus the platform on which the temple stands, correspond to the 365 calendar days. According to the Maya, the planets (and segments of time itself) were ruled by gods, usually represented in Maya art as men and women carrying burdens on their shoulders. The Maya and the various Meso-American peoples that followed them believed in the cyclical creation and destruction of the world, and they prudently entrusted the sacred mission of time-keeping to their priests.

The Empires of the Inkas and the Aztecs

In 1000 C.E., the Inkas were only one of many small warring peoples but, by the fifteenth century, they had become the mightiest power in South America. Indeed, at its height in the late fifteenth century, the Inka settlement consisted of an astounding sixteen million individuals. Located amidst the mountains of the Andes in Peru, the Inka flourished in the rich soils of earlier Peruvian cultures noted for their fine pottery, richly woven textiles (Figure 19.20), and sophisticated goldwork (see Figure 19.11). Like that of ancient Rome, Inkan civilization imposed its political might, its gods, and its customs over lands that extended almost three thousand miles from present-day Ecuador to Chile (see Map 19.3).

Small by comparison with the Inka civilization, that of the Aztecs—the last of the great Meso-American

Figure 19.20 Tapestry weave Inka tunic, from the south coast of Peru, 1440–1540. Camelid fiber and cotton, 35⅞ × 30 in. Dumbarton Oaks Research Library and Collections, Washington, D.C.

Figure 19.21 Aztec peoples, *Coatlique, Mother of the Gods*. Photo: Ancient Art and Architecture Collection, Middlesex, U.K.

practice of blood sacrifice to the staggering numbers of victims captured in their incessant wars. They preserved the native Meso-American traditions of temple construction, ceramics, weaving, metalwork, and stone-carving. During the fifteenth century, the Aztecs raised to new heights the art of monumental stone sculpture, carving great basalt statues that ranged from austere, realistic portraits to ornate, abstract, and terrifying icons of gods and goddesses such as Coatlique, Lady of the Skirt of Serpents and ancient earth mother of the gods (Figure 19.21). Shaped like a mountain, "she-of-the-serpent-skirt" bears a head consisting of two snakes, clawed hands and feet, and a necklace of excised hearts and severed hands. Renaissance Europeans, whose idea of female divinity was shaped by Raphael's gentle madonnas, found these usually blood-drenched "idols" outrageous and destroyed as many as they could find.

The Aztecs carried on the traditions of timekeeping begun by the Maya. Like the Maya, they devised a solar calendar of 365 days and anticipated the cyclical destruction of the world every fifty-two years. They produced the famous "Calendar Stone," a huge votive object that functioned not as an actual calendar, but as a symbol of the Aztec cosmos (Figure 19.22). The four square panels that surround the face of the sun god represent the four previous creations of the world. Arranged around these panels are the twenty signs of the days of the month in the eighteen-month Aztec year, and embracing the

Figure 19.22 Aztec sun disc, known as the "Calendar Stone," fifteenth century. Diameter 13 ft., weight 24½ tons. Museo Nacional de Antropologia, Mexico. Photo: South American Pictures, Woodbridge, Suffolk, U.K.

empires—is estimated to have numbered between three and five million people. In their earliest history, the Aztecs (who called themelves "Mexica") were an insignificant tribe of warriors who migrated to Central Mexico in 1325. Driven by a will to conquer matched perhaps only by the ancient Romans, they created in less than a century an empire that encompassed all of central Mexico and the lands as far south as Guatemala. Their capital at Tenochtitlán, a city of some 250,000 people, was constructed on an island in the middle of Lake Texcoco. It was connected to the Mexican mainland by three great causeways and watered by artificial lakes and dams. Like the Romans, the Aztecs were masterful engineers, whose roads, canals, and aqueducts astounded the Spaniards who arrived in Mexico in 1519. Upon seeing Tenochtitlán for the first time, Spanish soldiers reported that it rivaled Venice and Constantinople, cities that were neither so orderly nor so clean.

Both the Aztec and the Inka civilizations absorbed the cultural traditions of earlier Meso-Americans, including the Maya. They honored the pantheon of nature deities centering on the sun and extended the

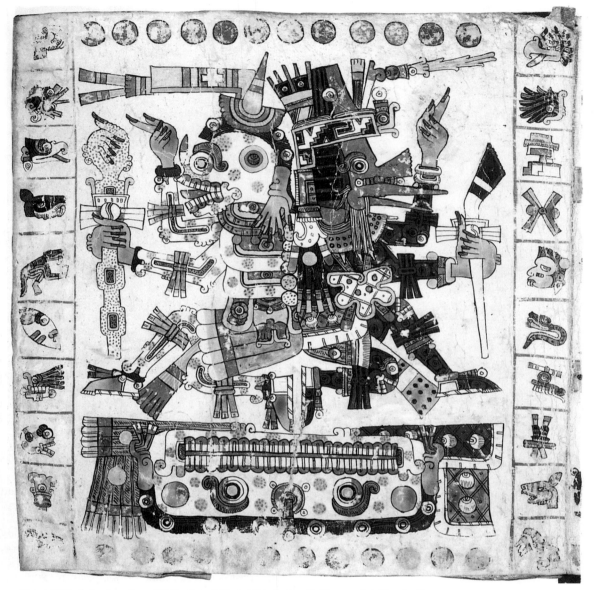

Figure 19.23 Aztec peoples, *Mictlantecuhtli and Quetzalcoatl*. Manuscript illumination. Vatican Library, Rome, Codex Borgia, f.56.

entire cosmic configuration are two giant serpents symbolizing the sky. The stone is the pictographic counterpart of Aztec legends that bind human beings to the gods and to the irreversible wheel of time.

Some of the most interesting records of Aztec culture are preserved in the form of codices, that is manuscripts—usually made of deer hide—with pictographic representations that recount tribal genealogy, history, and mythology. The most complex surviving Meso-American codex, which is housed today at the Vatican Library in Rome, illustrates the history of Quetzalcoatl in the underworld. A page showing the dual aspects of the universe—life and death—in the form of a pair of fantastically arrayed deities includes an inverted skull or earth monster (below) and twenty pictographic day signs on either side (Figure 19.23).

Cross-Cultural Encounter
The Spanish in the Americas

Columbus made his initial landfall on one of the islands now called the Bahamas, and on successive voyages he explored the Caribbean Islands and the coast of Central America. At every turn, he encountered people native to the area—people he called "Indians" in the mistaken belief that he had reached the "Indies," the territories of India and China. Other Spanish explorers soon followed and rectified Columbus' misconception. Spanish adventurers, called *conquistadores*, sought wealth and fortune in the New World. Although vastly outnumbered, the small force of six hundred soldiers under the command of Hernán Cortés (1485–1574), equipped with fewer than twenty horses and the superior technology of

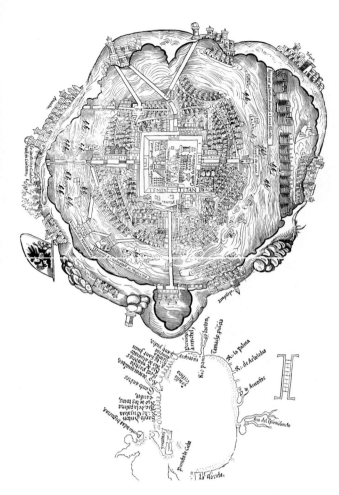

Figure 19.24 Plan of Tenochtitlán which appeared in the Latin edition of Cortés' Second Letter, Nuremberg, 1524. Rare Books Division, The New York Public Library. Astor, Lenox and Tilden Foundations.

gunpowder and muskets, overcame the Aztec armies in 1521. Following the thirty-five-day siege, the Spanish completely demolished the island city of Tenochtitlán (Figure **19.24**), from whose ruins Mexico City would eventually rise. While the technology of gunpowder and muskets had much to do with the Spanish victory, other factors contributed, such as religious prophecy (that Quetzalcoatl would return as a bearded white man), support from rebellious Aztec subjects, and the outbreak of smallpox among the Aztecs.

The Spanish destruction of Tenochtitlán and the melting down of most of the Aztec goldwork left little tangible evidence of the city's former glory. Consequently, the description that is the subject of Cortés' second letter to Queen Isabella of Spain is doubly important: Not only does it offer a detailed picture of Aztec cultural achievement, but it serves as a touchstone by which to assess the conflicted reactions of Renaissance Europeans to their initial encounters with the inhabitants of strange and remote lands.

READING 3.25
From Cortés' Letters from Mexico

This great city of Temixtitan[1] is built on the salt lake, and no matter by what road you travel there are two leagues from the main body of the city to the mainland. There are four artificial causeways leading to it, and each is as wide as two cavalry lances. The city itself is as big as Seville or Córdoba. The main streets are very wide and very straight; some of these are on the land, but the rest and all the smaller ones are half on land, half canals where they paddle their canoes. All the streets have openings in places so that the water may pass from one canal to another. Over all these openings, and some of them are very wide, there are bridges made of long and wide beams joined together very firmly and so well made that on some of them ten horsemen may ride abreast. 1 / 10

Seeing that if the inhabitants of this city wished to betray us they were very well equipped for it by the design of the city, for once the bridges had been removed they could starve us to death without our being able to reach the mainland, as soon as I entered the city I made great haste to build four brigantines, and completed them in a very short time. They were such as could carry three hundred men to the land and transport the horses whenever we might need them. 20

This city has many squares where trading is done and markets are held continuously. There is also one square twice as big as that of Salamanca,[2] with arcades all around, where more than sixty thousand people come each day to buy and sell, and where every kind of merchandise produced in these lands is found; provisions as well as ornaments of gold and silver, lead, brass, copper, tin, stones, shells, bones, and feathers. They also sell lime, hewn and unhewn stone, adobe bricks, tiles, and cut and uncut woods of various kinds. There is a street where they sell game and birds of every species found in this land: chickens, partridges and quails, wild ducks, flycatchers, widgeons, turtledoves, pigeons, cane birds, parrots, eagles and eagle owls, falcons, sparrow hawks and kestrels, and they sell the skins of some of these birds of prey with their feathers, heads and claws. They sell rabbits and hares, and stags and small gelded dogs which they breed for eating. 30 / 40

There are streets of herbalists where all the medicinal herbs and roots found in the land are sold. There are shops like apothecaries', where they sell ready-made medicines as well as liquid ointments and plasters. There are shops like barbers' where they have their hair washed and shaved, and shops where they sell food and drink. There are also men like porters to carry loads. There is much firewood and charcoal, earthenware braziers and mats of various kinds like mattresses for beds, and other, finer ones, for seats and for covering rooms and hallways. There is every sort of vegetable, especially onions, leeks, garlic, common cress and watercress, borage, sorrel, teasels and artichokes; and there are many sorts of fruit, among which are cherries and plums like those in Spain. 50

[1]Tenochtitlán.
[2]A Spanish university town.

They sell honey, wax, and a syrup made from maize canes, which is as sweet and syrupy as that made from the sugar cane. They also make syrup from a plant which in the islands is called *maguey*,[3] which is much better than most syrups, and from this plant they also make sugar and wine, which they likewise sell. There are many sorts of spun cotton, in hanks of every color, and it seems like the silk market at Granada, except here there is a much greater quantity. They sell as many colors for painters as may be found in Spain and all of excellent hues. They sell deerskins, with and without the hair, and some are dyed white or in various colors. They sell much earthenware, which for the most part is very good; there are both large and small pitchers, jugs, pots, tiles, and many other sorts of vessel, all of good clay and most of them glazed and painted. They sell maize both as grain and as bread and it is better both in appearance and in taste than any found in the islands or on the mainland. They sell chicken and fish pies, and much fresh and salted fish, as well as raw and cooked fish. They sell hen and goose eggs, and eggs of all the other birds I have mentioned, in great number, and they sell *tortillas* made from eggs.

Finally, besides those things which I have already mentioned, they sell in the market everything else to be found in this land, but they are so many and so varied that because of their great number and because I cannot remember many of them nor do I know what they are called I shall not mention them. Each kind of merchandise is sold in its own street without any mixture whatever; they are very particular in this. Everything is sold by number and size, and until now I have seen nothing sold by weight. There is in this great square a very large building like a courthouse, where ten or twelve persons sit as judges. They preside over all that happens in the markets, and sentence criminals. There are in this square other persons who walk among the people to see what they are selling and the measures they are using; and they have been seen to break some that were false.

There are, in all districts of this great city, many temples or houses for their idols. They are all very beautiful buildings, and in the important ones there are priests of their sect who live there permanently; and, in addition to the houses for the idols, they also have very good lodgings. All these priests dress in black and never comb their hair from the time they enter the priesthood until they leave; and all the sons of the persons of high rank, both the lords and honored citizens also, enter the priesthood and wear the habit from the age of seven or eight years until they are taken away to be married; this occurs more among the first-born sons, who are to inherit, than among the others. They abstain from eating things, and more at some times of the year than at others; and no woman is granted entry nor permitted inside these places of worship.

Amongst these temples there is one, the principal one, whose great size and magnificence no human tongue could describe, for it is so large that within the precincts, which are surrounded by a very high wall, a town of some five hundred inhabitants could easily be built. All round inside this wall there are very elegant quarters with very large rooms and corridors where their priests live. There are as many as forty towers, all of which are so high that in the case of the largest there are fifty steps leading up to the main part of it; and the most important of these towers is higher than that of the cathedral of Seville. They are so well constructed in both their stone and woodwork that there can be none better in any place, for all the stonework inside the chapels where they keep their idols is in high relief, with figures and little houses, and the woodwork is likewise of relief and painted with monsters and other figures and designs. All these towers are burial places of chiefs, and the chapels therein are each dedicated to the idol which he venerated.

There are three rooms within this great temple for the principal idols, which are of remarkable size and stature and decorated with many designs and sculptures, both in stone and in wood. Within these rooms are other chapels, and the doors to them are very small. Inside there is no light whatsoever; there only some of the priests may enter, for inside are the sculptured figures of the idols, although, as I have said, there are also many outside.

The most important of these idols, and the ones in whom they have most faith, I had taken from their places and thrown down the steps; and I had those chapels where they were cleaned, for they were full of the blood of sacrifices; and I had images of Our Lady and of other saints put there, which caused Mutezuma[4] and the other natives some sorrow. First they asked me not to do it, for when the communities learnt of it they would rise against me, for they believed that those idols gave them all their worldly goods, and that if they were allowed to be ill treated, they would become angry and give them nothing and take the fruit from the earth leaving the people to die of hunger. I made them understand through the interpreters how deceived they were in placing their trust in those idols which they had made with their hands from unclean things. They must know that there was only one God, Lord of all things, who had created heaven and earth and all else and who made all of us; and He was without beginning or end, and they must adore and worship only Him, not any other creature or thing. And I told them all I knew about this to dissuade them from their idolatry and bring them to the knowledge of God our Saviour. All of them, especially Mutezuma, replied that they had already told me how they were not natives of this land, and that as it was many years since their forefathers had come here, they well knew that they might have erred somewhat in what they believed, for they had left their native land so long ago; and as I had only recently arrived from there, I would better know the things they should believe, and should explain to them and make them understand, for they would do as I said was best. Mutezuma and many of the chieftains of the city were with me until the idols were removed, the chapel cleaned and the images set up and I urged them not to sacrifice living creatures to the idols, as they were accustomed,[5] for, as well as being most abhorrent to God, Your Sacred Majesty's laws forbade it and ordered that he who kills shall be killed.

---

[3]Fermented aloe or *pulque*, a powerful liquor still popular today in Mexico.

[4]Moctezuma II, the last Aztec monarch, who ruled from 1502 to 1520.
[5]In 1488, at the dedication of the Great Pyramid at Tenochtitlán, Aztec priests sacrificed more than twenty thousand war captives.

And from then on they ceased to do it, and in all the time I stayed in that city I did not see a living creature killed or sacrificed.

The figures of the idols in which these people believe are very much larger than the body of a big man. They are made of dough from all the seeds and vegetables which they eat, ground and mixed together, and bound with the blood of human hearts which those priests tear out while still beating. And also after they are made they offer them more hearts and anoint their faces with the blood. Everything has an idol dedicated to it, in the same manner as the pagans who in antiquity honored their gods. So they have an idol whose favor they ask in war and another for agriculture; and likewise for each thing they wish to be done well they have an idol which they honor and serve.

There are in the city many large and beautiful houses, and the reason for this is that all the chiefs of the land, who are Mutezuma's vassals, have houses in the city and live there for part of the year;⁶ and in addition there are many rich citizens who likewise have very good houses. All these houses have very large and very good rooms and also very pleasant gardens of various sorts of flowers both on the upper and lower floors.

Along one of the causeways to this great city run two aqueducts made of mortar. Each one is two paces wide and some six feet deep, and along one of them a stream of very good fresh water, as wide as a man's body, flows into the heart of the city and from this they all drink. The other, which is empty, is used when they wish to clean the first channel. Where the aqueducts cross the bridges, the water passes along some channels which are as wide as an ox; and so they serve the whole city.

Canoes paddle through all the streets selling the water; they take it from the aqueduct by placing the canoes beneath the bridges where those channels are, and on top there are men who fill the canoes and are paid for their work. At all the gateways to the city and at the places where these canoes are unloaded, which is where the greater part of the provisions enter the city, there are guards in huts who receive a [percentage] of all that enters. I have not yet discovered whether this goes to the chief or to the city, but I think to the chief, because in other markets in other parts I have seen this tax paid to the ruler of the place. Every day, in all the markets and public places there are many workmen and craftsmen of every sort, waiting to be employed by the day. The people of this city are dressed with more elegance and are more courtly in their bearing than those of the other cities and provinces, and because Mutezuma and all those chieftains, his vassals, are always coming to the city, the people have more manners and politeness in all matters. Yet so as not to tire Your Highness with the description of the things of this city (although I would not complete it so briefly), I will say only that these people live almost like those in Spain, and in as much harmony and order as there, and considering that they are barbarous and so far from the knowledge of God and cut off from all civilized nations, it is truly remarkable to see what they have achieved in all things. . . .

180
190
200
210
220
230

———————◆———————

⁶Provincial lords were required to spend part of each year at the capital.

The Aftermath of Conquest

Mexican gold and (after the conquest of the Inkas) Peruvian silver were not the only sources of wealth for the conquerors; the Spanish soon turned to the ruthless exploitation of the native populations, enslaving them for use as miners and field laborers. During the sixteenth century, entire populations of Native Americans were destroyed as a result of the combined effects of such European diseases as smallpox and measles and decades of inhumane treatment, such as that described in the following eyewitness account from a *History of the New World* (1565) by the Italian Girolamo Benzoni (1519–1570), who spent fifteen years in the Americas:

After the death of Columbus, other governors were sent to Hispaniola;* both clerical and secular, till the natives, finding themselves intolerably oppressed and overworked, with no chance of regaining their liberty, with sighs and tears longed for death. Many went into the woods and having killed their children, hanged themselves, saying it was far better to die than to live so miserably serving such ferocious tyrants and villainous thieves. The women terminated their pregnancies with the juice of a certain herb in order not to produce children, and then following the example of their husbands, hanged themselves. Some threw themselves from high cliffs down precipices; others jumped into the sea and rivers; others starved themselves to death. Sometimes they killed themselves with their flint knives; others pierced their bosoms or sides with pointed stakes. Finally, out of two million inhabitants, through suicides and other deaths occasioned by the excessive labour and cruelties imposed by the Spaniards, there are not a hundred and fifty now to be found.

Such reports of Spanish imperialism in the Americas, brought to life by the illustrations of the Flemish engraver Theodore de Bry (1528–1598; Figure **19.25**), fueled the so-called "Black Legend" of Spanish cruelty toward the "Indians" and fed the heated debate that questioned the humanity of so-called "savage" populations. In this debate, the Spanish missionary-priest, Bartolomé de Las Casas (1474–1566), author of the infamous *Very Brief Account of the Destruction of the Indies* (1552), roundly denounced Spanish treatment of the "Indians." His humanitarian position prompted Pope Paul III to declare officially in 1537 that "the said Indians and all other people who may later be discovered by Christians, are by no means to be deprived of their liberty or . . . property." (The papal edict, it is worth noting, failed to extend such protection to Africans.) Las Casas, known

*The name Columbus gave to the island in the West Indies that now comprises Haiti and the Dominican Republic.

Figure 19.25 Theodore de Bry, *Spanish Cruelties Cause the Indians to Despair*, from *Grands Voyages*. Frankfurt, 1594. Woodcut. The John Carter Brown Library, Providence, Rhode Island.

as the "Apostle to the Indians," pleaded, ". . . all the peoples of the world are men, and the definition of all men collectively and severally, is one: that they are rational beings. All possess understanding and volition, being formed in the image and likeness of God. . . ."

Unlike the civilizations of India, China, and Africa, which have each enjoyed a continuous history from ancient times until the present, none of the empires that once flourished in ancient America has survived into modern times. The European invasion of the Americas severely arrested the cultural evolution of native tribal populations. Remnants of these populations, however, remain today among such groups as the Hopi and the Pueblo of the Southwestern United States, the Maya of the Yucatán, and the Inuit of the Pacific Northwest. Among these and other tribes, the ancient crafts of pottery, weaving, beadwork, and silverwork still reach a high degree of beauty and technical sophistication. In terms of the humanistic tradition, however, the most important legacy of the European conquest may be said to lie in the creation of new cultures and new peoples

that resulted from contact between Old and New World populations. Out of the biological and cultural mix of Europeans, Native Americans, and Africans came the *mestizo* (a European and Native American genetic blend) and the many *creole* ("mixed") populations of the Americas. The Columbian exchange also generated new developments in all aspects of life, ranging from technology to diet and dance. On the threshold of modernity, the Euro-African and Euro-American encounters opened the door to centuries of contact and diffusion that shaped the mixed culture of a brave new world.

SUMMARY

The civilizations of Africa and the Americas offer some startling features that set them apart from the culture of the West. Tribal organization and an animistic view of nature were primary characteristics of the many diverse peoples who flourished in both of these vast regions. The literature, music, and art of the first kingdoms of West Africa reflect the communal and deeply spiritual nature of African society. The great body of African literature, from *Sundiata* to the tales, proverbs, and poems of various African tribes, emerges out of an oral tradition that, like African music and art, is characterized by strong rhythmic patterns. African music, dance, poetry, and the visual arts are often integrated in ceremonial performance. African sculpture, usually made of wood, takes the form of masks, ancestor figures, and reliquaries, many of which function as fetishes. While some regions in Africa produce art marked by great realism, others show a preference for expressive abstraction. The honesty and vitality of the African artistic heritage, particularly in the domains of poetry, sculpture, and music, have exercised a powerful influence on language, the visual arts, and the development of modern musical styles.

By comparison with Africa, the rich traditions of Native American cultures have almost disappeared. However, extant ceramics, textiles, baskets, metalwork, and sculpture, as well as the remains of pueblo architecture, testify to the vitality and originality of tribal people throughout the Americas. Among these, only the Maya left a system of writing, though the oral traditions of other early Native American cultures are known to us thanks to records of more recent vintage. The genius of the Maya, the Aztecs, and the Inkas—the three most notable of the Meso- and South American cultures—is still visible in the ruins of their great palaces, temples, and ballparks. An impressive record of these imperial civilizations, their nature deities, and

their religious rituals remains in the form of technically sophisticated goldwork, polychrome ceramics, and vividly carved stone sculptures.

Although they lived in different parts of the world and under different circumstances, ancient African and early Native American people shared a similar view of the world: They held that the universe and all natural objects were infused with spiritual power and that the community of the living was shared by the dead. They viewed time as cyclical rather than as moving toward a specific end or goal. Essentially, they sought the roots of their social order in nature and in the communion of human beings with nature. Such attitudes, closer in spirit to those of ancient India and China than to those of Renaissance Europe, would struggle to survive the aggressive momentum of European expansion and the critical scrutiny of the Christian world.

GLOSSARY

anaphora the repetition of a word or words at the beginning of two or more lines of verse

animism the belief that the forces of nature are inhabited by spirits

fetish an object believed to have magical power

griot a special class of poet-historians who preserved the legends and lore of Africa by chanting or singing them from memory

kiva the underground ceremonial center of the Southwest Indian pueblo community

scarification the act or process of incising the flesh as a form of identification and rank, and/or for aesthetic purposes

totem an animal or other creature that serves as a heraldic emblem of a tribe, family, or clan

MUSIC LISTENING SELECTIONS

Cassette I Selection 19 African music, "Greetings from Podor" (from Senegal).

Cassette I Selection 20 Native American music for male chorus with gourd rattles, "Navajo Night Chant."

SUGGESTIONS FOR READING

Bierhorst, John. *The Mythology of Mexico and Central America*. New York: William Morrow, 1990.

Brody, J. J., et al. *Mimbres Pottery: Ancient Art of the American Southwest*. New York: Hudson Hills Press, 1983.

Feder, Norman. *American Indian Art*. New York: Abradale Books, 1995.

Fraser, Douglas. *African Art as Philosophy*. New York: Interbook, 1974.

Laude, Jean. *The Arts of Black Africa*. Berkeley, Calif.: University of California Press, 1971.

Levathes, Louise. *When China Ruled the Seas: The Treasure Fleet of the Dragon Throne, 1405–1433*. New York: Oxford University Press, 1996.

Levenson, Jay A., ed. *Circa 1492: Art in the Age of Exploration*. New Haven: Yale University Press, 1991.

Lewis, Bernard. *The Muslim Discovery of Europe*. New York: Norton, 1985.

Mbiti, John S. *African Religions and Philosophy*. New York: Doubleday, 1969.

Moctezuma, Eduardo M. *The Aztecs*. New York: Rizzoli, 1989.

Penney, David, and George Longfish. *Native American Art*. New York: Scribners, 1994.

Prussin, Labelle. *African Nomadic Architecture: Space, Place, and Gender*. Washington, D.C.: Smithsonian Institution Press, 1995.

Schele, Linda, and Mary Ellen Miller. *The Blood of Kings: Dynasty and Ritual in Maya Art*. New York: Braziller, 1986.

Sieber, Roy, and R. A. Walker. *African Art in the Cycle of Life*. Washington, D.C.: Smithsonian Institution Press, 1987.

Stierlin, Henri. *The Art of the Aztecs and Its Origins*, translated by Betty and Peter Ross. New York: Rizzoli, 1982.

Stannard, David E. *American Holocaust: The Conquest of the New World*. New York: Oxford University Press, 1993.

Weaver, Mildred P. *Aztecs, Maya and Their Predecessors: Archeology of Mesoamerica*. New York: Academic Press, 1981.

Willett, Frank. *African Art: An Introduction*. New York: Praeger, 1971.

Selected General Bibliography

Anderson, Bonnie S., and Judith P. Zinsser. *A History of Their Own: Women in Europe from Prehistory to the Present*. Vol. 1. New York: Harper, 1988.

Baker, Herschel. *The Image of Man: A Study in the Idea of Human Dignity in Classical Antiquity, the Middle Ages, and the Renaissance*. New York: Harper, 1961.

Braider, Christopher. *Refiguring the Real: Picture and Modernity in Word and Image, 1400–1700*. Princeton, N.J.: Princeton University Press, 1993.

Bronowski, Jacob, and Bruce Mazlish. *The Western Intellectual Tradition: From Leonardo to Hegel*. New York: Harper, 1960.

Brown, Howard *M. Music in the Renaissance*. Englewood Cliffs, N.J.: Prentice-Hall, 1975.

Clark, Kenneth. *Civilisation: A Personal View*. New York: Harper, 1970.

———. *The Nude: A Study in Ideal Form*. Princeton, N.J.: Princeton University Press, 1956.

Coe, Michael D. *The Maya*, 5th ed. London: Thames and Hudson, 1994.

De la Croix, Horst, Richard G. Tansey, and Diane Kirkpatrick. *Gardner's Art Through the Ages*. 10th ed. San Diego: Harcourt, 1996.

Devisse, Jean, and Michel Mollat. *The Image of the Black in Western Art*. Vol. 2, *From the Early Christian Era to the "Age of Discovery,"* translated by William G. Ryan. Houston, Tex.: Menil Foundation, 1990.

Ferguson, George. *Signs and Symbols in Christian Art*, rev. ed. New York: Oxford University Press, 1989.

Floyd, Samuel A. *The Power of Black Music: Interpreting its History from Africa to the United States*. New York: Oxford University Press, 1995.

Harman, Carter. *A Popular History of Music*, rev. ed. New York: Dell, 1973.

Kaufmann, Thomas DaCosta. *The Mastery of Nature: Aspects of Art, Science, and Humanism in the Renaissance*. Princeton, N.J.: Princeton University Press, 1991.

Khapoya, Vincent B. *The African Experience*. Englewood Cliffs: Prentice-Hall, 1994.

King, Margaret L. *Women of the Renaissance*. Chicago: University of Chicago Press, 1991.

Kostoff, Spiro. *A History of Architecture: Settings and Rituals*. New York: Oxford University Press, 1985.

Ladis, Andrew. *The Craft of Art: Originality and Industry in the Italian Renaissance and Baroque Workshop*. Athens, Ga.: University of Georgia Press, 1995.

Levathes, Louise. *When China Ruled the Seas: The Treasure Fleet of the Dragon Throne, 1405–1433*. New York: Oxford University Press, 1996.

Lund, Erik, Mogens Pihl, and Johannes Sløk. *A History of European Ideas*, translated by W. G. Jones. Reading, Mass.: Addison-Wesley, 1962.

May, Elizabeth, ed. *Music of Many Cultures*. Berkeley, Calif.: University of California Press, 1980.

Miller, Mary Ellen. *The Art of Mesoamerica from Olmec to Aztec*. New York: Thames and Hudson, 1986.

Nuttgens, Patrick. *The Story of Architecture*. Englewood Cliffs, N.J.: Prentice-Hall, 1983.

O'Faolain, Julia, and Lauro Martines, eds. *Not in God's Image: Women in History from the Greeks to the Victorians*. New York: Harper, 1973.

Prussin, Labelle. *Hatumere: Islamic Design in West Africa*. Berkeley, Calif.: University of California Press, 1995.

Pumfrey, Stephen, et al., eds. *Science, Culture and Popular Belief in Renaissance Europe*. New York: St. Martin's Press, 1994.

Rabb, Theodore K. *Renaissance Lives: Portraits of an Age*. New York: Pantheon Books, 1993.

Roston, Murray. *Renaissance Perspectives in Literature and the Visual Arts*. Princeton, N.J.: Princeton University Press, 1987.

Scher, Stephen K. *The Currency of Fame: Portrait Medals of the Renaissance*. New York: Abrams, 1996.

Sorrell, Walter. *The Dance Through the Ages*. New York: Grosset and Dunlap, 1967.

Spencer, Harold. *The Image Maker: Man and His Art*. New York: Scribner, 1975.

Sternfeld, F. W. *Music from the Middle Ages to the Renaissance*. Vol. 1 of *The History of Western Music*. New York: Praeger, 1973.

Sullivan, Michael. *The Arts of China*, 3rd ed. Berkeley, Calif.: University of California Press, 1984.

Tidworth, Simon. *Theatres: An Architectural and Cultural History*. New York: Praeger, 1973.

Townsend, Richard. *The Aztecs*. London: Thames and Hudson, 1994.

Wilson, Katharina M., ed. *Women Writers of the Renaissance and the Reformation*. Athens, Ga.: University of Georgia Press, 1987.

BOOKS IN SERIES

Daily Life in the Five Great Ages of History. The Horizon Books of Daily Life. New York: American Heritage Pub. Co., 1975.

Great Ages of Man: A History of the World's Cultures. New York: Time-Life Books, 1965–1969.

Time-Frame. 25 vols. (projected). New York: Time-Life Books, 1990–.

Credits

The author and publishers wish to thank the following for permission to use copyright material. Every effort has been made to trace the copyright holders, but if any have been inadvertently overlooked the publishers will be pleased to make the necessary arrangement at the first opportunity.

Reading 3.3 (p. 11) Excerpts from Christine de Pisan, *The Book of the City of Ladies*, trs. Earl Jeffrey Richards. Copyright © 1982 by Persea Books, Inc., by permission of Persea Books, Inc.

Reading 3.8 (p. 30) Excerpts from *The Albertis of Florence*, trs. Guido A. Guarino. Copyright © Associated University Presses 1971, by permission of Associated University Presses

Reading 3.18 (p. 101) Introduction and footnotes by David Bevington to "Tragedy of Othello, the Moor of Venice" from *Complete Works of Shakespeare*. Copyright © 1980, 1973 by Scott, Foresman and Company, by permission of Addison-Wesley Educational Publishers Inc.

Reading 3.19 (p. 139) Excerpts from Djibul Nione, *Soundjata ou L'Epopée Mandingue (Sundiata: An Epic of Old Mali)*, 1960, by permission of Présence Africaine

Reading 3.21 (p. 144) Selections from *African Poetry: An Anthology of Traditional African Poems*, compiled and edited by Ulli Beier, Cambridge University Press, 1966, by permission of Ulli Beier

Reading 3.22 (p. 149) Excerpts from *The Travels of Ibn Battuta A.D. 1325–54*, vol. IV. trs. H. A. R. Gibb, The Hakluyt Society, 1994, by permission of David Higham Associates on behalf of the author

Reading 3.25 (p. 164) Excerpts from *Hernan Cortés: Letters from Mexico*, ed. Anthony Pagden, 1986, by permission of Yale University Press

Index